THE BETROTHAL CONTRACT IN THE CODE OF CANON LAW

(Canon 1017)

The Catholic University of America
Canon Law Studies
No. 326

The Betrothal Contract in the Code of Canon Law

(Canon 1017)

A DISSERTATION

SUBMITTED TO THE FACULTY OF THE SCHOOL OF CANON LAW OF THE CATHOLIC UNIVERSITY OF AMERICA IN PARTIAL FULFILLMENT OF THE REQUIREMENTS FOR THE DEGREE OF DOCTOR OF CANON LAW

BY THE
REV. CHESTER F. WRZASZCZAK, A.B., S.T.L., J.C.L.
Priest of the Diocese of La Crosse

The Catholic University of America Press
Washington, D. C.
1954

NIHIL OBSTAT:

HUGO C. KOEHLER

Censor Librorum

Crossae, Wisconsin, die 17a iunii, 1953

IMPRIMATUR:

✠ JOANNES P. TREACY

Ordinarius Crossensis

Crossae, Wisconsin, die 19a iunii, 1953

MURRAY AND HEISTER
WASHINGTON, D. C.

PRINTED BY
TIMES AND NEWS PUBLISHING CO.
GETTYSBURG, PA., U.S.A.

TABLE OF CONTENTS

TABLE OF CONTENTS—(Continued)

TABLE OF CONTENTS—(Continued)

TABLE OF CONTENTS—(Continued)

PAGE

Section II

Section III

Section IV

TABLE OF CONTENTS—(Continued)

TABLE OF CONTENTS—(Continued)

FOREWORD

In a military age such as this, when men are called away from their homes to serve on foreign shores, the temptation to secure a spouse before departure is often impelling. Regrets and repudiation are as often as not a common aftermath. Solemn espousals can prevent such tragedy and unhappiness and are capable of acting as a curb and brake upon hasty and ill-advised unions. Betrothment assures one of a partner and of fidelity in absence by way of a formal promise and pledge to enter into future nuptials, a promise and pledge, binding unless and until renounced for a just and reasonable cause by one or the other or both the contracting parties.

Apart from these extraordinary considerations, betrothal compacts provide ample and excellent opportunity for proper preparation and anticipation of the many marital obligations, cares and responsibilities with which the sacrament of matrimony is fraught. In the primitive Church the early Christians adopted the concept and custom of espousals because they saw in them a fitting preliminary and prelude to the great step in life—marriage. In the beautiful language of St. Thomas, betrothment for the faithful became a "quasi-sacramental" annexed to the sacrament of matrimony. In the later Middle Ages it served as a practical expediency to insure marriage and to allow for sufficient time for investigation into the fitness of the parties wishing to be wedded.

Today in many parts of the world solemn engagements are utterly obsolete, deemed archaic. In other portions of the globe they retain their traditional rôle in the drama of life. In the United States during the second World War they were revived in certain quarters. The practice still survives here and there as the old war gives way to the new. A widespread revival would indeed aid somewhat in stemming the awful tide of betrayed love and broken lives.

Substantially, the law of the Church on espousals is that

which is found in Roman law, but modified to a degree and influenced by Germanic and Hebraic legal concepts. However, as found today in Canon 1017 of the Code of Canon Law, betrothals, i.e., engagements, represent a transformation undergone, first, in the Decree of Gratian, secondly, in the Decretals of Popes Gregory IX and Boniface VIII and, thirdly, in the pontifical and conciliar legislation before and after the great Council of Trent. They have also been a constant object of commentary by canonists and the subject of continuous clarification by the Sacred Congregations in Rome. Final legislation comes with the Code.

The writer wishes to avail himself of the opportunity presented here to express his sincere gratitude to his Bishop, the Most Rev. John P. Treacy, Ordinary of the Diocese of La Crosse, Wisconsin, for graciously granting him the rare privilege of pursuing higher studies at the renowned Catholic University of America in the School of Canon Law. Thanks are also extended here to the Rev. Theophilus Wojak, former pastor of the writer, for encouraging him to do graduate work in canon law.

Lastly, grateful acknowledgments are here accorded to the members of the Faculty of the School of Canon Law at The Catholic University of America, Washington, D. C., for their valuable advice, guidance and assistance in the writing of this dissertation.

IESU CHRISTO
CANAE GALILAEAE
HOSPITI DIVINO

PART ONE

Historical Development

CHAPTER I

Early Civil Law Sources

SECTION I. ROMAN LAW

Article 1: Derivation and Definition of Roman Betrothals

For the etymology of *sponsalia,* betrothals, Roman jurisprudence is indebted to a second century jurist, Ulpian. This eminent authority in order to arrive at the origin of the term hearkened back to early Roman custom and legal practice. He described these in a rather lapidary style, stating simply that "it was customary among the ancients to stipulate and to pledge to one another those who would be their future wives."[1]

Now, the infinitive *stipulari,* to stipulate, as used by Ulpian, refers to one of the four verbal contracts common to Roman law. To stipulate signified to assume an obligation orally, to bind oneself by the spoken word, to enter into a unilateral contract by word of mouth.[2] In its earliest days, however, prior to its appearance about the middle of the fifth century B.C., *stipulatio* was known as *sponsio.*[3] This term was founded on the legalities observed by the early Romans when they contracted betrothals. A suitor seeking the hand of a maiden in marriage asked the father or lawful guardian of the girl with all due solemnity of legal form: *Spondesne* (Do you promise, viz., to give this woman as my betrothed)? To which question the equally formalistic called for reply, in the absence of cause of a contemplated refusal, was *Spondeo* (I promise).[4]

---

[1] "Nam moris fuit veteribus stipulari et spondere sibi uxores futuras."—D. (23.1) 2.

[2] G. III, 92. Cf. also Leage, *Roman Private Law* (2. ed., London: Macmillan, 1948), p. 299.

[3] Muirhead, *The Law of Rome* (2. ed., London, 1899), p. 214.

[4] Thus, v.g., Richeri, *Universa Civilis et Criminalis Iurisprudentia* (2. ed., 12 vols., Taurini, 1824), I, 210; and Wernz-Vidal, *Ius Canonicum* (7 vols. in 8, Vol. V, 3. ed., a P. Aguirre recognita, 1946, Romae: apud Aedes Uni-

Hence Ulpian declared that *sponsalia* is derived from *spondere,* i.e., to promise or pledge.[5] From this same root are derived *sponsa* and *sponsus,* i.e., spouses, another Roman jurist, Florentinus (died circa 161) asserted.[6]

As for the classical definition of *sponsalia,* Justinian (527-565) selected the above-mentioned Florentinus as his authority: "Betrothals are the mention and promise of future marriage."[7]

Article 2: Form

Except for the formalities expressed in the question and answer form, mentioned previously, there is no evidence of any other juridic requirements for early Roman espousals. However, various solemnities gradually did appear, but these were not regarded

versitatis Gregorianae, 1923-1946), V, 100-101. Gaius (2nd century) gave this form together with other formularies as employed by the Romans for different transactions.—G. III, 92.

[5] D. (23.1) 2. Aulus Gellius in the second century (*Noctes Atticae,* lib. IV, cap. IV) pointed to a non-legal source, Servius Rufus Sulpicius (+ 43 B. C.), who wrote: "Is contractus stipulationum sponsionumque dicebatur sponsalia." —Rolfe, *The Attic Nights of Aulus Gellius* (3 vols., London, 1927), I, 324. As for the significance of *spondeo* itself there is much discussion among authors in civil and canon law both. Cf. Muirhead, *The Law of Rome,* pp. 214-216; also Cappello, *De Sacramentis* (5 vols., Vol. I-II, 4. ed.; Vol. III-IV, 2. ed.; Vol. V, 5. ed., Romae: Marietti, 1942-1947), V, 81, footnote 1, who, for instance, definitely disagrees with such authors as Vecchotti and Gasparri, who held to *sponte* as the root of *sponsio;* Cappello derives the term from Greek sources, alluding to the libations (from which he states *sponsio* is derived) that took place in the forum on the occasion of ancient Roman betrothals. Gaius himself wrote that the word was said to be of Grecian origin.—G. III, 93.

[6] D. (23.1) 3. Varro (*De Lingua Latina,* lib. VI, no. 70) explained: "[Si] spondebatur pecunia aut filia nuptiarum causa, appellabatur et pecunia et quae desponsata erat sponsa; quae pecunia inter se contra sponsum rogata erat, dicta sponsio; cui desponsa quae erat, sponsus; quo die sponsum erat, sponsalis." Cf. Kent, *Varro on the Latin Language* (2 vols., New York: Putnam, 1938), I, 236.

[7] "Sponsalia sunt mentio et repromissio futurarum nuptiarum."—D. (23.1) 1. However, Mommsen (*Digesta Iustiniani Augusti* [2 vols., Berolini, 1870], I, 656, n. 1) stated that *conventio* rather than *mentio* is the more correct reading.

as essential to the contract.[8] When they were observed certain liabilities were incurred on breach of the contract, as will be later explained. The sending of an iron ring to the affianced by her fiancé became a common practice, but the use of the ring was by no means confined to betrothment agreements. It was also used in other contracts of sale.[9]

With the growth of the empire the observance of a set form came to have greater legal value. The giving of the *arrha*[10] or

---

[8] De Smet, *De Sponsalibus et Matrimonio* (4. ed., Brugis, 1927), n. 14.

[9] D. (19.1) 11. The early Christians finding the custom of ring-giving free of superstitious ties adopted the practice, as will be shown in the next chapter, in which reference will be made to Tertullian's statement in his treatise on Idolatry.—*Liber de Idolalatria,* c. XVI—*Patrologiae Cursus Completus, Series Latina* (221 vols., Parisiis, 1844-1855), I, 685 (hereafter cited as *MPL*). The Christian ring, called *annulus* or *pronubus,* was probably of gold, as may be surmised from Tertullian's observation that the Christian woman knows no gold save that on her finger.—*Apologeticus,* c. VI—*MPL,* I, 302.

[10] "Dicta autem arrha a re pro qua traditur," is the explanation given by St. Isidore in his *Etymologiarum Libri XX.* "Est autem arrha non solum sponsio conjugalis sed etiam pro qualibet promissa re data ut compleatur."—*MPL,* LXXXII, 365. Traces of the *arrha* can be found in all parts of the world. The roots lie probably in the view, common still to some savage races, that marriage is simply the sale of a wife, to which sale the betrothals stand in the relation of contract to delivery. Cf. Smith, "Arrha," *Dictionary of Christian Antiquities* (2 vols., Hartford, 1880), I, 142. *Arrha* could consist of mobile and immobile goods exchanged mutually by the contracting parties or their parents in sign of contract and as pledge of non-breach. As will be shown below, violation of the betrothal contract resulted in a loss of the *arrha.*—Cf. also Ferraris, s.v. *Sponsalia, Prompta Bibliotheca, Canonica, Iuridica, Moralis, Theologica, necnon ascetica, Polemical Rubricistica, Historica* (9 vols., Romae, 1885-1899), VIII, 417. (Hereafter this work will be cited simply: *Bibliothcca*). "*Arrha* is not to be confused with the later medieval *iocalia,* given as a token of love and hence not inherently subject to surrender in the event one failed to keep his troth, unless a private stipulation to the contrary was drawn up. This also applied to the other *munera* and the *donatio* inasfar as they were not regarded as the *arrha.* Likewise *dos, dowry,* is not to be confused with *arrha,* since *dos* properly belongs to the marriage contract as distinct from the betrothment agreement. It represents the bride's contribution toward the household expenses. Cf. Sherman, *Roman Law in the Modern World* (2. ed., 3 vols., New York, 1924), n. 478. Cf. pp. 175-176 of this thesis.

earnest money in pledge of fulfillment of the agreement and even the passing of the kiss[11] between the affianced parties became repeated subjects of Constantine's legislation. In 336, for example, this Emperor instructed his vice-regent in Spain, Tiberianus, that if gifts had been exchanged and the kiss given in betrothals the property thus passed was to be equally divided between the espoused woman and the suitor's heirs should death intervene before the promised marriage took place. If the kiss was not bestowed, the donation was null and void, to be returned to the heirs of the deceased. In the rare occurrence in which the woman herself had given the gift, the act was to be annulled and the gifts to be returned to the woman or her heirs in the event of premature death in this regard.[12]

Witnesses were not required for the validity of the contract, and it did not matter whether the espousals were made in writing or orally.[13] Even the very presence of the couple was not deemed necessary, "as this takes place every day," Ulpian observed,[14] provided however that the absent parties subsequently ratified the agreement made in their absence.[15]

Article 3: Consent

"Mere consent" Ulpian again ruled, "is sufficient to constitute espousals."[16] Paulus (died after A.D. 222) pointed out that in espousals consent is mandatory of those from whom it will be demanded in marriage.[17] Judged from what Justinian enacted both

---

[11] A solemn ratification of espousals. The kiss is also mentioned by Tertullian in his *De Velandis Virginibus,* c. XI, as an old heathen custom. —*MPL,* II, 897.

[12] C. (5.3) 16. This legislation is substantially that of the earlier Emperors Valentinian II (375-392) and Theodosius II (408-450). Theodosius advised Eutropius: "Arrhis sponsaliorum nomine datis, si interea sponsus vel sponsa decesserit, quae data sunt, iubemus restitui nisi causam ut nuptiae non celebrantur defuncta iam praebuit."—C. Th. (3.5) 5.

[13] D. (23.1) 7.

[14] D. (23.1) 4, 1.

[15] D. (23.1) 6.

[16] "Sufficit nudus consensus ad constituenda sponsalia."—D. (23.1) 4.

[17] D. (23.1) 7.

in the *Digest* and in the *Code,* it appears, in reference to a son's consent, that neither in the sixth century nor in the classical period could a father troth his son against the latter's will.[18] This certainly was true of the son *in potestate,* and hence *a fortiori* of the emancipated son, for Julian (died before A.D. 169) was quoted by Paulus to the effect that when the son became betrothed the father's consent was always presumed unless it was clear that he withheld it.[19]

It is not clear, however, whether this also obtained for the daughter *in potestate.* Perhaps in late imperial times the *filia familias* was unrestricted in the use of her rights, but earlier such re-occurring expressions as *in matrimonium dare, collocare, tradere,* etc., in reference to betrothments arranged by fathers for their *daughters* as contrasted with such terminology as *uxorem duci, pati,* etc., as used of *sons,* seems to indicate a lack of liberty in this regard.[20]

A presumption of law was invoked by Ulpian when he declared that consent is understood as given when the girl does not resist her father's will,[21] hence the *paterfamilias* could send notice to his daughter's affianced, if he so desired, and herein annul the betrothment as long as she was under his control.[22]

Insanity incapacitated persons from contracting and rendered their acts null and void according to the ruling of Gaius.[23]

Article 4: Age

"In contracting betrothals there is no limit to the age of the parties as in the case of marriage," Justinian legislated, following the authority of Modestinus (died after A.D. 244). "Wherefore espousals can be made at a very early age, provided that what is being done is understood by both persons, that is to say, when

---

[18] D. (23.1) 13; (23.2) 2; C. (5.4) 12, 14.

[19] D. (23.1) 7.

[20] Corbett, *The Roman Law of Marriage* (Oxford: Clarendon Press, 1930), p. 2.

[21] D. (23.1) 12.

[22] D. (23.1) 10.

[23] D. (23.1) 18.

they are not under seven years of age."[24] Hence, contracting parties could not be *infantes* nor *infantiae proximi* but needed to be of sufficient age so as to be capable of intelligent acts, presumed by Justinian to be at the age of seven. That espousals occurred at an early age, approximating even the minimum, may be inferred from the Theodosian Code, for example, where an express ruling was enacted regarding different penalties to be incurred for breach of contract according as the girl was below or above the age of ten, and another penal measure according as the maiden was not yet twelve.[25]

Article 5: Impediments

Capacity to contract betrothals required freedom from the bond of consanguinity. Hence, those who could not intermarry could not be betrothed,[26] but possibly in classical law espousals were allowed in view of the expiration of a temporary obstacle.[27] Affinity, too, acted to disbar betrothal agreements.[28] Legal relationship also fell under proscription. Thus a guardian was not permitted to betroth his own ward, or unite her in marriage to his son, in the judgment of Modestinus.[29] The *Lex Julia* (passed in A.D. 9) forbade senators, their sons, nephews and the sons' nephews to become espoused to a freedwoman or to one whose parents practiced the profession of actors. The prohibition extended, *mutatis mutandis*, to the daughters and nieces as well.[30]

---

[24] D. (23.1) 14: "In sponsalibus contrahendis aetas contrahentium definita non est ut in matrimoniis, quapropter et a primordio aetatis sponsalia effici possunt, si modo id fieri ab utraque persona intellegatur, id est, si non sint minores quam septem annis." Corbett, *The Roman Law of Marriage*, p. 3, however, is of the opinion that the words ". . . si modo . . . septem annis . . ." at the end of the passage is probably an interpolation.

[25] C. Th. (3.5) 12.

[26] D. (23.2) 53-55.

[27] D. (23.1) 15, 16.

[28] D. (23.2) 12.

[29] D. (23.1) 5; (23.2) 60 (5).

[30] D. (23.2) 44. Cf. also D. (23.1) 16.

Article 6: Breach of Contract

Throughout the long period of Roman history liabilities resulting from violation of the betrothal promise varied considerably before the law. Thus, Justinian accepted the strict principles set forth in the laws of Severus and Antoninus and legislated that immorality in an espoused woman was to be looked upon as adultery and punished with the same penalties.[31] Nonetheless, he ruled that the contract might be dissolved at any time by mutual consent and that it was optional to either party to terminate it by means of a *repudium.*[32] If the agreement had been accompanied by the traditional formalities with the presentation of the ring, the exchange of gifts and the giving of the kiss, repudiation was allowable only on certain specified grounds. Should no such grounds be forthcoming the party sending the *repudium* incurred a pecuniary liability.[33] Where the formalities had been neglected no cause needed to be assigned. Moreover, if an affianced woman married another man at the desire of her father, no charge of adultery could be brought against her.[34] To be betrothed to two persons simultaneously was branded an infamy at law (*infamia iuris*) by pretorian edict.[35] Failure on the part of the prospective bridegroom to carry out his promise within a *two-year period* relieved the woman of her obligation, as she was not obliged, in the language of the legislator, "to suffer her vows to be treated with contempt."[36] Gaius allowed protraction for one, two or three years when a just cause was present, as illness, death, accusation of capital crimes and long journey. This was incorporated into Justinian law.[37]

Multiple damages in respect to *arrha* for breach of contract was the subject of much legislation in both the Theodosian and Justinian Codes. Double and quadruple damages were inflicted

---

[31] C. (9.13) 1.
[32] D. (24.2) 2.
[33] C. (5.1) 1.
[34] D. (23.1) 6.
[35] D. (3.2) 1.
[36] C. (5.1) 2. The engagement ceased *ipso facto.*
[37] D. (23.1) 17.

according to various circumstances of age and dignity of the contracting parties, the mode of contract, the value and the specific character of gifts bestowed, and according to other reasons too numerous to enumerate here.[38]

Of interest, however, is Constantine's treatment of cases relating to those who were desirous of consecrating themselves to God after betrothment. By a rescript to a certain John, pretorian prefect, Constantine abrogated in 354 the previous legislation which had imposed the penalty of loss of property given by the man and which demanded double the value of the *arrha* received by the woman should there occur the renunciation of the world, *post factum* to the prenuptial arrangement. The reason for the abrogation given by the Emperor was that the former law "seemed contrary to the benign spirit of our religious belief."[39] Then, by newly enacted legislation he provided that any affianced man who wished to enter the religious state or receive Holy Orders after espousals was to receive all the property that had passed without any diminution whatsoever, and the betrothed woman who was intent on plighting her troth to God was to surrender only what she had received from her former lover.[40]

Other exceptions were also acknowledged. Thus exempting from penalties were such factors as repugnance on the part of the woman toward her betrothed because of his low character, shameless conduct, spendthrift habits, or adherence to another creed. Impotency and other similarly reasonable causes giving legal grounds for repudiation were likewise admitted.[41]

Creditors were disallowed action at court and could not sue a betrothed woman in order to obtain her property accruing from

---

[38] Cf., v.g.: C. Th. (3.5) 11; C. (5.1) 1-20.

[39] "Nostrae mansuetudini satis religioni esse contrarium visum est."—C. (1.3) 54 [56].

[40] *Loc. cit.*

[41] C. (5.1) 5. Ignorance of the repellent or disqualifying features in the affianced person was a necessary condition for the exemption to void the contract. The former quadruple damages were thereby eliminated by this ruling. The legislation did not provide for any exemptions from private agreements even though these stipulated double or quadruple damages contrary to or outside the common law.

her espousals—unless they could prove that it was previously encumbered to them.[42]

Betrothals when accompanied with sexual intercourse constituted marriage, Justinian finally legislated. As no formal expression of consent was required, at least by the early Roman law, for the marriage itself, and even though marriage was a distinct entity from espousals, the consent of betrothals was considered as passing automatically into a consent to the actual present union.[43]

SECTION II. GERMANIC LAW

Article 1: Nature of Germanic Betrothals

From the fifth century onward, the Church was thrown into contact with the Germanic tribes then overrunning the empire. It was inevitable that the impact would produce some effect on the Church's attitude toward betrothals, as these peoples brought with them marriage laws and customs differing from those of the Romans.[44] In time, however, the Germans merged their legislation with that of the empire, as will be pointed out below, influencing to an extent subsequent ecclesiastical practice.

Among the Teutons betrothals (*beweddung*)[45] occupied a place of prominence quite unlike anything in Roman law. The Barbarian codes, i.e., the *Leges Romanae Barbarorum*[46] regarded es-

---

[42] C. (5.3) 13.

[43] N. (74.5).

[44] For an accurate analysis of the complexity of Germanic law on marriage and espousals, cf. von Hörmann, *Quasiaffinität* (2 vols., Innsbruck, 1897-1906), II, 457 ff.

[45] From the Anglo Saxon. The root is *wed,* meaning a pledge or a surety. The English word *wedding* is derived from this source as betrothals, originally preceding the actual marriage, became in time part of the nuptial ceremony itself.—Joyce, *Christian Marriage* (2. ed., London: Sheed and Ward, 1948), p. 50; Pollock-Maitland, *The History of English Law Before the Time of Edward I* (2. ed., 2 vols., Boston, 1899), II, 364-366.

[46] Three such Teutonic codes of *"Leges Romanae"* are of historical importance. The first, that of the Ostrogoths in Italy, was compiled by King Theodoric in 500, and is embodied in what is known as the *Edictum Theodorici* with the *Sententiae Pauli* and the Theodosian Code as the source. The second, that of the Visigoths in Southern France, was published at Aire,

pousals more than a mere promise of marriage. Betrothal was tantamount to wife-purchase, common to all tribal customs,[47] which made it legally binding, although dissolution was possible. Thus, King Flavius Recesvinth in 654 ruled for his subjects that there was not to be any separation between betrothed persons unless the consent of all concerned was obtained; penalties were to be imposed for all unwarranted violation of the betrothment pact.[48]

Article 2: Form

Meager information is had as to the formalities employed in Germanic espousals. As the underlying theory was that of wife-purchase, the ceremony, so it appears, called for some form of transfer of authority over the girl, as observed in the actual mar-

---

Gascony, in 506, and is recognized as the Code of Alaric II, or the *Breviarium Alaricianum,* with the same sources as the Ostrogothic code. The third, the laws of the Burgundians, was promulgated by King Sigismund in 517; these laws are embodied in the *Lex Burgundionum* (or *Burgundiorum*), utilizing the Roman sources indicated above together with the Breviarium of Alaric.—Sherman, *Roman Law in the Modern World,* I, n. 133.

[47] Smith, "Betrothals," *Dictionary of Christian Antiquities,* I, 203. Cf. also "Betrothal" and "Marriage," *The Catholic Encyclopedia* (15 vols., Index and two Supplements, New York, 1907-1922), II, 537-538; IX, 703-707.

[48] *Leges Visigothorum-Monumenta Germaniae Historica* (Hannoveriae, 1835-1927-*Leges,* 5 vols.; Vol. I, *Capitularia Regum Francorum* (ed. G. H. Pertz, 1835); Vol. II, *Constitutiones et Acta Regum Germanicorum* (ed. G. H. Pertz, 1837), Vol. III, *Leges Nationum Germanicarum*: *Lex Alamannorum* (ed. J. Merkel); *Lex Baivwariorum* (ed. J. Merkel); *Leges Burgundionum* (ed. Fr. Bluhme); Lex Frisionum (ed. K. de Richtofen, 1863-Neudruck, 1925); Vol. IV, *Leges Longobardorum* (edd. Fr. Bluhme et A. Boretius, 1868-Neudruck, 1925); Vol. V, *Leges Saxonum* (edd. K. de Richthofen et K. F. de Richthofen); *Lex Thuringorum* (ed. K. F. de Richtofen); *Edictum Theodorici Regis* (ed. Fr. Bluhme); *Remedii Curiensis Episcopi Capitula* (ed. G. Haenel); *Lex Ribuaria* (ed. R. Sehm); *Lex Francorum Chamavorum* (ed. R. Sehm); *Lex Romana Raetica Curiensis* (ed. K. Zeumer, 1889)-*Legum Sectio I,* tom. I, *Legis Visigothorum,* pars 1, ed. K. Zeumer, 1902); tom. II, pars 1, *Leges Burgundiorum* (ed. L. R. de Salis, 1892); tom. V, pars 1, *Leges Alamannorum* (ed. K. Lehman, 1888; pars 2, *Lex Baiwariorum* (ed. E. von Schwind, 1927)—*Legum Sectio II, Capitularia Regum Francorum,* tom. I (ed. A. Boretius, 1883)-*Legum Sectio I,* tom. I, pars 1, p. 170 (hereafter cited *MGH*).

riage ceremony and known as the *mundium*. Undoubtedly, since it was the father or the guardian of the girl who exercised strict authority (*mundim*) in the Teutonic home, it was he who acted in the capacity of making the transfer. Within the Lombard Kingdom in Italy (568-774) it was customary for the betrothed couple to make a formal declaration of their consent in the presence of the local assembly. At this ceremony a layman, chosen by the pair or their kinsmen,[49] asked for and received the consent of the parties to the union. Gradually, however, among the Germanic people betrothals were merged with the nuptial ceremonies.[50] The contract could be made even with the contractants absent, as in the celebrated case of Chlodowig (Clovis), who espoused Chlotilda through his envoys.

The exchange of gifts was customary. The bestowal of the ring was an innovation adopted from Roman law, conforming to the concept of espousals and marriage as a sale, i.e., a pecuniary, civil transaction, in which the ring represented value in the absence of money.[51] Visigothic law spoke of the ring-bestowal as constituting a marriage contract enforceable at law on failure to deliver. "When a ring has been given or accepted in the name of earnest," the law read, "even though nothing has been committed to writing, the promise must in no wise be broken."[52] Lombard

---

[49] In Lombard law he is designated as the orator, whereas modern German writers speak of him as the *Fürsprecher*. This last term Joyce (*Christian Marriage*, p. 49) regarded as not synonymous with the Anglo-Saxon *Forspreca* since the *Fürsprecher's* office was different.

[50] The famous *Sarum Ritual* still retains vestiges of the distinction between betrothment and marriage, as does the *Roman* Ritual. The *Salisbury* custom calls for the exchange of promise outside the church doors (*coram Ecclesia*, literally). The Nuptial Mass followed within the body of the church. The *Roman* ceremonial calls for the plighting of the troth first and then for the mutual exchange of marital consent. Cf. also Dodwell, *The Time and Place for the Celebration of Marriage*, The Catholic University of America Canon Law Studies, n. 154 (Washington, D. C.: The Catholic University of America Press, 1942), pp. 36-40; Carberry, *The Juridical Form of Marriage*, The Catholic University of America Canon Law Studies, n. 84 (Washington, D. C.: The Catholic University of America, 1934), pp. 13-14.

[51] Hence, the Teutonic term: *ring-money*.—Smith, "Betrothals," *Dictionary of Christian Antiquities*, I, 203.

[52] *MGH, Legum Sectio I*, tom. I, *Leges Visigothorum*, pars I, 123.

legislation was to the same effect, viz.: "When a man betroths himself to a woman with a ring only, he gives earnest for her and makes her his own, and if afterward he marries another, he is liable to the amount of six hundred solidi."

Writing out the contract and calling in witnesses was the customary practice. The presence of the witnesses was required by law, as may be indirectly inferred from the general legislation on this subject.[53]

Article 3: Consent and Requisite Age

With the *patria-potestas* strongly entrenched in Germanic tribal life, it is not surprising to find the father's authority safeguarded by law also in the matter of his daughter's espousals. Hence, Flavius Recesvinth (649-672) decreed that under no circumstances should a daughter be permitted to marry, in defiance of her father's or guardian's will, any other than the one betrothed to her by her father or guardian.[54] Even should the father die, by the same ruling the girl was held to her father's original choice.[55] When a girl married without parental or tutelary consent, then by Thuringian law she stood to lose all her property.[56] An offending suitor in the realm of the Frisians was liable to a fine of twenty solidi or sixty denarii when the father's wish was so contravened.[57] However, Christian influence reacted in the girl's favor in due course of time. King Chlothachar I, in 560, by a royal constitution forbade marriage (hence, analogously, betrothment) of maidens and widows when such an act was contrary to their wills.[58] When the ring had been given or received

[53] *Cartularium,* n. 16—*MGH, Leges, Leges Longobardorum, IV,* 599.

[54] *MGH, Legum Sectio I,* tom. I, *Leges Visigothorum,* pars 1, 122-123. The prohibition is categoric: ". . . nullo modo permittimus. . . ."

[55] *Loc. cit.*

[56] "Si libera femina sine voluntate patris aut tutoris cuilibet nupserit perdat omnem substantiam quam habuit vel habere debuit."—*Lex Thuringorum,* n. 47—*MGH, Leges,* V, 135.

[57] *Lex Frisionum,* n. 11—*MGH, Leges,* III, 665.

[58] "Nullus per auctoritatem nostram matrimonium viduae vel puellae sine ipsarum voluntate praesumat expetere."—*Chlothacarii I Regis Constitutio,* n. 7—*MGH, Leges, Constitutiones et Acta Regum Germanicorum,* II, 2.

in Visigothic espousals, it was deemed unlawful for either party to withhold consent or change his or her mind as to the consummation of the contract.[59]

As for the age necessary for the validity of the prenuptial contract, the laws of Liutprand (717) were most severe against espousals of girls who had not reached the age of puberty: "If anyone betroths or takes to wife a maiden under the age of twelve, he is to compound, pay in satisfaction, according to the edict on rape, ninety solidi."[60] The Roman computation of twelve years as constituting the *aetas minor* for girls, and fourteen for boys, was also followed by Germanic law.

Article 4: Legal Effects

Enslavement and pecuniary fines were the usual punishments inflicted for the violations of betrothal contracts and their infringements. Enumeration of the penalties to be inflicted according to various circumstances attendant upon the breach fill many a page of the Barbarian codes.

To sin with a betrothed person was styled adultery, as in marriage, and merited the same liabilities. Marriage to another than the betrothed came under the same category. Hence, in punishment the guilty parties were delivered as slaves to the injured suitor and his gifts returned as compensation.[61] Abductors and ravishers of an espoused maiden lost half their property to the woman violated and half to her intended husband. If the delinquent had few or no possessions, he was sold as a slave and the price delivered to the affianced pair.[62] Should the abductor or ravisher be slain in the chase, no charge of homicide could be preferred against the pursuers.[63] Parents consenting to the abduction of their daughter espoused to another were liable to

---

[59] *MGH, Legum Sectio I,* tom. I, *Leges Visigothorum,* pars I, 124.

[60] *Lex Alamannorum, LII,—MGH, Leges,* III, 149.

[61] ". . . desponsata . . . una cum adultero puniatur, aut certe si qui isponsus [sponsus] fuerat ambo tradatur . . . et pretium ad illum sponsum qui dederat revertatur."—*MGH, Legum Sectio I,* tom. I, *Leges Visigothorum,* pars I, 148.

[62] *Ibid.,* p. 142.

[63] *Loc. cit.*

quadruple damages in relation to the value of the dowry. The criminal was delivered into the power of the woman's betrothed.[64]

By the *Lex Alamannorum*, whoever took to himself a partner already promised to another was to be fined two hundred solidi and made to return the affianced to her fiancé. Failure to restore the woman doubled the fine.[65]

It was permissible to delay fulfillment of the betrothal agreement. Lombard law, for example, following Roman law, allowed a two-year period to intervene before obligating the parties to consummate their contract, as can be seen from King Rathar's decree issued about the year 638.[66]

Incestuous relations with an espoused woman called for the immediate separation of the sinning kinsman and his confinement to a monastery for perpetual, i.e., life-time penance.[67]

Breach was allowable if the betrothed woman consequent upon her espousals was struck down with leprosy, became possessed by the devil, or was blinded in both eyes, as Rothar in his one hundred and eighth edict declared.[68]

SECTION III. HEBREW LAW

Article 1: Nature of Hebrew Betrothals

Complete legislation on espousals is lacking in the Old Testament. The Pentateuch, in particular, though dealing with the subject, is silent as to whether or not betrothment had legal significance. Nevertheless, the institution was a common and a well

[64] "Si parentes raptori consenserint, pretium filie [filiae] sue [suae] quod cum priore [priori] sponso definisse [definivisse] in quadruplum eidem sponso cogatur [cogantur] absolvere. . . ."—*Op. cit.*, p. 141.

[65] "1. Si quis sponsatam alterius contra legem acceperit reddat eam et 200 solidis componat. 2. Si autem reddere noluerit solvat eam cum 400 solidis. . . ." —*MGH, Leges*, III, 62.

[66] *MGH, Leges*, IV, 41.

[67] *MGH, Legum Sectio I*, tom. I, *Leges Visigothorum*, pars I, 159.

[68] "Si contigerit, postquam puella aut mulier sponsata fuerit, lebrosa [leprosa] aut demoniaca aut de ambos [ambobus] occulos [occulis] excaecata apparuerit, tunc sponsus recipiat res suas et non compellatur [compelletur] ipsam invitus tollere ad uxorem nec pro hac causa calomnietur [calumnietur]." —*MGH, Leges*, IV, 42.

recognized proceeding among the Hebrew people, arising not so much from law as from tradition and custom.[69]

However, the Jews did not look upon betrothals as did the occidental nations. Although in itself betrothment was perhaps nothing more than a customary and mutual declaration that a marriage was in the process of being arranged, the *solemn rite* for the Jew carried with it all the juridic effects of marriage. Once the prenuptial pact had been entered into, it was definitely binding upon both parties, who then and there were considered man and wife in all legal as well as religious aspects save that of cohabitation. The very etymology of the Hebrew root from which the Talmudic abstract *erusin* is derived must be understood in this sense, viz., a contract of an actual but unconsummated marriage.[70]

Thus, in two of the passages where the words occur in the Old Testament, the betrothed woman is explicitly designated as *wife*.[71] In the New Testament the celebrated example is Mary, whom the angel terms *wife* (*coniugem*),[72] even though the Evangelists speak of her as *espoused* (*desponsatam*)[73] to Joseph, whom in turn they style as her *husband, vir*.[74] Hence in strict accordance with this sense rabbinical law declared that betrothals are equivalent to actual marriage.[75]

---

[69] Neufeld, *Ancient Hebrew Marriage Law* (New York: Longmans, 1944), p. 94.

[70] Cf. "*Betrothals*," *The Jewish Encyclopedia* (12 vols., New York: Funk and Wagnalls, 1903), III, 125. The *Talmud* also uses the more common *Kiddushim*, i.e., a consecration whereby the bride is rendered holy or consecrated in the same sense as the objects within the sanctuary. The meaning is mystical and calls attention to the solemn character of marriage as envisaged by Judaism.—Epstein, *The Babylonian Talmud, Kiddushim* (London: Sancino Press, 1936), introd.

[71] II Kings, III, 13; Deut., XXII, 24.

[72] Matt., I, 20.

[73] Matt., I, 18.

[74] Matt., I, 19; Luke, I, 27.

[75] Neufeld, *Ancient Hebrew Marriage Laws*, pp. 94, 142-143.

Article 2: Form

Among the ancient Hebrews *Kiddushim,* espousals, were arranged by means of *Mohar,* i.e., the bride-price.[76] The prospective groom or his father or guardian paid the price as agreed to the future father-in-law, and thus acquired by purchase or sale the bride-to-be. Upon completion of the formalities by payment of the *Mohar,* the marriage was already legally effective, i.e., inchoate but not yet consummated.[77] The *Talmud* also allowed espousals by means of a debt,[78] by law of surety,[79] with proceeds from unusable tokens[80] and with many other items too numerous to mention here.

As among other nations, the presence of the contracting parties was not obligatory. The *Mishna* ruled: "A man can betroth [a woman] through himself or through an agent."[81] From the scanty information available, it appears that the ceremonies surrounding espousals consisted mainly of a banquet[82] at which the families of the betrothed couple and their more intimate friends were assembled. Gifts in addition to the *Mohar* were presented by the groom or his friends to the bride or her family.[83] A benediction was pronounced over the woman by her father or guardian with the prayer that she might be blessed with children.[84]

This private and personal observance in Talmudic days gave way in later times to a formal practice accompanied with great pomp. It became customary to make out in writing a legal con-

---

[76] For the various opinions as to the precise juridic implications of *Mohar,* cf. Neufeld, *Ancient Hebrew Marriage Laws,* pp. 95-96.

[77] Neufeld, *op. cit.,* p. 94.

[78] Kid. 6b; 13a. All references to the Talmud are from Epstein, *The Babylonian Talmud, Kiddushim.*

[79] Kid. 7a.

[80] Kid. 56b.

[81] Kid. 41a.

[82] Cf. Judges, XIV, 10.

[83] Gen. XXIV, 23. The gifts were called *siblonot* or *sablonot,* meaning *payment* or *token* (according to the Greek root). The presents offered to both the bride and groom to defray the wedding costs were known as *shoshbinut.* Cf. "Betrothals," *The Jewish Encyclopedia,* III, 128.

[84] Gen., XXIV, 60; Ruth, IV, 12; Tob., X, 11-12.

tract of marriage (*Ketubah*), containing various stipulations in the event of breach or infidelity.[85]

The nuptials did not follow immediately despite the juridic fact that an inchoate marriage had already been contracted on espousal. There was usually a short period between the two ceremonies of *Mohar* payment and the actual hometaking of the bride.[86] The servant of Abraham, for instance, wished to hasten his marriage, but Laban and Bathuel requested him to "let the maiden stay at least ten days with us and afterward she will depart."[87] *Deuteronomy* confirms the custom of having an interval of time intervene between the two ceremonies of betrothment and marriage, declaring that when a man had plighted his troth he should not immediately go to war but continue in peace until after the nuptials.[88]

In David's case betrothment and marriage were concurrent because of a military factor present, scil., prowess in battle. The second King of Israel sent word to Isboseth saying: "Restore my wife Michol whom I espoused to me for a hundred foreskins of the Philistines."[89]

The *Talmud* fixed a thirty-day period for widows and widowers as a sufficient interval between espousals and marriage.[90] Twelve months, however, was the usual period of waiting.[91]

Witnesses were customary, although Sacred Scripture is silent on the matter. Rabbinical law mentions that the testimony of one witness to espousals is insufficient.[92] Selden's *"Uxor Hebraica"* gives the schedule of later betrothments and recounts how the prenuptial pact was written out by the men before witnesses and given to the woman.[93]

---

[85] "Betrothals," *The Jewish Encyclopedia,* III, 127.

[86] In Hebrew called: *erusin* and *niss'in;* in Latin: *traductio in domum;* in Anglo-Saxon: *gifta.*

[87] Gen., XXIV, 54-55.

[88] Deut., XX, 7.

[89] II Kings, III, 13. This passage and I Kings, XVIII, 25, show that for the customary monetary payment for the bride, the *Mohar,* a substitution could be made through deeds of valor.

[90] Kid. 58b.

[91] "Betrothals," *The Jewish Encyclopedia,* III, 126.

[92] Kid, 65a.

[93] Cf. Smith, "Betrothals," *Dictionary of Christian Antiquities,* I, 202.

The use of a ring was undoubtedly an importation from the outside Gentile world, for no mention is made of it either in Biblical or early Talmudic times. Nor is anything said in regard to the *osculum,* the kiss.

As for the parties' consent, little is known. It is implied in the father's consent on the principle: *Qui tacet, consentit.* This was probably true when the girl was not quite twelve years of age. It appears that consent was asked of her, probably by way of ratification of the espousals, already contracted in her name prior to her attaining the necessary age, i.e., when she reached the age of puberty.[94] Selden (1584-1654), in the passage quoted above, states that when a betrothment contract had been committed to writing, the woman needed to know its import, and hence had to give at least an implicit consent.[95] The Babylonian rabbi Rab (Abba Arika, + 247) pointed to serious punishment for anyone who married his betrothed partner without her consent.[96]

Article 3: Effects

Unfaithfulness on the part of the betrothed woman, or an attack on her virginity, was likened to adultery; it called for capital punishment.[97] Apart from this legal sanction the Bible, unlike the legal system of other Semitic peoples, provided no penalties for breach of contract. It seems improbable, however, in the light of the solemnity of the espousals and of the severity of the punishment attaching to interference by a third party, that no liabilities would have been stipulated by either of the contracting parties. The last was undoubtedly the case. In post-Talmudic days, as noted before, the betrothal contract became a formal affair, in which express penalties were implemented for failure to fulfill its terms.[98] Hence, the silence of the Pentateuch is not to be construed as precluding all applicable punishments. To become betrothed a second time called for formal divorce proceedings first.

---

[94] "Betrothals," *The Jewish Encyclopedia,* III, 125.

[95] *Loc. cit.*

[96] Kid. 13a.

[97] Deut., XXII; 23-27.

[98] These agreements were called *shiddukin* (consent to marry) and *tenaim* (conditions).—"Betrothals," *The Jewish Encyclopedia,* III, 127.

One happy effect, already referred to, was exemption of the betrothed man from military service until marriage had ensued, "lest he die in war and another take her [i.e., his espoused]."[99]

Article 4: Levirite Espousals

A word must be said about this institution, peculiar to the Hebrews alone. Like the ordinary betrothment of a later period in Jewish history, these levirite betrothals consisted of the levir giving his late brother's widow a ring or some object of value in the presence of witnesses, or by writing an instrument containing the formula: "Be thou betrothed unto me according to the law of Moses and Israel."[100] Legally this sufficed to constitute the contract, but later more elaborate ceremonies grew out of various social customs.[101]

Levirite espousals were not called *erusin* or *kiddushim,* terms which imply conveyance and consecration, for the reason that the levirite woman was not conveyed, since original conveyance was still in effect, nor was she consecrated or sanctified anew, as her sanctification still perdured from her first marriage,[102] the theory being that her original status and condition remained unchanged by her husband's death. The technical term for levirite betrothment was ma'amar, signifying promise or pronouncement.[103]

As *ma'amar* was post-Biblical, it did not enjoy the legal effects of Biblical betrothals. It did not make the widow the wife of the *levir.* In regard to adultery, the act was not held different after the espousals than before. Furthermore, even after levirite espousals the woman could become betrothed to another man and marry him. These second betrothals were regarded even more valid at law than the former, since the levirite institution had only rabbinical standing, whereas the subsequent betrothal was vested with Biblical validity.[104]

---

[99] Deut., XX, 7.

[100] Cf. Deut., XXV, 5-10.

[101] Epstein, *Marriage Laws in the Bible and in the Talmud* (Cambridge: Harvard University, 1924), p. 117.

[102] Analogical to the Church's practice of not granting the nuptial blessing to widows at their marriage.

[103] *Op. cit.*, p. 117.

[104] Epstein, *Marriage Laws in the Bible and in the Talmud,* p. 118.

CHAPTER II

Early Canon Law

SECTION I. PRE-GRATIAN PERIOD

Article 1: Nature and Notion of Betrothals in the Western Church

Since betrothment by nature was so convenient an adjunct to marriage, the early Christians readily accepted the traditional Roman conception of it, purified it, sanctified it. The Church exerted its influence to enhance its binding force and raised it to the dignity of a sacred, liturgical rite. It became in practice what St. Thomas Aquinas (1225-1274) later styled a *"quasi-sacramental"* annexed to the sacrament of marriage.[1]

On Tertullian's authority at the end of the second and the beginning of the third century the formalities not incompatible with Christian piety, such as the bestowal of the ring,[2] the exchange of gifts, the joining of hands and the kiss, were all retained.[3] In his book of sermons St. Augustine in the fourth century even mentions the *tabulae* or instrument, i.e., the written contract, the signatory of which (among others) was the bishop himself.[4] What had been purely a civil transaction thus became an ecclesiastical ceremony. St. Ignatius (+ c. 107), in his letter to Polycarp, wrote: "It is the fitting thing for men and women when they

---

[1] *St. Thomas, Supplementum,* q. 43, a. 1.—*Summa Theologica* (1st American ed., 3 vols., New York: Benziger, 1948), III, 2719.

[2] "Touching the ceremonies, however . . . as those of espousals . . . I should think no danger need be guarded against from the breath of the idolatry which is mixed up with them. . . . Those above-named I take to be clean in themselves because . . . neither the marital ring or union descends from honors done to any idol."—*Liber de Idololatria,* Cap. XVI—*MPL,* I, 685. Translation taken from: Roberts-Donaldson, *Ante-Nicene Fathers* (14 vols., New York, 1925), III, 71.

[3] *De Virginibus Velandis,* c. XI—*MPL,* II 904.

[4] "Istis tabulis subscripsit episcopus." *Sermo CCCXXXIII—MPL,* XXXVIII, 1463.

wed, to marry with the consent of the bishop."[5] Moreover, at Rome Pope Siricius (384-398) spoke of a blessing pronounced by the priest at what appears to have been a betrothal ceremony rather than a marriage celebration.[6]

Veiling the bride-to-be (at least in Africa) was also customary already in Tertullian's time. The affianced woman continued to wear the veil given her at espousals until the day of her wedding.[7]

Hence, by the fourth century at the latest, betrothals were recognized by the Church as an acceptable custom and as perfectly lawful and fully binding contracts. In the East, betrothments needed no introduction, as they survived from Roman law. They continued their legal existence and leaped into great prominence under Theodosius II (408-450) and Justinian, as seen in the previous chapter.

However, *two* remarkable and most significant changes gradually evolved in the West. There was first a growing tendency in many places to combine the betrothal ceremony with the marriage rite itself. The period between promise and fulfillment became more and more foreshortened. Frequently *sponsalia* occurred simultaneously with the nuptials proper. The plighting of troth in many instances was followed almost immediately by an exchange of consent or its equivalent: the *traductio* of the bride to the home of her espoused with subsequent cohabitation and *copula*. As a result, a second phenomenon emerged. There was a gradual

---

[5] *Ep. ad. Polycarpum,* V. 3—Migne, *Patrologiae Cursus Completus, Series Graeca* (161 vols., Parisiis, 1857-1866), V, 723 (hereafter cited as *MPG*).

[6] *Ep. I,* cap. 4—*MPL,* XIII, 1136. The precise meaning of the terminology employed by the Pope is questioned by some authors. It is asked whether betrothals were actually meant. Cf. Dodwell, *The Time and Place for the Celebration of Marriage,* pp. 3-5; Carberry, *The Juridical Form of Marriage,* p. 12. A discussion on the ambiguity of the terms appearing at that time will be discussed below. Freisen (*Geschichte des Canonischen Eherechts* [2. ed., Paderborn, 1893], p. 129) denied that a blessing was given by a priest at the time of espousals by way of a general and universal custom. He admitted, however, that the fact is not entirely clear historically. Wernz-Vidal (*Ius Canonicum,* V, 103, n. 15) pointed to the absence of such a blessing in the *Roman Ritual* and in the customs of Italy. The Oriental Church has such a blessing.

[7] *De Virginibus Velandis,* cap. XI—*MPL,* II, 905.

change in terminology, in concept and in meaning behind the language employed in connection with these two institutions. Some Christian writers, though not consistently or universally, commenced using the terms *desponsatio* and *desponsare* to signify marriage, and began to speak of the *sponsa* as *wife*, i.e., as an already wedded bride prior to the consummation of her marriage. The words *nuptiae* and *nubere* began to mean the commencement of cohabitation and could even imply consummation; hence the woman was *uxor* and *coniux*, as conjugal life, duties and privileges become fully hers. Von Hörmann (1865-1946) seemed to be the first, at least in modern times, to point out this remarkable fact.[8] He enumerated Tertullian, Cyprian, Ambrose, Augustine, Jerome, Pelagius I, Isidore, Nicholas I, the Council of Tribur (held in 895), Gratian and Panormitanus in support of his theory.[9]

Notwithstanding all this, these *same* writers and others (the ones to be mentioned in this chapter) continued to use *desponsatio* and *sponsa*, particularly *sponsalia*, in their original meaning. The ambiguity and confusion, however, as thus created were sure to mount in the meantime—to culminate in the famous controversy among the medieval jurists on marital consent, to which Gratian was a leading witness.[9a]

Article 2. Betrothals in the Eastern Church

In the East, betrothals retained their distinct identity; they did not coalesce with the nuptial rites. Since the civil law accentuated their legal significance, it was not surprising that ecclesiastical legislation on this subject also evolved. The first such legislation of note is that of the Council held at Ancyra in 314. This Council

[8] Von Hörmann, *Quasiaffinität*, II, 1-223.

[9] For the pertinent passages of these writers cf. Von Hörmann, *op. cit.*, II, 24, 33, 80 sqq. Joyce (*Christian Marriage*, p. 46) adopted von Hörmann's views and defended them rather strenuously. He quoted the same pertinent passages in the Appendix (pp. 610-611) of his work. He admitted, however, that neither the change in custom nor the change in language was necessarily universal.

[10] Cf. pp. 31-35 of this dissertation.

decreed that betrothed maidens when seized and carried off were to be returned to their espoused partners even though they had been ravished by their abductors.[10] At the same time a case that was brought before the assembled Church Fathers, for the reason that it involved an unfortunate woman who had taken her life after her sister's betrothed had rendered her pregnant, evoked a sentence of ten years' penance upon the culprit and upon all who were responsible for the deed.[11]

B. The Statutes of St. Basil

Some years later St. Basil (330-379) in a letter to Amphilochius, Bishop of Iconium, excluded abductors from communion until they had restored the betrothed women they had carried away.[12]

Elsewhere clerics (readers and subdeacons) were debarred from exercising their office for a year's duration, and were forbidden to advance to Holy Orders upon an act of fornication with their betrothed.[13]

Towards the end of the seventh century the historical Trullan Council met at Constantinople in 692. It appears that at that time the Church in the East was attempting to assert its independence of the civil law which allowed dissolution of both betrothal and nuptial contracts, as was noted above in reference to Justinian's *Corpus Iuris Civilis.* Consequently, in canon ninety-eight the Council proclaimed: "If any man take as his wife a woman who has already been betrothed to another, let him be charged with adultery."[14]

At first sight this canon seems to have declared all betrothals without exception to be absolutely indissoluble. This, however, was not the case. It appears most likely that the passage referred only to those espousals in which formalities had been employed—

---

[10] *Council of Ancyra,* can. 11—Bruns, *Canones Apostolorum et Conciliorum Saeculorum IV-VII* (2 vols., Berolini, 1839), I, 68 (hereafter cited as Bruns).

[11] Can. 24—Bruns, I, 70.

[12] *Epistola CXCIX,* can. 22—*MPG,* XXXII, 721-722.

[13] *Epistola CCXVII,* can. 69—*MPG,* XXXII, 799, 802.

[14] Bruns, I, 63.

to solemn betrothment. The reason for this interpretation is that the Eastern Church, while allowing divorce as it did on the grounds assigned in civil law, was equally prepared to permit dissolution of the betrothals for similar causes. The scope of the decree was, first of all, to disallow dissolution by mutual consent, and then to deny that betrothals could be extinguished through the mere lapse of time, and lastly, to deny that a man could free himself of his prenuptial pact simply by means of the payment of a pecuniary fine.[15]

Article 3: Legislation in the Western Church

On this matter in the Western Church the first conciliar legislation appeared at Elvira in Spain. There, in the year 305, it was ruled that parents breaking off the engagement of their daughters were to be excluded from communion with the faithful for three years.[16] A serious crime on the part of either of the affianced parties was conceded as an exception whereby parents were freed of the penal measure,[17] but even then the betrothment contract had to be upheld inviolate, though immoral relations had existed between the affianced pair.[18]

Toward the middle of the fourth century Pope Julius I (337-352)) was the first purportedly to attempt establishing a new marriage impediment. The Pope prohibited a brother or a relative

---

[15] Thus Joyce, *Christian Marriage,* p. 100. Concerning papal ratification of this Council, cf. Van Hove, *Commentarium Lovaniense in Codicem Iuris Canonici,* Vol. I, tom. I, *Prolegomena ad Codicem Iuris Canonici* (2. ed., Mechlinae—Romae: H. Dessain, 1945) I (1), n. 166 (hereafter the work will be cited *Commentarium*). Cf. also Marbach, *Marriage Legislation for the Catholics of the Oriental Rites in the United States and Canada,* The Catholic University of America Canon Law Studies, n. 243 (Washington, D. C.: The Catholic University of America Press, 1946), pp. 4-5.

[16] Can. 54: "Si qui parentes fidem fregerint sponsaliorum, trienni tempore abstineatur. . . ."—Bruns, II, 9.

[17] ". . . si tamen idem sponsus vel sponsa in gravi crimine fuerint deprehensi, sunt parentes excusati."—Bruns, II, 9.

[18] *Loc. cit.*

to marry his deceased kin's betrothed after solemn betrothals—or his wife, if consummation had not taken place.[19]

In the sixth century the question of relationship arising out of betrothals was being widely discussed. However, the letter of Pope Benedict I (575-579), supposedly written to the Bishop of Grado and stating that, since it is the *copula coniugalis* that makes the two to be one in marriage, mere betrothment would not prevent a man from entering wedlock with the sister of his espoused, is apocryphal and cannot be held authentic in this regard.[20]

Some time later there appeared a decree of Pope Gregory the Great (590-604) allowing a woman who had plighted her troth to her fiancé to sever her engagement in order to enter a convent.[21]

It was at some time during this same period that the famous statement (borrowed from St. Augustine)[22] in reference to consummated and non-consummated marriage appeared from the pen of St. Isidore of Seville (560-636). "The name of 'married persons' is most correctly given to people in view of the initial plighting of troth," he declared, "even though consummation had not taken place."[23]

Legislation in the seventh century included that of Theodore of Canterbury (668-690). His alleged Penitential provided that, if a woman after betrothment refused to take her affianced as her husband or to cohabit with him after marriage, she was to be forced to restore whatever property or money he had given her

---

[19] Mansi, *Sacrorum Conciliorum Nova et Amplissima Collectio* (53 vols. in 59, Parisiis, 1901-1927), II, 1266 (hereafter cited as Mansi). Mansi stated that the decree can be found only in Ivo and Gratian. Cf. also von Hörmann, *Quasiaffinität,* II, 303, n. 1.

[20] "Apocrypha est-apud Jaffé deest."—Richter-Friedberg, *Corpus Iuris Canonici* (2. ed., 2 vols., Lipsiae, 1879-1881) in c. 18, C. XXVII, q. 2—Vol. I, pars 2, p. 1066, footnote 135 (hereafter cited as Friedberg).

[21] Cf. Gratian's *Decretum*—c. 27, C. XXVII, q. 2; Friedberg, *in eodem,* Vol. I, pars 2, p. 1066, ftn. 284a.

[22] *De Nuptiis et Concupiscentiis,* lib. I, c. 11—*MPL,* XLIV, 420.

[23] "Conjuges verius appellantur a prima desponsationis fide, quamvis adhuc inter eos ignoretur concubitus."—Linsay, *Isidori Hispalensis Episcopi Libri XX* (2 vols., Oxonii, 1911), lib. IX, cap. VII, 6. Cf. also *MPL,* LXXXVIII, 365.

and to add to it another third. In a later canon parents were forbidden to give an espoused daughter to another suitor, "if she resists altogether."[24]

In the next century the Council of Compiègne, convoked in 787 in Gaul, ordained,[24a] when dealing with and referring to relationship arising out of fornication, that if a father had carnal relations with his son's betrothed, the son could not consummate his marriage with the maiden. Such a union, the assembly declared, was incestuous. Hence extra-marital intercourse, i.e., the *copula illicita,* became a basis of affinity in the same wise as licit relations.

More than a century later the Carlovingian Capitularies ruled that an affianced girl had to be given back to her betrothed, but in the event of his refusal to accept her she could marry any one else (save her ravisher, under pain of anathema).[25]

Prevalent at that time and slowly gaining momentum was the practice of child-betrothments. Parents frequently betrothed their sons and daughters as part of a family compact when these children were still *impuberes.* The practice was influenced by the Germanic customs outlined earlier. The Teutonic father in his capacity as *mundualdus* was free to contract marriage for his son or daughter as long as either one was under his *patria-potestas.*[26] Whenever this occurred, it was not uncommon for the full ceremony, betrothals and marriage both, to be performed. However, the rite had only the force of a betrothment, for the ratification with a new consent or with a renewal of the old consent was necessarily forthcoming when the affianced child

---

[24] *Theodori Poenitentiale,* cc. X, XI—*MPL,* XCIX, 954-955, 986-987. For legislation in Ireland concerning the father's authority over his daughter's choice in marriage, cf., v.g., *The Synod of St. Patrick*—Mansi, VI, 526.

[24a] Can. 13—Hardouin, *Acta Conciliorum et Epistolae Decretales ac Constitutiones Summorum Pontificum* (12 vols., Parisiis), III, 2006 (hereafter cited Hardouin).

[25] Cf., v.g., the Carlovingian Capitularies passed circa 818-819—*MGH, Legum Sectio II, Capitularia,* I, 279, n. 24.

[26] Cf. pp. 12-14 of this dissertation.

reached the age of puberty.[27] To correct this abuse (together with others) the Council of Friuli met in 791 at Aquileia. Under the direction of its leading prelate, Paulinus, the Council issued a strong condemnation of such marriages on the score that these unions frequently led to disastrous results.[28] The Council also banned marriages between relatives within the forbidden degrees and called for the intervention of the betrothal pacts as a *remedy* against clandestine and hasty marriages of persons related by blood. The purpose of betrothment thus became a very practical one, namely, to allow sufficient time for investigation into the genealogy of the contracting spouses.[29]

That espousals still remained a distinct entity even in the ninth century, despite their concurrence with the nuptial ceremony, is clearly demonstrated by the celebrated *"Responsa ad Consulta Bulgarorum"* of Pope Nicholas I (858-867). In reply to a series of questions put to the Pontiff by the Bulgarian Christians, Nicholas explained the customs connected with the marriage rite as they were observed at Rome.[30] He made the process to consist of four stages. There was first the betrothal proper, for which the Pope gave what was to become the standard medieval definition, namely: "Sponsalia, quae futurarum sunt nuptiarum

---

[27] This practice, too, will add to the debate on consent in a later period, as will be seen in the next section. It corroborates von Hörmann's view as to earlier coalescence of the two ceremonies; there is general agreement among all writers that *by this time* the merger of betrothal with marriage rites was widespread, yet *the espousals* as such were still recognizable, and never were mistaken for marriage itself.

[28] Can. 9: ". . . prohibere decrevimus ut nullus praesumat ante annos pubertatis, id est, infra aetatem puerum vel puellam in matrimonium sociare nec in dissimili aetate sed coaetaneos sibique consentientes."—Mansi, XIII, 848.

[29] Can. 8: ". . ut nemini liceat furtim raptimque nuptias contrahere. . . . Sed interventis pactis sponsalibus per aliquam dilatationis moram requisiti, quin etiam diligenti cura vicini vel majores natu loci illius qui possunt scire lineam generationum utrorumque, sponsi scilicet et sponsae."—Mansi, XIII, 847-848.

[30] Cf. Joyce, *Christian Marriage,* p. 47.

promissa foedera."[31] Secondly, there was the actual marriage rite (*desponsatio*) at which the *arrha* was given, the ring placed on the woman's finger, and the deed of settlement delivered to her.[32] Thirdly, Mass was celebrated either immediately (*mox*) or at some other convenient time (*aut apto tempore*),[33] at which time the bride received a blessing while a veil was held over the heads of both.[34] Lastly, the crowning of the couple took place as they were leaving the church.[35]

Having thus described the rites, Nicholas I expressly insisted that these external observances were not essential for validity, "as the Greeks, you tell us, would have you believe, especially since it often happens that some are so hampered by extreme poverty that they remain without the help that should enable them to prepare for such celebrations."[36] But once the formalities of betrothal were observed, espousals were strictly binding, and their violation was subject to recognized ecclesiastical penalties. Hincmar himself (+ 882) was a witness to this.[37]

---

[31] *"Responsa ad Consulta Bulgarorum,"* C. III—Mansi, XV, 402. Cf. also Jaffé, *Regesta Pontificum Romanorum ab condita Ecclesia usque ad annum post Christum natum MCXCVIII* (2. ed. [by F. Kaltenbrunner (to the year 590), P. Ewald (from 590-882), and S. Loewenfeld (from 882 to 1198) and so referred to as JK, JE and JL], 2 vols. in 1, Lipsiae, 1885-1888), JK, n. 2312.

[32] ". . . et postquam arrhis sponsam sibi sponsus per digitum fidei a se annulo insignitum desponderit, dotemque utrique placitam sponsus ei cum scripto pactum hoc continente coram invitatis ab utraque parte tradiderit. . . ." —Mansi, XV, 402.

[33] Hence there was an interval of time possible between the two acts—particularly if the parties were children.

[34] ". . . demum benedictionem et velamen caeleste suscipiunt. . . ." *Ibid.*, p. 403.

[35] "Post haec autem de Ecclesia egressi coronas in capitibus gestant, quae semper in Ecclesia ipsa sunt solitae reservari."—*Loc. cit.*

[36] *Loc. cit.*

[37] *Epistola XXI*: ". . . ecclesiasticae regulae de his etiam definitionis sententiam proferunt qui sponsalitiorum fidem fregerunt."—*MPL,* CXXVI, 143.

SECTION II. THE DECREE OF GRATIAN

Article 1: The Medieval Problem on Marital Consent

It was almost the middle of the twelfth century when Gratian wrote. The great problem in Gratian's time, that is, the relationship between the factors of consent and consummation in marriage, had reached a high point of discussion and debate. There was an imperative need to define with certainty and to decide with finality whether marriage is effected with consent alone or whether in addition it postulated the *copula carnalis* for its realization and completion. The teaching of the great doctors of the Church had become obscure. These had strongly affirmed the sufficiency of consent.[38] They maintained that the marriage of Mary and Joseph, which stand acknowledged as an integral part of Christian tradition, afforded an incontrovertible proof for this doctrine.

At Paris the school of theology held to this traditional view that mutual consent sufficed for and constituted marriage.

The Bolognese canonists, however, maintained that the consent given at the time of marriage did not constitute marriage in the full sense. They espoused the *copula* theory by insisting that consummation was necessary to complete marriage.

Gratian (c. 1140), whose view the school at Bologna adopted, had concluded that marriage is effected by consent on the strength of the teaching of St. Ambrose[39] and on the authority of St. Isidore.[40] However, this great canonist was unwilling to admit that consent could effect anything more than a *matrimonium initiatum,* carnal action was essential to make it *ratum,* i.e., indissoluble.[41]

---

[38] Thus, v.g., St. Augustine in his treatise, *De Nuptiis et Concupiscentia,* lib. I, c. 11—*MPL,* XLIV, 420. Cf. also St. Ambrose, *De Institutione Virginiis,* C. VI, n. 42—*MPL,* XVI, 316.

[39] "Cum initiatur coniugium, tunc coniugii nomen assciscitur. Non enim defloratio virginis facit matrimonium sed pactio coniugalis . . ." c. 5, C. XXVII, q. 2.

[40] "Coniuges verius appelantur a prima desponsationis fide, quamvis adhuc inter eos ignoretur coniugalis concubitus." c. 6, C. XXVII, q. 2.

[41] "Sed sciendum est, quod coniugium desponsatione initiatur, commistione [commixtione] perficitur. Unde inter sponsum et sponsam coniugium est, sed

The reason why Gratian fell into this error was because he followed Hincmar's mistake by accepting the words erroneously attributed to St. Augustine[42] and the misunderstood passage from St. Leo's letter to Rusticus which Hincmar knew only in its altered form.[43] He advanced certain other reasons for his conclusions, e.g., one who is bound to the obligation of conjugal life may not enter a religious order without the permission of his partner, whereas this may be done by one whose marriage is not yet consummated, even against the will of the other party. He concluded that though it is customary to speak of those who have gone through the ceremony of marriage as man and wife even before the consummation of the union, the terms are applied to them only by *anticipation.*[45]

For a time this opinion prevailed even at Rome. Hence if, after a marriage which had not been consummated a woman pledged herself to another man and consummated the union, the first contract was set aside and the second was adjudged to be a true marriage. In France, on the other hand, an unconsummated marriage was held as a sacramental union and a subsequent marriage was treated as null and void.

Furthermore, Gratian decided that the consent given at betrothals had the same force as that given in marriage. It effected, so he thought, a *matrimonium initiatum.* Hence for him the term *desponsatio* was equivalent to an inchoate, i.e., non-consummated marriage.[46]

---

initiatum, inter copulatos est coniugium ratum."—c. 34, C. XXVII, q. 2 et c. 35, C. XXVII, q. 2. Rufinus (wrote c. 1157), one of the earliest admirers of Gratian, spoke of this distinction as "sacred" and in rather strong language condemned those who opposed Gratian's view.—Rufinus, Summa Decretorum (ed. H. Singer, Paderborn, 1902), C. XXVII, q. 2, p. 440.

[42] "Non est dubium, illam mulierem non pertinere ad matrimonium cum qua commistio [commixio] sexus non docetur fuisse."—Cf. c. 17, C. XXVII, q. 2.

[43] *MPL,* LIV, 1204. This passage has no reference to the consummation of marriage. Hincmar thought that the words *spirituale coniugium* used by Leo referred to sexual intercourse. The passage is found in its altered form, which requires this last meaning, in c. 17, C. XXVII, q. 2.

[45] Cf. c. 26, C. XXVII, q. 2.

[46] Cf. all of C. XXVII, q. 2 and Joyce, *Christian Marriage,* pp. 58-62.

Article 2: Solution to the Problem

A clarification of this problem came with the appearance of a clear-cut distinction. By Gratian's time (1140) it was known in many places in Europe. The distinction called for a consideration of consent *per verba de futuro* in reference to betrothal, and of consent *per verba de praesenti,* which properly constituted marital consent and made the union of spouses a true though unconsummated marriage. A mutual exchange of consent by the couple to take each other here and now as husband and wife sufficed to establish an indissoluble union. Consummation merely perfected and completed the union, and thus achieved the symbolic representation of the mystical union of Christ and His Church, which union the medieval theologians felt to be symbolized solely in the union of the bodies in marriage.

William of Champeaux (+ 1121) is accredited as the originator of this differentiation. He used, however, the terms *fides pactionis* and *fides coniugii* when distinguishing between betrothment and matrimony, and insisted that the *fides pactionis* does not invalidate a subsequent marriage whereas the *fides coniugii* does, in that it constitutes a true marital consent.[44] There is no doubt that this distinction was of real service in clearing men's minds and helping them to grasp the difference between the consent given at espousals and those given at the nuptials as expressed by one and the same word, *desponsatio.*

Soon after, Pope Innocent II (1130-1143) put the distinction to use in deciding a case sent to Rome for settlement. When a legitimate consent has been given, the papal pronouncement read, and as soon as the woman of her own volition has declared herself wife, she is at once the man's wife. For the promise was not given as something of the *future,* but a *present* fact was established, so the Pope proclaimed.[47]

---

[44] The original text can be found in a Paris manuscript of William of Champeaux's *Sentences.* It is quoted by P. Fournier in *Revue d'histoire et de litterature religieuses,* III (1898), 115. Cf. Joyce, *Christian Marriage,* p. 63, ftn. 1.

[47] C. 10, Comp. I, IV, 1: "Dico quod legitimo consensu interveniente, ex eo statim conjunx sit quo spontanea concessione sese conjugem esse asserit.

Hugh of St. Victor (+ 1141)[48] had also by this time given an adequate solution when treating of the problem theologically. He declared that betrothment confirmed by an oath does not invalidate a subsequent marriage. It is otherwise, he added, when the union has not been promised as something in the *future,* but is confirmed by means of the attestation of an assent in the *present.*[49]

About ten years after the appearance of Gratian's *Decretum,* Peter Lombard (+ 1160 or 1164) undertook to express the distinction in unmistakable language. Treating of marriage in his *Book of Sentences,* written between 1150 and 1152, he indicated the essential difference between the pledges given at betrothals and at marriage respectively. In both of these the parties agree to take each other as husband and wife; but, whereas the one is consent given in the *future* tense, the other is assent concerning the *present.*[50]

Article 3: Final Papal Pronouncement

Among the eminent canonists who accepted Gratian's conclusions there was, surprisingly enough, Roland Bandinelli, afterward the great Pope Alexander III (1159-1181). In his *Summa,* written prior to his elevation to the papal dignity, he was entirely on Gratian's side. Subsequently, however, when it was necessary for him as Roman Pontiff to legislate on the matter, he followed the opposite doctrine and thereby brought the discussion to a final

---

Non enim futurum promittebatur sed praesens firmabatur." Agustin, *Quinque Compilationes Antiquae* (Ilerdae, 1576), p. 59; JL, n. 8274.

[48] Wernz-Vidal (*Ius Canonicum,* V, p. 102, ftn. 15) claimed that this theologian was the first to originate the famous distinction between *sponsalia de futuro* and *sponsalia de praesenti.* Freisen (*Geschichte des canonischen Eherechts,* pp. 179 ff.), on the other hand, gave the credit to Peter Lombard.

[49] *De Sacramentis,* lib. 2, p. XI, C. 5: "Non autem sic est quando sacramentum coniugii, non quidem, ut supra dictum est, mutua sponsione futurorum promittitur, sed praesentis assensus attestatione firmatur."—*MPL,* CLXXVI, 486.

[50] *IV Sent.,* dist. XXVII, 3: "Efficiens autem causa matrimonii est consensus non quodlibet sed per verba expressus nec de futuro sed de praesenti." —*MPL,* CXCII, 910.

settlement. Even shortly before his election to the See of Peter in 1159, his *Sententiae,* written between 1150 and 1153, already reflected a shifting of his position away from Gratian.[51] As Alexander III he made the distinction between *consensus de praesenti* and *de futuro.* He declared for the sufficiency of marital consent, as is evidenced by his replies to the Archbishop of Salerno (with a slight reservation, however, namely, that the exchange of the consent take place in the presence of a priest)[52] and to the Bishops of Winchester, Bath and Hereford.[53] Final, unreserved and explicit law on this subject was given to the Bishop of Norwich. The Pope made no reservations in this reply, the consent of the parties rank as valid marriage. It differs from betrothal consent.[54]

Article 4: Betrothals in Gratian's Decretum

A. Juridic Capacity to Contract Betrothals

Most of Gratian's decrees under the title of *sponsalia* deal with *matrimonum initiatum,* since this famous canonist understood this term and "desponsatio" to mean also inchoate marriage. Some decrees, however, explicitly refer to *sponsalia* as betrothment proper. Thus, when speaking of juridic capacity Gratian had only betrothals in mind. He gave the unaltered law on age as handed down by Roman jurisprudence: "Sponsalia ante septennium contrahi non possunt; soli enim consensu contrahuntur."[55] This consent, Gratian's dictum continues, cannot be had unless both par-

---

[51] Gietl, *Die Sentenzen Rolands* (Friburgi Brisgoviae, 1891), pp. LXII, 274, as cited by Joyce, *Christian Marriage,* p. 64, footnote 2.

[52] C. 3, X, *de sponsa duorum,* IV, 4; JL, n. 14091.

[53] C. 3, X, *de matrimonio contracto contra interdictum ecclesiae,* IV, 17.

[54] Cf. C. 6, Comp. I, IV, 4 (Agustin, *Quinque Antiquae Collectiones Decretalium*), p. 55.

[55] C. unic., C. XXX, q. 2. O'Dea (*The Matrimonial Impediment of Nonage,* The Catholic University of America Canon Law Studies, n. 205 [Washington, D. C.: The Catholic University of America Press, 1944], p. 9) remarks: "While Gratian did not make any clear-cut distinction between *sponsalia de futuro* and *sponsalia de praesenti,* it seems obvious that the age here referred to was not marriage itself but rather a promise of a future marriage."

ties are aware of the steps they are taking. Hence, betrothment is impossible among children whose very age precludes consent. Consequently, those who betroth children still in their cradles (*in cunabilis*) effect nothing unless their consent is obtained on their attaining the age of reason.[56]

B. Breach of the Betrothal Contract

When commenting on breach of contract Gratian also unmistakably had betrothals in view. The decree which condemns parents to three years' exclusion from communion with the faithful for breaking off their daughter's espousals, he took from the fifty-fourth canon of the Council of Elvira.[57] Moreover, Gratian emphasized the parents' possession of authority in arranging matrimonial matters for their charges when these were not yet *sui iuris*. However, freedom and personal choice in these matters were not made subject to restriction for virgins and widows.[58]

C. Abduction

The question of abduction also was treated in Gratian's decrees. One such decree referred specifically to betrothed virgins who were allowed to marry their repentant abductors. After the death of an abductor who had married a maiden, formerly betrothed to another, his widow was barred from marrying again. This law was taken from the Council of Meaux, held in France in 845; it represents an advancement and a change in the law over the ancient legislation, which had forbidden ravishers to take as their own those whom they had violently defiled.[59]

---

[56] *Loc. cit.*

[57] C. 1, C. XXXII, q. 3; Bruns, II, 9.

[58] C. 16, C. XXXII, q. 2. The decree is taken from the III Council of Toledo (canon 10), held in 589.—Cf. Bruns, I, 215.

[59] C. 10, C. XXXVI, q. 2. For the ruling of the Council of Meaux, cf. Mansi, XIV, 834. The *Glossa Ordinaria* in the *Casus* calls the woman *sponsa de futuro*.

D. Dissolution of the Betrothal Contract

Although Gratian did not treat of the dissolution of betrothals, the *Glossa Ordinaria* listed seven causes as furnishing acceptable grounds for the non-fulfillment of the betrothal promise. They are: the desire to enter the religious life,[60] desertion or disappearance of one of the parties,[61] infection with leprosy or the sustaining of some physical deformity after the plighted faith,[62] affinity, the mutual desire and agreement to break off the engagement, a subsequent marriage even *per verba de praesenti,* and lastly the foregoing of ratification in the cases of children betrothed below the age of seven.[63]

SECTION III. DECRETAL LAW

Article 1: Decretals of Gregory IX

A. The Binding Force of the Betrothal Contract

Pope Gregory IX (1227-1241) opened his decretals[64] on *sponsalia* with the decretal proclaiming that the betrothment agreement when entered into purely and absolutely, or under oath, always called for fulfillment. The contracting parties were to be induced and even threatened (if necessary) to keep their prenuptial pledge.[65] However, if the contracting parties refused to marry, the Church was ready to tolerate the dissolution of the

[60] Cf. c. 27, C. XXVII, q. 2, s.v. *tamen quaeritur.*

[61] Gregory's Decretals will treat of this under c. 5, X, *de sponsalibus et matrimoniis,* IV, 1.

[62] Also found in the Decretals of Gregory IX. Cf., v.g., c. 2, X, *de coniugio leprosorum,* IV, 8.

[63] These questions will be treated at greater length in the next section on decretal law.

[64] The Decretals of Gregory IX were published September 5, 1234.

[65] "Praeterea hi qui de matrimonio contrahendo pure et sine conditione fidem dederunt (aut) iuramentum fecerunt, commonendi sunt et diligentius exhortandi et modis omnibus inducendi ut praestitam fidem vel iuramentum factum observent et se, sicut promiserint, coniungant."—C. 2, X, *de sponsalibus et matrimoniis,* IV, 1. Cf. also c. 10, X, IV, 1.

agreement, "lest worse evils ensue."[66] A dissolution of the *sponsalia de futuro,* so Gregory announced, was effected when *sponsalia de praesenti* or *copula* followed in the wake of the betrothals. Sex-union after *sponsalia de futuro* was for the mutually betrothed the equivalent of marriage. The occasion for such a law arose out of a case presented to Alexander III. A man who had been betrothed to a woman by whom he already had a child was forced into marriage *per verba de praesenti* with another woman with whom he was apprehended in sin. The Pontiff adjudicated the second union unlawful, because of the existing previous bond which was a true marriage, inasmuch as a carnal union had followed upon the previous betrothal.[67] In other words, copulation on the part of the engaged couple implied the mutual exchange of marital consent.

In another decretal the *sponsalia de futuro* were adjudged dissolved by the *sponsalia de praesenti,* even though the former had been executed under oath. Thus ruled Gregory IX (1227-1241) when answering the Bishop of Le Mans. Penance was imposed upon the violating party.[68] However, subsequent *sponsalia de futuro* did not dissolve the earlier betrothal executed in the nature of *sponsalia de futuro.* This was a decision of Pope Innocent III to the Bishop of Ferentino, who submitted to Rome a case in which the plaintiff complained that five years after espousals her fiancé became engaged to another woman and subsequently married her in contempt of his first pledge. It was the marriage, of course, and not simply the *sponsalia* exchanged in relation to it, that nullified the previous betrothment.[69]

---

[66] C. 2, X, IV, 1. The Decretals erroneously attribute this law to Innocent II (1130-1143), whereas it is that of Alexander III (1159-1181). Cf. Friedberg in c. 2, X, IV, 1, Vol. I, pars 2, p. 661, ftn. 2. Cf. also JL, n. 13903. The glossator's heading for this decretal explicitly qualifies the term *sponsalia* with the phrase *de futuro.*

[67] C. 15, X, *de desponsalibus et matrimoniis,* IV, 1.

[68] C. 30, X, *de sponsalibus et matrimoniis,* IV, 1; Potthast, *Regesta Pontificum Romanorum inde ab anno post Christum natum MCXCVIII ad annum MCCCIV* (2 vols., Berolini, 1874-1875), n. 9661 (hereafter cited as Potthast).

[69] C. 22, X, *de sponsalibus et matrimoniis,* IV, 1; Potthast, n. 24.

Those who deserted their betrothed by leaving for parts unknown gave cause before the law for a dissolution of the espousals. However, Alexander added a new ruling to this old law by imposing a penance upon the deserted women in proportion to her guilt in failing to bring about the promised union in as far as she was capable of so doing.[70]

Returning to the problem of the presumed status of marriage consequent upon sexual relations after *sponsalia de futuro,* Pope Gregory expressly legislated, when writing to the Bishop of Le Mans, that against this presumption of law no contrary proof was (directly) admissible. This legislation was the result of a decision rendered by the Pope in a case involving a man who had engaged in marital relations with his betrothed, but later left her and publicly (*in facie ecclesiae*) married someone else.[71]

B. Capacity to Contract Betrothals

Concerning the capacity to contract espousals, Pope Hormisdas (514-523) allegedly in his reply to Eusebius had ruled that the father is to supply the consent for his son when the latter is still below the age of puberty as the boy is legally incapable of doing this himself. Once the boy had attained that age, it was no longer allowable for the father to perform this function unless the son's consent concurred.[72] The age of puberty was reached at fourteen years by boys, and at twelve years by girls.[73]

---

[70] C. 5, X, *de sponsalibus et matrimoniis,* IV, 1; JL, n. 14043.

[71] "Is, qui fidem dedit . . . mulieri super matrimonio contrahendo, carnali copula subsecuta, et si in facie ecclesiae ducat aliam et cognoscat, ad primam redire tenetur, quia, licet praesumptum primum matrimonium videatur, contra praesumptionem tamen huiusmodi non est probatio admittenda. . . ."—C. 30, X, *de sponsalibus et matrimoniis,* IV, 1; *Potthast,* n. 9661. Hostiensis (*Commentaria in Quinque Libros Decretalium* [5 vols. in 3, Venetiis, 1581], lib. IV, tit. 1, cap. 30 [hereafter cited Hostiensis], s.v. *admittenda*) stated the presumption to be *iuris et de iure.* Cf. Dillon, *Canon Law Marriage,* The Catholic University of America Canon Law Studies, n. 153 (Washington, D. C.: The Catholic University of America Press, 1942), pp. 115-116.

[72] C. 1, X, *de desponsatione impuberum,* IV, 2. Friedberg (in eod. cap., II, 672) states this chapter is a *caput incertum.*

[73] Cf. Hostiensis, lib. IV, tit. II, cap. 2, s.v. *adulto;* Panormitanus, *Commentaria super Quinque Libros Decretalium* (5 vols. in 7, Venetiis, 1588), lib. IV, tit. II, cap. 2 (hereafter cited as Panormitanus).

Once the betrothment pact had been concluded by the parents in behalf of their children, if these were under the age of puberty, the agreement continued without subjection to change until both the children attained the necessary age. The contractant who reached the age of puberty prior to the other had to wait, before ratifying or rejecting the betrothal, until the other had also reached the requisite age. Another possibility envisioned by the supreme legislator in the Church was that of a disparity relative to the fact of puberty at the time of the engagement. The party who at that time had not yet reached the age of puberty could at his own volition recede from the espousals on reaching the age of puberty, even though the other party might be unwilling.[74]

Sometimes affianced children lived under the same roof. Hence, Alexander III enacted that upon reaching the age of puberty the youthful pair should separate, unless perchance in the meantime there had intervened an act of carnal intercourse.[75] However, Pope Urban III (1185-1187) decided that a mere *attempt* at sex-union (*conatus*) was not to be construed or presumed to constitute marriage.[76] About forty years later Gregory IX declared that *attempted* relations even by betrothed *adults* did not constitute marriage.[77]

---

[74] C. 7, X, *de desponsatione impuberum* IV, 2; also c. 11 of the same title. The former of these contains a decision of Pope Alexander III given to the Bishop of Bath in England. Cf. JL, n. 13767.

[75] C. 8, X, *de desponsatione impuberum,* IV, 2; JL, n. 13765.

[76] C. 10, X, *de desponsatione impuberum,* IV, 2. Cf. Panormitanus, lib. IV, tit. II, cap. 10. In speaking of this and related decisions he remarked: "Nota mirabilem decisionem: minor pubertate, major tamen septennio contrahens sponsalia vel matrimonium, potest adveniente aetate legitima sine alia causa resilere a talibus sponsalibus sive matrimonio, licet mulierem saepe nixus [nisus] fuerit corrumpere."

[77] C. 32, X, *de sponsalibus et matrimoniis,* IV, 1. Cf. Panormitanus, lib. IV. tit. I, cap. 32, and Hostiensis, *eod. loco,* s.v. *conatus.* It was pointed out by them that an attempted carnal union was not the act of consummation, and therefore did not effect the marriage: "Nisi perfecte sponsus cognoscat sponsam, non transeunt sponsalia in matrimonium."—Panormitanus, *loc. cit.*

C. Freedom in Contracting Betrothals

Regarding the question of liberty of choice, Gregory IX declared that both the betrothals and the nuptials must be free of coercion. Then the Pope went further by declaring that penalties exacted for breach of contract could not be of such a nature as to bind one to the contract, since "marriage must be altogether free." The case that occasioned this decree concerned a woman named Teberga, who was betrothed to a certain Peter of Alferio when she was below the age of seven. The parents of the two parties stipulated at the time of the espousals that a breach of the agreement would carry with it financial liabilities. When Teberga had married someone else on reaching puberty, the disappointed suitor appealed to Rome and pressed his claims for pecuniary compensation. The Pontiff set aside the claim and declared that marriages must be contracted with full liberty, and that all stipulations of a financial nature are to be regarded as not having been invoked, since they hinder the freedom of choice. Under pain of excommunication, the formerly affianced lover was ordered to forego all insistence on payment.[78]

The final legislation concerning the betrothals of persons under the age of puberty invoked another presumption of law. Innocent III decreed that, when persons over the age of puberty enter a contract with persons under the age of puberty per *verba de praesenti,* the contract was to be regarded not as a contract of marriage but as one of *betrothment.* The fact that ratification pledges (*subarrhatio*) had been exchanged made no difference. The presumption stood as a *presumptio iuris et de iure,* i.e., it was not open to rebuttal nor could any but direct proof to the contrary dislodge it.[79]

---

[78] C. 29, X, *de sponsalibus et matrimoniis,* IV, 1: "Cum itaque libera matrimonia esse debeant, et ideo talis stipulatio propter poenae interpositionem sit merito improbanda: Mandamus, quatenus, si ita sit, eundem B [Petri Patrem], ut ab extorsione praedictae poenae desistat, ecclesiastica censura compellas." The *Glossa Ordinaria* s.v. *stipulatio* adds: "Stipulatio poenae in sponsalibus non tenet propter rationem quae redditur in littera; sed arrhas datas pro sponsalibus perficiendis amittit qui resilit sine iusta causa."

[79] C. 14, X, *de desponsatione impuberum,* IV, 2. Potthast, n. 2775. In regard to the *subarrhatio,* the *Glossa* explains, s.v. *subarrhavit*: ". . . fit

D. The Impediment of Public Propriety

Definite legislation is found in Gregory's Decretals on the new diriment impediment arising out of betrothals. By the eleventh and twelfth century it was definitely felt that marriage was improper if one of the contracting parties had been previously betrothed to a relative of the other party. This impediment was termed quasi-affinity or public propriety (*publica honestas*) and was held to arise from espousals as well as from unconsummated marriages. It was based on certain spurious decretals embodied by Gratian in his *Decretum,*[80] the purpose of which, it appears, was to oppose a change then taking place in the law of affinity. The Roman Church had held that the impediment rose only out of valid marriage that had been consummated. In Germanic law this impediment was regarded as a consequence of the *unitas carnis,* affinity resulting also from the *copula illicita.* Italian canonists at the time more and more adopted this juridic concept until it became part of the Church's legislation under Alexander III.[81] The extent of the impediment, however, was not specified. Until 1215 it was understood to be the same as that resulting from affinity and consanguinity. The decree of Pope Innocent III in that year[82] reduced it to the fourth degree, i.e., to third cousins.[83]

Sponsalia de futuro, if never actually ratified, or if null for

---

quandoque per immissionem annuli . . . quandoque per dotationem aliarum rerum vel aliorum insignium, et quandoque fit talis subarrhatio interveniente consensu expresso ut hic, quandoque etiam non interveniente: sed sive interveniat sive non, dummodo constet de subarrhatione, praesumitur matrimonium." Hence, by this time the ring was bestowed quite universally at the nuptials rather than at the espousals.

[80] Cc. 11, 12, 14, 15, C. XXVII, q. 2.

[81] Cf. C. 4, X, *de sponsalibus et matrimoniis,* IV, 1. Freisen (*Geschichte des canonischen Eherechts,* p. 502) maintained that the law at the time, while prohibiting the *sponsa* from marrying the kindred of her betrothed, did not impose a similar obligation upon the *sponsus.* This was possibly the reason why Alexander III earlier did allow marriage when the impediment seemed present (cf. c. 2, Comp. I, IV, 1) ; but sufficient evidence is lacking for this statement. Cf. Joyce, *Christian Marriage,* p. 94, footnote 1.

[82] C. 8, X, *de consanguinitate et affinitate,* IV, 14.

[83] Cf. Panormitanus, lib. IV, tit. 14, cap. III.

lack of consent, did not create the impediment. This was a further clarification of the law made by Alexander III.[84]

E. The Impediment of Affinity

Another impediment flowing out of espousals, affinity, known as *affinitas superveniens,* was also touched upon in decretal law. If one of the parties to a valid betrothment had sexual intercourse with a blood relative of the other party, this dissolved the engagement, giving rise to an impediment of *affinity* between the *betrothed themselves* and an impediment of *public propriety* between the *guilty espoused party and a relative of the other party* in the first degree of the collateral line.[85] Further, affinity which arose from illicit sex relations, so Pope Innocent III declared, not only invalidated espousals but also deprived the parties involved of the right to contract marriage in the future. Prompting this declaration was the flagrant immorality of a man who had committed acts of sexual intercourse with both the mother of his betrothed and with his fiancée, once she had come of age. The case was widely divulged in the Diocese of Gerona where it occurred. The Pope forbade all three parties concerned ever to be wedded to anyone. Only ignorance of her mother's deed could have permitted the daughter to contract marriage with any other save her betrothed. A severe penance was likewise imposed upon all.[86]

Similarly the same Pontiff adjudged a case in which a man had committed fornication with two sisters (one being his espoused) before and after marriage. For these misdeeds a heavy penance

---

[84] C. 5, X, *de desponsatione impuberum,* IV, 2. JL, n. 13887.

[85] Cf. cc. 1, 2, 4, 6 X, *de eo qui cognovit consanguineam uxoris suae vel sponsae,* IV, 13.

[86] C. 8, X, *de eo, qui cognovit consanguineam uxoris suae vel sponsae,* IV, 13. Potthast, n. 1942. *Glossa Ordinaria,* s.v. *separatis*: "Et nota quod affinitas superveniens sponsalia de futuro rumpit . . . secus in matrimonio." For further discussion on affinity, cf. Wahl, *The Matrimonial Impediments of Consanguinity and Affinity,* The Catholic University of America Canon Law Studies, n. 90 (Washington, D. C.: The Catholic University of America, 1934), pp 78-79.

was imposed together with the command that the man thereafter contain himself from both women.[87]

A further advance in legislation on this matter can be seen in a decree attributed to Urban III (1185-1187), but actually enacted by Alexander III.[88] The decree made clear that affinity when publicly known, as in the case adverted to above, rendered espousals null and void.[89] The factor of adverse publicity was to be reckoned with relation to the locality in which the impediment was incurred.[90]

F. Conditional Betrothals

For *conditional* espousals Alexander III informed the Archbishop of Palermo that a fulfillment of the condition was necessary if marriage was to follow. If the betrothed party failed to fulfill the given pledge, the espousals ceased to bind unless either a consent *de praesenti* or the fact of *copula* intervened.[91]

G. Simple Vow

Simple vows also dissolved *sponsalia de futuro,* but not subsequent marriage, in decretal law. Thus legislated Pope Celestine III (1191-1198), as may be seen from his letter to the Archbishop of Sens.[92]

---

[87] C. 9, X, *de eo, qui cognovit consanguineom uxoris suae vel sponsae,* IV, 13; Potthast, n. 2000. The marriage in question was invalid because of the then existing impediment of affinity.

[88] Friedberg, c. 9, X, *de eo, qui cognovit consanguineam uxoris suae vel sponsae,* IV, 13, p. 701. JL, n. 13790.

[89] *Loc. cit.*

[90] ". . . quodsi manifestum est iuvenem cognovisse propinquam praedictae puellae vel si non est manifestum, fama tamen loci hoc habet: cum esset sponsa tantummodo de futuro, idem ab eius impetitione debet absolvi."—*Loc. cit.*

[91] C. 3, X, *de conditionibus appositis in desponsatione vel in aliis contractibus,* IV, 5: JL, n. 14043.

[92] C. 6, X, *qui clerici vel voventes matrimonium contrahere possunt,* IV, 6; JL, n. 17649.

H. Interdicted Betrothals

At times it happened that espousals were directly forbidden for some grave reason, for instance, when there was present an impediment to the forthcoming marriage or when one or both parties had a case pending in court. However, if it could be established that the purported exchange of consent *per verba de praesenti* was after all an exchange of promise *per verba de futuro,* the subsequent marriage undertaken by either of the parties to someone else was to be regarded as valid even though this marriage was interdicted the while the investigation was in progress. This was the situation when Pope Alexander III wrote to the bishops of Winchester and Hereford. Gregory IX incorporated the law into his decretals.[93]

Article 2: Betrothals in the Liber Sextus of Boniface VIII

A. The Problem Concerning Terminology

Pope Boniface VIII (1294-1303) issued his decretals under the title of *Liber Sextus* at the end of the thirteenth century.[94] By that time Gregory's decretals and the intervening conciliar legislation (which will be treated in the next chapter) had clarified the relation, nature and juridic effects of betrothals, largely through the distinction of sponsalia *de futuro* and *sponsalia de praesenti.* However, the distinction as such still remained ambiguous in the sense that the term *sponsalia* was still applied to marriage unless followed by the phrase, *de praesenti,* whereas properly it referred only to espousals.[95]

---

[93] C. 2, X, *de matrimonio contracto contra interdictum ecclesiae,* IV, 6; JL, n. 14311.

[94] March 3, 1298.

[95] Wernz-Vidal (*Ius Canonicum,* V, 102, ftn. 15) found the distinction ambiguous: "Divisio sponsalium in sponsalia de praesenti et de futuro quae iure Decretalium obtinebat non est vere logica participatio sponsalium proprie dictorum in duas species coordinatas et sub eadem notione generica comprehendens." Schmalzgrueber, *Ius Ecclesiasticum Universum* (5 vols. in 12, Romae, 1843-1845), lib. IV, tit. 1, n. 1, desired that the term *sponsalia de praesenti* be eliminated altogether since it was so confusing. Hereafter Schmalzgrueber will be cited *Ius Ecclesiasticum.*

The same obtained for the word *desponsatio*. St. Raymond explained that this was a popular term for the technical *subharratio* or ring-bestowal, common at the time to the nuptials rather than to the betrothment rite.[96]

B. Child Betrothments and the Impediment of Public Propriety

Added to this was the difficulty arising out of the all too frequent practice of child-marriage, rampant in the eleventh and twelfth centuries. The entire system manifestly was open to the gravest of abuses, as already glimpsed in the Decretals of Gregory. Alexander III had legislated, it is true, that all betrothments arranged by parents before the child had attained the age of puberty were altogether void of effect unless ratified by the child on reaching the age of puberty.[97] However, the law was not being observed. Hence Boniface repeated this law in clear and unambiguous terms in the fourth book of his decretals. The Pontiff declared that the mere fact that the parties had attained the age of puberty and did not express any desire to annul the contract, that fact did not make them husband and wife; for this it was necessary that they exchange a true marital consent. This, the Pope insisted, was requisite even though as children they had given their consent *per verba de praesenti* and with the intention of entering matrimony.[98] Further, the impediment of public propriety could *not* arise from the espousals of children below seven years in age. Betrothals of this kind did not become valid simply with the lapse of time, the Pontiff pointed out, and hence could not give rise to the impediment in question. They were null and void *ab initio* because of deficiency as to consent.[99]

---

[96] "De annuli subarrhatione quae vulgo dicitur desponsatio, sed proprie subarrhatio nuncupatur . . . etc."—Sanctus Raymundus de Pennafort, *Summa* (Veronae, 1744), lib. IV, tit. I, n. 1, p. 463.

[97] Cf. the preceding article of this work.

[98] C. unic., *de desponsatione impuberum,* IV, 2, in VI°.

[99] ". . . sponsalia huiusmodi, quae ab initio nulla erant, per lapsum dicti temporis minime convalescunt, et ideo quum sint nulla, ratione defectus consensus publicae honestatis iustitiam [impedimentum] non inducunt." *Loc. cit.*

Once the betrothals had been ratified by the children when of age, they became so binding that only through an episcopal sentence could a dissolution be effected. However, even when thus dissolved, the espousals entailed the impediment of public propriety in respect to the relatives and kinsmen of the betrothed. Boniface VIII re-enacted the statutes of his predecessors by decreeing that from absolute (*puris*) and definite (*certis*) betrothals, even though null because of consanguinity, affinity, frigidity, religious disparity, etc., there arises an impediment of public propriety sufficiently efficacious to impede and invalidate subsequent, but not to dissolve antecedent, espousals as well as nuptials. He made one exception, specifically the lack of consent. Espousals entered into without the consent of the parties did *not* create the impediment.[100] Wherefore, the Supreme Legislator continued, if anyone plighted his troth without any condition whatever and subsequently offered a similar pledge of betrothal to a relative of his betrothed, the second betrothal was void and he remained bound to his initial contract of betrothal, unless consent was lacking in the first espousal.[101]

The second part of Boniface's decretal allowed for the necessary exception to the law. Conditional espousals did not give rise to the impediment *prior* to the fulfillment of the condition. Hence, so the Pope explained, a consent *per verba de praesenti* with a relative of the betrothed did not result in an invalid marriage so long as the condition had not been fulfilled.[102]

With this ends the decretal legislation on betrothal pacts. It remains now to consider the law of the Council of Trent. This will be the burden of the following chapter.

---

[100] C. 1, *de sponsalibus et matrimoniis,* IV, 1, in VI°.

[101] *Loc. cit.* The *Glossa Ordinaria,* s.v. *consanguinitas,* calls attention to the extent of the impediment, namely, the *fourth degree,* and s.v. *aliqua quavis* [*ratione*] lists spiritual as well as legal relationship, solemn vows and the rest of the usual diriment impediments. Worthy of note too is the observation of the glossator that even a *monk* could occasion the impediment *publicae honestatis iustitiae* (public propriety) by contracting espousals and thereby making it impossible for anyone of his kin to have the woman thus betrothed for his own.—*Glossa Ordinaria,* s.v. *dissolvendum,* ad *de sponsalibus et matrimoniis,* c. 1, IV, 1, in VI°.

[102] *Loc. cit.* Cf. the *Glossa Ordinaria* in *Casum,* in which there is an admirable summation in six points of the entire title.

CHAPTER III

Tridentine and Post-Tridentine Period

SECTION I. TRIDENTINE LEGISLATION

Article 1: The Provisions of the Council of Trent

A period of eighteen years elapsed between the convocation and the adjournment of the Church's Nineteenth Ecumenical Council—The Council of Trent. The first session was held in 1545, the last in 1563. Ten years intervened between the twenty-third and twenty-fourth sessions alone.[1] It was at this twenty-fourth session that legislation on marriage was finally enacted which, together with the other decrees of the Council, was promulgated on January 26, 1564, by Pope Pius V, who had reconvened the General Assembly.[2]

Various proposals for reform with reference to clandestine marriages were considered as early as 1562, when the first minor session was held on March 11th of that year.[3] The first draft for such reform was presented to the General Council for discussion four months later—on July 20, 1563.[4] Since it was felt, however, that opposition to reform measures would be too vehement if they were embodied within the framework of the dogmatic decrees, the lawmakers decided to append them to the dogmatic canons on marriage as *disciplinary* legislation.[5]

---

[1] Pastor, *History of the Popes* (38 vols., St. Louis: Herder, 1923-1952), XV, 264.

[2] *Concilii Tridentini Diariorum, Actorum, Epistolarum, Tractatuum, Nova Collectio* (13 vols., Friburgi Brisgoviae (1901-1938), IX, 1152 (hereafter cited as *Conc. Trident., Nova Collectio*).

[3] Le Plat, *Monumentorum ad Historiam Concilii Tridentini Amplissima Collectio* (7 vols., Lovanii, 1781-1787), V. 104.

[4] *Conc. Trident., Nova Collectio,* IX, 639.

[5] Pallavicini, *Historia Concilii Tridentini* (trans. by Joannes Baptista Giattini, 3 vols. in 1, Antverpiae, 1670), III, lib. 22, cap. 4, n. 2 (hereafter cited *Pallavicini*).

The proposed reforms were opposed until the very end.[6] Few escaped bitter controversy and heated debate. One such proposal that did not evoke violent opposition concerned betrothals. The Fathers discussed the feasibility of prescribing a form for espousals as well as for nuptials. Many of the eminent members present considered necessary some sort of solemnity whereby the validity of the *sponsalia* might be juridically determinable in the external forum. They asked for a certain *regula* or *modus* to be enacted into law.[7] Nothing, however, resulted. Although the Council legislated much on marriage, little was enacted in respect to *sponsalia* proper. The older law, that of the Decretals largely, was deemed sufficient and was destined to remain fully operative except for *two* notable changes. The first provision abrogated former laws on the impediment of *public propriety* or *decency* (*publicae honestatis iustitiae*), whereas the second indirectly (through the statutes requiring a canonical form for a valid marriage) no longer left standing the presumption at law that marriage resulted as the consequence of an act of carnal union following on *sponsalia de futuro.*

A. The Impediment of Public Propriety

In regard to public propriety, the Council in its "Decree on the Reformation of Marriage" declared in the third chapter of that document: "The holy council completely removes the impediment of justice arising from public honesty where the betrothals are for *any* reason not valid. But where they are valid, the impediment shall not extend beyond the first degree, because in more remote degrees such a prohibition can no longer be observed without detriment."[8]

---

[6] Waterworth, *The Canons and Decrees of the Sacred and Oecumenical Council of Trent* (London, 1848), pp. CCXXI-CCLIII.

[7] Pallavicini, *op. cit.,* III, lib. 22, cap. 4, n. 4 et cap. 8, n. 8.

[8] *Conc. Trident.,* sess. XXIV, *De ref. matrim,* c. 3—Schroeder, *Canons and Decrees of the Council of Trent* (St. Louis: Herder, 1941), p. 457: "Iustitiae publicae honestatis impedimentum ubi sponsalia quacumque ratione valida non erunt, sancta synodus prorsus tollit. Ubi autem valida fuerint, primum

Hence, the great reformatory body at Trent defined, first, that the impediment of "justice arising from public honesty" was no longer in legal existence when the betrothment was invalid for any reason whatever. The laws of Alexander III, as embodied in the Decretals of Gregory IX,[9] as well as those of Boniface VIII,[10] which entailed the impediment even when the *sponsalia* were *invalid* for any reason save that of the lack of consent (the one exception) were thereby abrogated. Secondly, the impediment could not exceed the first degree when the betrothment was *de facto* valid. Hitherto, as Giraldi (1692-1775) pointed out, apparently no statute as to the extent of the canonical obstruction existed.[11] Nonetheless, it was commonly understood to be of the same extent as that of consanguinity and affinity, which the IV Council of the Lateran (1215) reduced, at least as far as marriage was concerned, to the fourth degree.[12] Thus, what was merely discussed at the II General Council of Lyons (1274), under Pope Gregory X,[13] scil., that the impediment should not exceed the first degree, was realized at the Council of Trent.

B. The Form of Marriage and Its Effect on Espousals

The other consideration given to betrothals resulted when the Tridentine law called for the presence of a priest and two witnesses

---

gradum non excedant, quoniam in ulterioribus gradibus jam non potest huiusmodi prohibitio absque dispendio observari." For the translation as here presented, cf. Schroeder, *op. cit.*, p. 186.

[9] C. 4, *de sponsalibus et matrimoniis,* IV, 1, et cc. 4, 5, 6, 8, X, *de desponsatione impuberum,* IV, 2.

[10] C. unic., *de sponsalibus et matrimoniis,* IV, 1, in VI°.

[11] "Plures DD. hanc decretalem exponentes, asserunt impedimentum publicae honestatis ortum ex sponsalibus contractis cum consanguinea, hic extendi a Pontifice [Alexandro III] usque ad quartum gradum quod etiam extensum inquiunt a Bonifacio VIII in cap. unic. ex Sponsalibus, hoc eodem titulo in VI°. De neutro tamen id satis constat, cum ne verbum quidem alteruter faciat huius extensionis, neque id colligatur ex ipsorum textu. . . ."—Giraldi, *Expositio Iuris Pontificii* (2 vols., Romae, 1769), II, 481.

[12] Can. 50—Mansi, XXII, 1038.

[13] Cf. Fagnanus, *Commentaria in Quinque Libros Decretalium* (4 vols., Venetiis, 1696), lib. IV, cap. IV, n. 7 et cap. VII, n. 26 (hereafter cited *Commentaria*) ; Feije, *De Impedimentis et Dispensationibus Matrimonialibus* (3. ed., Lovanii, 1885), n. 387 (hereafter cited *De Impedimentis*).

as part of the nuptial solemnity comprising the new and necessary form for the valid contracting of marriage.[14] The former presumption (*iuris et de iure*) that marriage was effected through a carnal union consequent upon betrothals, i.e., *sponsalia de futuro,* no longer obtained, at least not whenever the persons involved were over the age of puberty.[15] In other words, the act of carnal union between a betrothed couple no longer was regarded as of a marital character; in effect it was considered an act of fornication.[16]

This law of the Council of Trent as applicable to adults and persons over the age of puberty offered no difficulty. Its effect, however, on betrothed children under the age of puberty was not clear—as will be seen in a later article. The law, too, was applicable only where the decree *Tametsi* had been promulgated. This was the express will of the legislators, but, as is historically known, the decree for many conflicting reasons was given only a limited publication since it was never published, not only in certain dioceses but even within some states or countries. The Council had made provisions that the new legislation be promulgated several times during the very first year of its existence, and that it was to become effective in any given locality after *thirty days* from the day of its publication. Where the new law was not promulgated, the old law remained in force.[17]

Article 2: Interpretation of the Council's Legislation

Unfortunately, despite the care and circumspection of the legislators, the language of the law enacted at the Council of Trent

[14] Conc. Trident., sess. XXIV, *de ref. matrim.,* c. 1.

[15] Cc. 15, 30, X, *de sponsalibus et matrimoniis,* IV, 1.

[16] V.g., Schmalzgrueber, *op. cit.,* lib. IV, tit. 1, nn. 115-119; Barbosa, *Collectanea Doctorum tam Veterum quam Recentiorum in Ius Pontificium Universum* (6 vols. in 4, Lugduni, 1656), lib. IV, tit. 1, n. XXX (hereafter cited *Collectanea Doctorum*); Covarruvias, *Opera Omnia* (Antverpiae, 1638), pars 1, cap. IV, n. 1; Pirhing, *Ius Canonicum* (5 vols. in 4, Dilingiae, 1674-1678), lib. IV, tit. 1, n. XXVII.

[17] Conc. Trident., sess. XXIV, *de ref. matrim.,* c. 1. For an enumeration of places where the decree *Tametsi* was promulgated, cf. Wernz, *Ius Decretalium* (6 vols., Vol. IV, 1904, Romae, 1898-1905), IV, 237-244; also: Browne, *Handbook of Notes on Theology* (St. Louis: Ligourian Fathers, 1948), pp. 97-108.

was not entirely clear. First, the Council failed to define the term *sponsalia,* or at least to qualify it with the well-known phrase *per verba de futuro,* so as to free it from ambiguity. Secondly, although the assembly restricted the impediment of public property to the first degree, it failed to specify in what line. Thus, doubts were raised whether *sponsalia de praesenti* were also included in the orbit of the new decree, and whether the direct, the oblique, or both lines were embraced in the new ruling.

A. Definition of Terms

Consequently, the Holy See found it necessary to clarify the juridic problems thus occasioned. Pope Pius V resolved the first doubt on July 1, 1568, two years after the official appearance of the conciliar enactment, by issuing the constitution *Ad Romanum spectat.*[18] By this instrument the Pontiff expressed himself thus: "Of our own accord, in virtue of our Apostolic authority, we declare by these presents that the decree of the Council is to be understood absolutely in the sense that it applies to *sponsalia de futuro* only and not, as alleged, to marriage already contracted; with reference to the latter the impediment still exists in all cases and in all the degrees as established in the previous law before the aforesaid decree of the Council. And we hereby ordain and decree that all explain it thus."[19]

The supreme legislator, therefore, restricted the impediment to espousals and called attention to the fact that unconsummated marriage, which in an earlier passage had been styled *"sponsalia de praesenti,"* was still governed by decretal law.[20]

B. The Extent of the Impediment of Public Propriety

For the second *dubium,* which dealt with the extent of the impediment, no canonical interpretation was ever given explicitly. Canonists, however, always held that the Council, by not exclud-

---

[18] Pius V, const. *Ad Romanum spectat,* 1 iul. 1568—*Magnum Bullarium Romanum* (8 vols., Luxemburgi, 1727), II, 275. (Writer's translation.)

[19] *Loc. cit.*

[20] *Loc. cit.*

ing either line, meant to leave included both the direct and the transverse lines. Thus, for instance, taught Barbosa (1589-1649), Gonzalez-Tellez (+ after 1673), Sanchez (1550-1610), Giraldi (1692-1775), Pirhing (1606-1679), De Smet (1868-1927), etc.[21]

Article 3: Decisions of the S. Congregation of the Council

A. Juridic Form

As early as 1573, less than ten years after the close of the Council of Trent, the Sacred Congregation of the Council began answering a series of questions with responses that were eventually to crystallize the law and to pave the way to newer and more timely legislation on this matter. Some time that year (1573) the body of cardinals comprising the Congregation of the Council was approached with a problem arising out of the famous decree *Tametsi,* in which a specific form of celebration was prescribed for the contracting of valid unions.[22]

A marriage had taken place at Messina, where this decree of the Council had officially gone into effect. The ceremony had been witnessed by a notary and two other persons, but no proclamation of the banns had preceded and no priest was present at the ceremony. The question was asked of the Congregation whether the ceremony was equivalent at law to *sponsalia de futuro* in conse-

---

[21] A. Barbosa, *Collectanea Doctorum,* lib. IV, tit. I, cap. *ad audientiam,* n. 4: "At vero iure novissimo Concilii Tridentini . . . limitatur solummodo ad primum gradum, et cum indistincte loquatur, intellegi debet ut id impedimentum non excedat primum gradum consanguinitatis sive in linea transversa sive in recta. Quare iniens sponsalia non potest validum matrimonium contrahere cum patre, matre, fratribus, sororibus, vel filiis sponsi alterius vel sponsae; ut non potest cum consanguineis sive ascendentibus sive descentibus sive collateralibus." Similarly Gonzalez-Tellez, *Commentaria Perpetua in Singulos Textus Quinque Librorum Decretalium Gregorii IX* (5 vols., Lugduni, 1673), lib. IV, tit. I, n. 7 (hereafter cited *Commentaria*); Sanchez, *Disputationum de Sancto Matrimonii Sacramento Tomi Tres* (Antverpiae, 1626), lib. 7, dist. 68, n. 10 (hereafter cited *De Matrimonii Sacramento*); Giraldi, *Expositio Iuris Pontificii,* II, 481; Pirhing, lib. IV, tit. I, n. XXXIX; De Smet, *Betrothment and Marriage* (2 vols., St. Louis, 1912-1913), II, n. 310.

[22] Conc. Trident., sess. XXIV, *de ref. matrim.,* c. 1.

quence of the defect of the matrimonial form, and, secondly, whether the exchange of consent by words *de praesenti* sufficed for the validity of the marriage. To both questions the reply was in the negative. Neither promise, with reference either to the betrothal or the marriage, was valid before the law.[23]

A similar case occurred in 1857 and 1859 with this difference —the parties attempting the marriage were above the age of puberty. Two questions, accordingly, were put to the Congregation, viz., whether *sponsalia de futuro* were to be presumed (in the absence of the required form) in such a manner that the couple could be compelled through ecclesiastical censures to contract a valid marriage later, and, secondly, whether under similar circumstances, but with the added factor that a carnal union had occurred, the parties could be induced under threat of excommunication or other penalties to wed *coram ecclesia.* The Sacred Congregation decided negatively and disallowed the use of all threats and compulsion, since a betrothal was not juridically extant.[24]

Unfortunately, since no collection of the Congregation's cases had been edited prior to 1718, there are no *official* reasons accompanying the decision. A continuous commentary on the decrees of the Council of Trent would have been helpful perhaps in this regard, but the Constitution which confirmed the Council forbade this.[25]

---

[23] Pallottini, *Collectio omnium conclusionum et resolutionum quae in causis propositis apud Sacram Congregationem Cardinalium Concilii Tridentini Interpretum prodierunt ab eius institutione anno 1564 ad 1860, distinctis titulis alphabetico ordine per materias digesta* (17 vols., Romae, 1868-1893), s.v. *Sponsalia,* XVI, n. 19 (hereafter cited *Collectio*). Cf. also Benedictus XIV, *Opera Omnia* (12 vols., Romae, 1748), *De Synodo Diocesana,* lib. VII, cap. LXVII, n. 1.

[24] *Canones et Decreta Concilii Tridentini* (edidit sacerdos Joseph Pelella, Neapoli, 1859), p. 222, nn. 8, 9 (hereafter cited *Canones et Decreta C.* Tridentini a Pelella Edita). Cf. also Benedictus XIV (*Institutionum Ecclesiasticarum Libri Tres* [3 vols., Romae, 1784-1785], I, instit, XLIV, n. XII) for an identical decision, which he reports the Congregation handed down on December 19, 1596, Benedict XIV was Archbishop of Bologna when he wrote this work.

[25] Pius V, bulla *Benedictus Deus,* 26 ian. 1564—Magnum *Bullarium Romanum,* II, 3, n. 5. Cf. also Van Hove, *Commentarium,* Vol. I, tom. I, n. 392.

Regarding the marriage attempted by parties under the age of puberty, or by parties of whom one was under the age of puberty, a serious controversy arose after the Council of Trent. Canonists disputed among themselves whether or not the legislation of that General Council had destroyed the former presumption of law which recognized a *sponsalia de futuro* when the above-mentioned parties failed to qualify for marriage because of the impediment of nonage.[26]

The law had stated that, irrespective of the intention of children when attempting to contract matrimony, at law the *sponsalia de futuro* alone could juridically result. Engel (+ 1674), for example, claimed that this presumption was no longer tenable. His opinion, which he called probable, was based on two principles. First, he said, the actions of agents could not exceed the agents' intent, which in the given case was marital—hence not extendable to the contracting simply of a betrothal. Secondly, he argued, since the question centered about the factor of an obligation, volition and potentiality necessarily were involved. Consequently the rule: "Quod voluit, non potuit, et quod potuit, noluit," applied. In other words, what the person wished, namely, marriage in this instance, he was juridically unable to contract, and that which he was juridically able to contract, namely, betrothment, he had no will to contract.[27]

Schmalzgrueber (1663-1735) opposed this reasoning. If the parties in question did not exclude betrothal from their intention, the legal presumption in favor of betrothal remained, as was clear from Boniface's law.[28] In support of this view he cited Covarruvias (1512-1577), Sanchez (1550-1610), Laymann (1574-1635), Barbosa (1589-1649), Gonzalez-Tellez (+ after 1673), Fagnanus (1598-1678), Reiffenstuel (1642-1703), and others.[29]

---

[26] Cf. c. unic., *de desponsatione impuberum*, IV, 2, in VI°.

[27] Engel, *Collegium Universi Iuris Canonici* (9. ed., Beneventi 1760), lib. IV, tit. I, n. 10 (hereafter cited *Collegium Iuris Canonici*).

[28] C. unic., *uti supra*. Cf. also the *Glossa Ordinaria* in hoc caput s.v. *matrimonium*.

[29] Covarruvias, *Opera Omnia*, pars I, cap. I, § III, n. 3; Sanchez, *De Matrimonii Sacramento*, lib. I, dis. XXI, n. 2; Laymann, *Theologia Moralis in Quinque Libros Distributa* (ed. nova, Venetiis, 1630), lib. V, tract. X,

If the parties expressly *excluded sponsalia* from their intent, then Schmalzgrueber maintained that the legislator nonetheless presumed that the couple wished to bind themselves in whatever form was valid and licit to them. But in attempting marriage, the youthful pair could not bind themselves by an indissoluble bond because of the legal obstruction. Hence they bound themselves in the only legitimate way that the law allowed, namely, by betrothment.[30] If the two parties desired to escape from this juridic obligation, they could always do so when attaining the necessary age, as the law provided for this from the days of the decretals.[31]

Actually, the Congregation had decided the controversy before its very inception, namely, when it had been confronted with a problem along these lines at an earlier but unknown date. In a case presented to it, the Cardinals of this papal commission decreed that the older law was still operative in this regard, so that the attempt of marriage by persons under the age of puberty was to be presumed as connoting the intention of betrothment rather than the intention of marriage itself.[32]

Other pertinent questions pertaining to solemnities surrounding the espousals were also brought to the Congregation. Thus, in 1574, it was asked whether the older law obtained regarding the freedom to contract espousals in whatever manner the couple chose. The answer was in the affirmative.[33]

The Sacred Congregation remained adamantine in this policy

---

pars I, cap. I, n. 17 (hereafter cited as *Theologia Moralis*), Barbosa, *Collectanea Doctorum,* lib. IV, tit. II, cap. 1, n. 1 et 8; Gonzalez-Tellez, *Commentaria,* lib. IV, tit. II, n. 4; Fagnanus, lib. IV, *De Desponsatione Impuberum, in cap. Tua,* n. 1; Reiffenstuel, *Ius Canonicum Universum* (5 vols. in 7, Parisiis, 1864-1870), lib. IV, tit. II, n. 18 (hereafter cited *Ius Canonicum*).

[30] Schmalzgrueber, *op. cit.,* lib. IV, tit. II, n. 61.

[31] *Loc. cit.*

[32] Pallottini, XVI, p. 387, n. 25. The case involved a girl who was ten years of age when attempting marriage with a youth already in his majority. Apparently the canonists were not aware of this decision, since they nowhere mentioned it.

[33] Zamboni, *Collectio Declarationum Sacrae Congregationis Cardinalium Sacri Concilii Tridentini Interpretum* (4 vols., Atrebati, 1860-1868, Vol. IV, 1867), s.v. *Sponsalia,* III, 261 (hereafter cited Zamboni).

and was not to be swayed from its course for the next three centuries. Not even at the instance of the King of Spain, who was bent on stamping out clandestine espousals within his realm, did the Congregation yield in this regard when asked in 1591 for a declaration in favor of a definite form, whereby (at least for Spain) validity might be determinable at law.[34] The Cardinals comprising the Congregation did, however, allow local legislation to prohibit *clandestine* espousals under threat of spiritual and material penalties.[35] Five years later the Cardinals reiterated that the Council of Trent had not prescribed any form for the plighting of troth. All parties concerned were declared at liberty to make their promises in any form they saw fit.[36]

In the early eighteenth century the Archbishop of Braga asked whether he could demand some public document for the validity of the espousals to the exclusion of privately drawn up instruments (*apocas privatas*), in order to halt all possible fraud arising out of secret betrothals. The Congregation on January 26, 1715, did not accede to the Archbishop's wish for the enactment of such a statute within his archdiocese, or for any legislation requiring a set form for the validity of contract of betrothal.[37] Forty years afterward Benedict XIV gave a negative reply to the Archbishop of Cologne who made a similar request.[38] In 1789 the Bishop of Lausanne, and in 1852 the Archbishop of Quebec, were refused permission by the Holy Office to do the same.[39] The Cardinal Major Penitentiary presented a number of petitions to this effect as sent to the Holy See by several bishops in 1865, but the Holy Father did not deem it prudent to acquiesce.[40] Certain Italian bishops were also refused when approaching Rome with a like request.[41] In a rather severe manner Cardinal Consalvi

[34] Pallottini, XVI, p. 387, n. 26.

[35] *Loc. cit.* Cf. also *ibid.*, p. 430, n. 186, for a similar decision rendered the following year.

[36] Case described by Benedict XIV in *Institutionum Ecclesiasticarum Libri Tres,* instit. XLVI, n. XII. Cf. also Pallottini, XVI, p. 384, nn. 9-10.

[37] S.C.C., *Bracharen., Sponsalium,* 26 ian. 1715—*Pallottini,* XVI, p. 384, n. 8.

[38] Cf. Feije, *De Impedimentis,* n. 558, ftn. 6.

[39] Cf. Feije, *loc. cit.* also Wernz-Vidal, *Ius Canonicum,* V, p. 104, n. 36.

[40] Cf. Wernz-Vidal, *loc. cit.*

[41] Wernz-Vidal, *loc. cit.*

(1757-1824), acting for Pius VII, reprobated on October 16, 1817, the synodal constitutions which, contrary to the mind of the Church, Wessenberg, then the administrator of the Diocese of Constance, had imprudently promulgated in 1804.[42]

However, as circumstances offered more proof and the conditions of the times gave ampler evidence of the legitimate need for a set form, the Holy See began gradually to recede from its original position and to allow exceptions. Thus, on January 31, 1880, in the famous *Placentina* decision, the Congregation of the Council declared that betrothals contracted *in Spain* without the formalities of public documentation, i.e., without the signatures of the parties made before a notary or some other official, also other than a priest, were *invalid*.[43] The reason prompting the decision of the Congregation was this: Charles III by his pragmatic sanction on April 28, 1804, had established that only those betrothals would be recognized as legal which were formulated in a public document. Although this enactment was obviously devoid of any binding force, emanating as it did from a source incompetent to legislate in matters canonical by nature, it was, nonetheless, admitted in practice and followed within the Spanish confines. In time it obtained by custom the force of ecclesiastical law, and as such received recognition in the external forum of the Church in Spain.[44] As a consequence, when the Congregation was confronted with the problem in 1880 it ruled to retain the custom, as described above. It took only a few years for the custom to spread to Latin America, where it also obtained the force of law by papal decree in 1900.[45]

[42] Cf. Feije, *ibid.*, p. 435, n. 558; Wernz-Vidal, *ibid.*, n. 104. Other examples of a similar nature are listed *ibid.*, nota 37.

[43] S.C.C., *Placentina, Sponsalium,* 31 ian. 1800—*Thesaurus Resolutionum Sacrae Congregationis Concilii* (167 vols., Vols. I—V, Urbini, 1739-1740; Vols. VI ff., Romae, 1741 ff.; Urbini-Romae, 1718-1908), CXXXIX (1881), 33 (hereafter cited *Thesaurus*).

[44] Cf. the entire case, S.C.C., *Placentina Sponsalium,* 31 ian. 1880—*Thesaurus,* CXXXIX (1881), 33-41.

[45] *S. C. pro Neg. Eccles. Extraordin.,* 1 iul. 1900—*Analecta Ecclesiastica seu Romana Collectanea* (19 vols., Romae, 1893-1911), VIII (1900), 167-169 (hereafter the source for this congregation will be cited as *Analecta Ecclesiastica*).

When asked in the middle of the nineteenth century what constituted a satisfactory form for betrothment in the light of the prevailing decretal law, the Congregation replied that not merely a verbal promise, but signs, deeds and even nods sufficed.[46] The force of the espousal pledge, so the Congregation explained two years later, lies not so much in the wording as in the meaning. So long as mutual will is signified in the formulary, the pact is valid.[47]

B. Consent as the Basis for Betrothal

The problem of form necessarily involved the factor of consent. With this problem the Congregation also had to cope. With their work viewed in a somewhat systematic rather than chronological order, the Cardinals of this Congregation decided, first, that *sponsalia* consisted basically in the consent of the parties.[48] The Congregation referred to several decretalists in support of its decision, Devoti (1744-1820) being one of them.[49] The tacit acceptance of a suitor's promise by the woman was deemed sufficient for validity in the eyes of the Congregation in a case tried before it in 1860. An explicit acceptance was said to be not necessary when in some other way the acceptance was manifested.[50] Several decisions by this body brought to the fore a finer distinction relating to consent. The eminent members of the Congregation, in several cases which were appealed from epis-

---

[46] S.C.C., *Ostunen., Sponsalium,* 26 ian. 1850—*Thesaurus,* CIX (1850), 13. Cf. also Devoti, *Institutionum Canonicarum Libri IV* (Romae, 1830), § CV, p. 129 (hereafter referred to as Devoti); Schmalzgrueber, *Ius Ecclesiasticum,* lib. IV, tit. I, n. 47. The Congregation cited these two in support of its ruling.

[47] S.C.C., *Beneventana, Sponsalium,* 27 nov. 1852—Pallottini, XVI, p. 383, n. 1. The decision was repeated in S.C.C., *Theatina, Sponsalium,* 10 sept. 1853 —*Thesaurus,* CXII (1853), 422; S.C.C., *Atrien, Sponsalium,* 7 iun. 1856—Pallottini, *loc. cit.;* S.C.C., *Tranen., Sponsalium,* 24 nov. 1860—Pallottini, *loc. cit.*

[48] S.C.C., *Ostunen., Sponsalium,* 26 ian. 1850—*Thesaurus* CIX (1850), n. 13. For other decisions cf. Pallottini, *ibid.,* n. 2

[49] *Loc. cit.,* cf. Devoti, sect. VIII, *De Sponsalibus,* §§ CX, CXII.

[50] S.C.C., *Tranen., Sponsalium,* 24 nov. 1860—Pallottini, *ibid.,* n. 5.

copal curias in the nineteenth century, made clear the difference between mere *velleity,* or wish, to contract marriage, or, even more subtly, to become affianced, and the *promise* actually made in all seriousness to this effect. The first engendered a *desire,* the other a legal *obligation.*[51] That a betrothment be perfectly binding at law, the Cardinals in 1787 interpreted the legislation of the Church as embracing three fundamental requisites. First, there had to be given under oath a mutual and a voluntary promise of future marriage. Secondly, the promise had to be accepted by each of the parties. Thirdly, the promise had to be externalized in some particular manner. These three requirements were to concur simultaneously in the sense that, if one was lacking, the obligation no longer could be urged.[52] This was the express teaching of Sanchez and others, as the Congregation acknowledged.[53]

The sentence of *"Non constat de sponsalibus"* was frequently rendered whenever it was demonstrated to the Congregation that the *repromissio,* or counter-promise, was lacking in betrothal covenants. Thus, v.g., a case was decided in 1885, the Cardinals pointing to Schmalzgrueber's teaching as confirmatory of their interpretation.[54] In the event that the *repromissio* was given only after the other party had withdrawn his promise, the Congregation adjudged the contract no longer binding.[55] Hence, both by

---

[51] Thus, v.g., S.C.C., *Tarentina, Sponsalium,* 13 mart. 1852—Pallottini, *ibid.,* n. 11. Cf. this same n. 11 for other cases.

[52] S.C.C., *Romana seu Comenensen, Sponsalium,* 24 nov. 1781: "Ut enim sponsalia sint perfecta et obligatoria, tria debent copulative concurrere, et servari in Sponsalium contractu; primum, scilicet, quod inter contrahentes mutua ac voluntaria futuri matrimonii iurata promissio intercesserit; secundum, quod ea fuerit acceptata; ac tertium, quod ex aliquo externo signo manifestata fuerit. . . ."—*Thesaurus,* XLIX (1780), 164.

[53] Cf. Sanchez, *De Matrimonii Sacramento,* lib. I, disp. I, n. 7.

[54] S.C.C., *Ugentina, Sponsalium,* 31 mart. 1855—*Thesaurus,* CXIV (1885), 130; Schmalzgrueber (*op. cit.,* lib. IV, tit. I, nn. 40-46) mentioned three minor canonists who disagreed with the common teaching by saying that the *repromissio* was virtually contained in the mere acceptance of the other party's word. Cf. also Pirhing, *eod. tit.,* sec. I, n. IX.

[55] S.C.C., *Senogallien, Sponsalium,* 30 mart., 1737:—*Thesaurus,* VIII (1742), 30. Cf. also Sanchez, *op. cit.,* lib. I, disp. V, n. 14, seq., to whom the Congregation referred.

Roman and decretal law, the Congregation held that mutual consent was absolutely essential for a bilateral contract, such as was the betrothal contract when solemnly and absolutely entered into by the future spouses.[56]

Factors infringing on the validity of consent in espousals as considered by the Sacred Congregation were *fear*,[57] *fraud*,[58] and *error*.[59]

C. Conditional Consent

Factors relating to conditional consent in espousals formed a large portion of the Congregation's task of clarifying and interpreting the law in this respect. The basic principles on which its decisions were made were those enunciated in the law of Boniface VIII[60] and Alexander III.[61] In 1725, and again in 1731, the Congregation had handed down decisions declaring that conditional betrothals could have no effect until the realization or fulfillment of the interposed condition was had.[62] Wherefore it was ruled that no compulsion was to be used with a view to forcing

---

[56] S.C.C., *Veliterna, Sponsalium,* 9 iun. 1855: ". . . perfectio contractus, mutua scilicet contextualis ac deliberata promissio, quae sponsalia constituit. . . ."—*Thesaurus,* CXIV (1855), 206.

[57] S.C.C., *Tranen., Sponsalium,* 13 mart. 1852—Pallottini, *ibid.,* n. 52. The Congregation stated that since it was not clear in the case whether consent was freely given, and since probable fear was involved, the betrothment obligation was not to be urged. Cf. Sanchez, *op. cit.,* lib. 4, dist. 27, n. 1.

[58] S.C.C., *Senogalen., Sponsalium,* 30 mart. 1737—*Thesaurus,* VIII (1742), 29, 31. The decision was negative; other factors militating against consent were likewise present.

[59] S.C.C., *Tarentina, Sponsalium,* 30 oct., 1705—*Canones et Decreta C. Tridentini a Pelella Edita,* pp. 222-223, n. 17. The decision was: "*Constare de sponsalibus.*" The error was neither substantial, nor was it such as to redound to error of person. Consequently the consent was regarded as unimpaired.

[60] C. unic., *de desponsatione impuberum,* IV, 2, in VI°.

[61] C. 4, X, *de sponsalibus et matrimoniis,* IV, 1.

[62] S.C.C., *Mediolanen., Sponsalium,* 13 iul. 1725—*Thesaurus,* III (1739), 189; et S.C.C., *Wormatien., Sponsalium,* 21 apr. 1731—*Thesaurus,* V (1745), 151.

the parties into marriage, so long as the betrothment remained suspensive, pending the fulfillment of the condition.[63]

Authors treated of this question at great length. They defined the word *condition* in various ways. Schmalzgrueber stated that most commonly it was defined as "that circumstance annexed to a disposition whose validity we wish to make dependent on its existence."[64] A condition was to be designated as strict or broad, according as it regarded a future and contingent effect,[65] or included also other kinds of conditions.[66]

Many other divisions and categories are found listed in the authors. Most apropos and of immediate importance is the strictly accepted notion of a condition as a factor whose fulfillment is contingent on the future.[67]

Sanchez and Covarruvias had denied that a condition could be annexed or opposed to *sponsalia* or marriage, on the principle that these two juridic entities are legitimate acts which, as legitimate acts, did not leave room for conditions. So long as the condition was present, there was neither betrothment nor matrimony.[68] The principle they appealed to was Rule Fifty of the *Regulae Iuris* appended to the decretals of Boniface VIII.[69] Schmalzgrueber, however, refuted this argument by calling attention to the fact that espousals and nuptials follow the normal

---

[63] S.C.C., *Wormatien., Sponsalium—loc. cit.*

[64] ". . . communissime pro circumstantia dispositioni adjecta a cuius existentia dependere volumus valorem illius."—Schmalzgrueber, *op. cit.*, lib. IV, tit. V, n. 1. Cf. Reiffenstuel, *Ius Canonicum*, lib. IV, tit. V, n. 1.

[65] ". . . stricte, sive pro ea quae de futuro et contingente effectu est." Schmalzgrueber, *ibid.*, n. 2.

[66] ". . . prout includit etiam alia conditionum genera."—*Loc. cit.*

[67] "Proprie conditio solum est cuius eventus in futuro contingens est."—*Ibid.*, n. 9.

[68] Sanchez, *De Matrimonii Sacramento*, lib. IV, disp. I, n. 5: "Matrimonium ipsum conditionem non recipit, bene tamen eius consensus. Hoc est, consensus praestitus ad matrimonium potest ex conditione pendere, at matrimonium ipsum minime. Quia quamdiu conditio pendet, matrimonium non est." Covarruvias (*Opera Omnia*, pars II, c. III, n. 4) had taught substantially the same.

[69] "Actus legitimi conditionem non recipiunt, neque diem." Reg. 50, R. J., in VI°.

laws governing contracts. Contracts could rest on future conditions, except such as are contrary to the substance of the contract.[70]

That conditions *de futuro* suspended the obligation in *sponsalia* as well as in *matrimonium,* canonists generally admitted. The Sacred Congregation observed that they were unanimous in this respect,[71] whether that future implied something contingent or necessary, as long as the condition was not repugnant to the substance of betrothals or of marriage.[72]

Another question raised among the authors was whether or not a new consent was necessary between the espoused couple once the condition had become realized. The answer was affirmative, if it was clear that the original consent had been revoked.[73] Renewal was unnecessary if the invoked condition looked to an absolute fulfillment of the obligation inherent in betrothment.[74]

Controversy, likewise, centered around the problem of impossible conditions. Sanchez, for example, claimed that so many authors concurred in the teaching that impossible conditions were to be regarded as having not been attached, that the contrary opinion lacked rational support.[75] Schmalzgrueber, in opposing this view, stated that the opinion of Sanchez and his followers did not transcend the level of probability. The reason for its probability, so Schmalzgrueber insisted, rested on a negative point, namely, that the silence of the law seemed to favor it.[76] Lastly, scholars all taught that a base (*turpis*) condition, contrary to the substance of *sponsalia,* vitiated the betrothals.[77]

---

[70] Schmalzgrueber, *ibid.,* n. 14.

[71] S.C.C., *Nolana, Sponsalium,* 26 iun. 1847—*Thesaurus,* VCII (1857), 376. Schmalgrueber, *ibid.,* n. 29.

[72] Schmalzgrueber, *ibid.,* n. 26.

[73] Thus, Sanchez, *op. cit.,* lib. IV, disp. VIII, n. 1; Laymann, *Theologia Moralis,* lib. IV, tract. X, pars II, c. VII, n. 2; Pirhing, *Ius Canonicum,* lib. IV, tit. 1, n. 23.

[74] Sanchez, *loc. cit.* Cf. also c. unic., *de sponsalibus et matrimoniis,* IV, 1, in VI°.

[75] Sanchez, *op. cit.,* lib. IV, disp. XVII, n. 2.

[76] Schmalzgrueber, *ibid.,* n. 77.

[77] St. Thomas, lib. 4, dist. 27, q. 2, art. 1—*Commentaria in IV Libros Sententiarum* (4 vols. in 2, Parisiis, 1659), II, 477 (hereafter cited *Commentaria*).

If it was not contrary, then it was to be regarded as having not been placed.[78]

A frequent form of condition encountered in the decisions of the Sacred Congregation is the one that adverted to the impediments. Espousal pacts made with the condition, "provided that a dispensation from the impediment is granted," were to be regarded null and void and of no juridic consequence, according to several decisions of the Rota;[79] but with many eminent authorities a distinction had to be made. If the impediment was one from which the Roman Pontiff did not or could not dispense, then the betrothals were not binding; if a dispensation could be granted, then the juridical effects of the betrothal remained in suspense until the dispensation had been obtained.[80] The Congregation cited Sanchez, Engel, Pirhing and others, as the *Doctores* on this point.[81]

Another case involving a condition which for its fulfillment looked to the granting of a dispensation was adjudged in favor of the defendant. He had married someone else, having remained ignorant that in the meanwhile there had arrived the dispensation which would have allowed him to become betrothed to the party of the earlier attempted betrothal. The Congregation declared the earlier betrothal not binding. In the case as appealed, the man was regarded lawfully married to his present spouse.[82] Most

---

[78] Thus, v.g., Engel, lib. IV, tit. V, n. 15.

[79] Cf. the following article dealing exclusively with *Rota* decisions.

[80] ". . . sponsalia, canonico intercedente impedimento, inita, etiam sub spe obtinendae dispensationis, irrita esse, nec vinculum obligationis inducere, sed post impetratam dispensationem novum requiri consensum, ut priora sponsalia convalescant, docent Abbas . . . Rota decis. 2222 coram Coccinio . . . Alii tamen Doctores sic censent distinguendum, ut si impedimentum tale sit, ut Pontifex, vel non possit, vel non soleat illud tollere, tunc sponsalia nullam pariant obligationem. At si soleat Pontifex super eiusmodi impedimento dispensare, in hac hypothesi sponsalia valida sunt, non tamquam absolute inita sed tamquam contracta sub conditione. . . ."—S.C.C., *Ianuen.*, *Sponsalium,* 12 dec. 1733—*Thesaurus,* VI (1741), 205.

[81] For their references confer *Thesaurus,* VI (1741), 205, as above.

[82] S.C.C., *Bragaten.*, *Sponsalium,* ian. 1709—*Canones et Decreta C. Tridentini a Pelella Edita,* p. 220, n. 1.

cases of this nature involved the impediments of consanguinity and affinity.[83]

A case dealing with *mixed religion* will be treated in the article to follow.

D. Expressions of Consent

Negative and indeterminate forms of consent were scrutinized by the Sacred Congregation. One case in point may be cited here. A suitor promised his beloved that he would marry no one else except her. When questioned about the validity of the promise, the Congregation was unwilling to construe the pledge as one of betrothal, unless it could be proved that the man intended by these words to become betrothed to the woman.[84] The doctrine was one with what was contained in the law of the Decretals,[85] and taught by Panormitanus, Hostiensis, and other decretalists.[86]

Authors gave examples of what constituted certain consent and of what reflected doubtful consent. Certain consent was expressed in such formulas as: I promise, or obligate myself, or I give you my pledge that I *shall* marry you. . . . You may consider me untrustworthy, if I do not make you my spouse. . . . I *shall* marry you tomorrow. . . . I *will* become your consort (husband or wife) *in the future,* . . . etc.[87] Doubtful expressions of consent were such as the following: I shall *espouse* you (*Te desponsabo*). . . . I shall contract *sponsalia* with you. . . . I wish to contract marriage with you. . . . I promise you love and fidelity, . . . etc.[88] The

[83] For a brief description and the decisions in each, cf. Pallottini, XVI, pp. 388-390, nn. 28-34.

[84] S.C.C., *Ventimilien., Sponsalium,* 1 iun. 1709—*Canones et Decreta C. Tridentini a Pelella Edita,* pp. 221-222, n. 6. Also a good case in point can be found in S.C.C., *Mediolanen., Sponsalium,* 14 apr. et 13 iul. 1725—*Thesaurus,* III (1739), 152-153, 188-189. Cf. also Schmalzgrueber, *Ius Ecclesiasticum,* lib. IV, tit. I, n. 54, and for a concise and brief explanation, cf. Ferraris, s.v., *Sponsalia,* VIII, 294, nn. 30-34.

[85] C. 11, X, *de desponsatione impuberum,* IV, 2; cc. 14, 15, 28, X, *de sponsalibus et matrimoniis, IV, 1.*

[86] Cf. Panormitanus, lib. IV, *De desponsatione impuberum,* c. 11; lib. IV, *de sponsalibus et matrimoniis,* cc. 14, 15, 28; Hostiensis, *eod. tit.*

[87] Cf. Reiffenstuel, *Ius Canonicum,* lib. IV, tit. I, n. 30.

[88] Reiffenstuel, *loc. cit.*

doubt was engendered because the formulae were ambiguous and could signify a promise to enter espousals as well as to contract marriage. The specific intention to bind oneself was not found in these last expressions of consent, and for that reason was not to be acknowledged as present. For some the Latin terms *sponsalia* and *desponsatio* still signified marriage.[89] The Sacred Congregation decided in many instances against the validity of espousals when the consent had remained doubtful in view of any ambiguity of meaning that attached to whatever may have been promised.[90]

E. Parental Consent and Dissent

The factor of parental consent for the betrothal of their children loomed large in the deliberations of the Cardinals who made up the Congregation of the Council. Although these ecclesiastics conceded the law's rightful insistence on the essence of the prenuptial promise as being inherent in the consent of the contractants themselves, in counter-distinction to the civil law, which looked to the father or guardian for an indispensable acquiescence,[91] nevertheless the rights of the parents were upheld many times. Hence, just as parental consent was not really necessary but only desirable for marriage, as the Council of Trent had insisted,[92] so too in the matter of espousals. However, if a parental dissent was justifiable, then a dissolution of the espousals was deemed necessary. Benedict XIV actually listed a father's dissent among the just and reasonable causes for a dissolution of the betrothal agreement.[93]

---

[89] Cf. Ferraris, *ibid.*, pp. 295-296, nn. 36-38.

[90] Cf., v.g., S.C.C., *Ventimilien., Sponsalium,* 1 iun. 1709—*Canones et Decreta C. Tridentini a Pelella Edita,* p. 221, n. 6; S.C.C., *Mediolanen., Sponsalium,* 13 iul. 1725,—*Thesaurus,* III (1739), 152-153, 188-189.

[91] Cf. S.C.C., *Ostunen., Sponsalium,* 26 ian. 1850—*Thesaurus,* CIX (1850), 13.

[92] Conc. Trident., sess. XXIV, *de ref. matrim.,* c. 1. For a thorough discussion of this subject cf. O'Donnell, *The Marriage of Minors,* The Catholic University of America Canon Law Studies, n. 221 (Washington, D. C.: The Catholic University of America Press, 1945), pp. 41-54.

[93] Benedictus XIV, *Institutionum Ecclesiasticarum Libri Tres,* instit. XLVI, n. 11. Cf. Pallottini, XVI, p. 409, n. 104.

Particularly when disobedience to the parents seriously prejudiced the well-being of the contracting son or daughter, or occasioned harm to a third party, the Congregation deemed it advisable to act in favor of the parent. Thus a resolution of the Sacred Congregation in a certain case confirmed a local ordinary's dissolution of the *sponsalia* when it was proved that disinheritance would result in the event that the pact was kept.[94]

Another decision voided the espousals because of a tacit dissent on the part of the father of one of the affianced. The father testified that, as his son was of lower social standing than his betrothed, the contemplated union augured ill for both contractants. The woman, he said, would be unable to perform the menial, domestic tasks imposed upon her. The Congregation agreed on the inadvisability of allowing the nuptials to take place.[95] Parental consent, if appended to betrothals as a condition, rendered the compact null when the consent did not materialize. This was the judgment of the Congregation in a case appealed from the Diocese of Pistoia in the nineteenth century.[96]

F. Dissolution of Betrothals

Other causes for dissolving espousals, as acknowledged by the Congregation on the strength of the Decretals, besides parental dissent, were sacred orders received by the previously espoused man,[97] religious profession,[98] subsequent infirmity, physical[99] and

---

[94] S.C.C., *Neapolitana, Sponsalium,* 24 aug. 1723—*Canones et Decreta C. Tridentini a Pelella Edita,* p. 223, n. 21. The case is found, not under Aug. 24, 1723, but under Aug. 21, 1721—*Thesaurus,* II (1739), 70.

[95] S.C.C., *Viennen., Sponsalium,* 19 aug. 1730—*Thesaurus,* V (1740), 26.

[96] S.C.C., *Pistorien., Sponsalium,* 26 apr. 1856—Pallottini, *ibid.,* n. 110.

[97] S.C.C., *Portalegren., Ordinationis et Sponsalium,* 26 iun. 1704—Pallottini, XVI, p 392, n. 40.

[98] S.C.C., *Tudertina,* 9 maii 1719—*Thesaurus,* I (1739), 182, 191.

[99] S.C.C., *Spoletana,* 8 mart. 1678—Pallottini, *ibid.,* n. 152. The woman in the case became lame in the knee after her espousals. She was able, however, to walk and perform her household tasks. The local bishop declared the betrothal not binding, even though it had been entered *coram ecclesia* and with the bestowal of the ring. The woman appealed to the Congregation of the Council. The Council upheld the bishop.

mental.[100] Drunkenness was also declared a sufficient cause for a dissolution,[101] as well as infidelity[102] and scandalous conduct.[103]

In 1723 the Congregation also declared lawful the action of the Archbishop of Milan, who had proclaimed by edict that all betrothals ceased to bind if one of the parties left the country and the marriage did not take place within six months after the betrothal. If the party at home agreed to wait longer than six months, then that fact had to be proved by means of an authentic document before the betrothal contract was regarded as still binding.[104]

Time and again the Congregation of the Council warned against repudiations of the betrothal agreement undertaken without just cause. Hence any subsequent betrothal, while the first was still in effect, was declared with unmistakable reprobation invalid, even though the woman may have yielded to a defloration in the second espousals.[105]

G. Indemnity for Unjustifiable Breach

Compensation for unjustifiable breach was exacted by order of the Congregation in numerous instances.[106]

Other problems connected with espousals, as solved by the Sacred Roman Rota, will be treated in the following article.

Article 4: Decisions of the Roman Rota

A. Essence of the Betrothal Promise

In cases appealed from inferior courts to the Sacred Roman

---

[100] S.C.C., *Civitatis Ducalis,* 14 maii 1729—*Thesaurus,* IV (1740), 295.

[101] S.C.C., *Dubia Sponsalia,* 22 sept. 1725—*Thesaurus,* III (1739), 224-225.

[102] S.C.C., *Caietana,* 20 maii, 1854—*Thesaurus,* CXIII (1854), 239.

[103] S.C.C., *Beneventana,* 29 ian. 1859—Pallottini, *ibid.,* n. 157.

[104] S.C.C., *Mediolanen.,* 2 oct. 1723—*Thesaurus,* II (1737), 376-378.

[105] S.C.C., *Neapolitana,* 27 aug. 1853—*Thesaurus,* CXII (1853), pp. 346-353. To the question: "An priora sponsalia dissolvantur per posteriora iuramento firmata?" Sanchez (*De Matrimonii Sacramento,* lib. 1, disp. 50, n. 1) replied: "Aliqui existimant servandam esse posterius promissum et priori aliter satisfaciendum esse . . . Caeterum dicendum est praevalere priora, quia illud fuit de re iniqua et in praejudicium tertii, quo casu nullo modo obligat."

[106] Cf., v.g., S.C.C., *Colonien.,* 26 apr. 1732—*Thesaurus,* V (1740), 256-257.

Rota,[107] many of the constitutive elements of the betrothal contract came up for judicial examination and interpretation, as they did before the Sacred Congregation of the Council. Thus, for example, the nature of the espousals was declared to consist in the mutual consent of the contracting parties, rather than in the formulary employed.[108]

Several Rota decisions also called attention to the distinction between a promise to contract espousals and the espousal pledge itself. The first, as seen in the decisions of the Sacred Congregation of the Council in the previous article,[109] was to be regarded as mere velleity, whereas the second was the efficacious will to enter betrothals.[110] In a decision handed down by one Rota judge, it was declared: "*Non constat de Sponsalibus,*" unless *both* parties

---

[107] Prior to Pope Pius X and the reformation of the Roman Curia, decisions of the Rota were collected privately and edited privately. The first collection, called *Decisiones Antiquiores,* comprised the decisions handed down in 1336-1337 and from 1355 to 1365. The second group, called *Antiquae,* contain decisions passed in 1372-1374. A third compilation, the *Avenionenses,* take in the years 1374-1375 and 1377-1378. The fourth collection, known as *Novae,* covers the years 1376-1381. The fifth group, the *Aureae Decisiones,* include the decisions passed in the first half of the sixteenth century.

The modern period distinguishes the collections into *Novissimae* (sixteenth century decisions), *Recentiores* (for the years 1558-1683), *Nuperrimae* (from 1684 to 1706) and the *Volantes* (not a new collection, but merely subsequent decisions edited and bound). The last three collections give the text of the decisions with the intent that they be read by the party litigants, and tell before which auditor the case was tried. Cf. Van Hove, *Commentarium,* Vol. I, tom. I, n. 399.

[108] S.R.R., dec. III, *post Coscium—De Sponsalibus Filiorum Familias Votiva Decisiva Christophori Cosci* (Romae, 1763), p. 291, n. 7 (hereafter cited *De Sponsalibus*).

[109] S.C.C., *Tarentina,* 13 mart. 1852—Pallottini, XVI (1892), 384, n. 11; S.C.C., *Atrien.,* 7 iun. 1856—Pallottini, *loc. cit.*

[110] S.R.R., *Baren., Sponsalium,* 26 iun. 1711, *coram Lancetta,* dec. DCLXXXII—*Sacrae Rotae Romanae Decisiones coram Cyriaco Lancetta* (7 vols., Romae, 1732), III, p. 112, n. 4 (hereafter cited *Decisiones*): "Et licet deponant [testes] de aliquibus actibus, ex quibus videretur posse inferri ad probationem sponsalium, tamen cum sint equivoci, et possint verificari in quadam velleitate sponsalium de futuro, non sufficiunt ad hunc effectum, pro quo requiritur consensus et voluntas efficax. . . ."

mutually promised to contract marriage. The *repromissio* of the other party was necessary.[111]

When a lack of mutual consent was alleged by the parties before the Rota, the judges declared that mere statements asserting a lack of consent were insufficient proof. Cogent valid arguments, deeds, actions and various indications had to be adduced in proof, for or against the given exchange of consent.[112] These indications, another decision declared, could be of a relative character, accommodated to the particular regions where the betrothals had taken place. Hence, local custom and practice had to be consulted in every process that probed controverted espousal pacts.[113]

For solemn betrothals, inasmuch as these were legal bilateral contracts, *formal* promises necessarily had to intervene for the validity of the transaction. This was the decision of both judges cited above.[114]

In so far as betrothments "inflicted a wound on the liberty to contract marriage," in the language of the Rota, they accordingly needed to be rigidly, perfectly and clearly provable at law, so that no doubt remained.[115]

B. Witnesses to Betrothals

Witnesses had to be *"omni exceptione maiores,"* i.e., trustworthy, competent and above suspicion, if their testimony was to

---

[111] S.R.R., *Melevitana, Matrimonii,* 1 iul. 1695, *coram Emerix,* dec. MDCCCXXV—*Decisiones Sacrae Romanae Rotae coram Jacobo Emerix* (3 vols., Romae, 1701), III, p. 387, n. 3 (hereafter cited *Decisiones*).

[112] Thus, v.g., S.R.R., *Colonien., Sponsalium,* 26 iun. 1711, *coram Molines,* dec. MCCCXXV—*Sacrae Rotae Romanae Decisiones coram Josepho Molines* (5 vols., Romae, 1728), V, p. 646, nn. 4-5 (hereafter cited *Decisiones*).

[113] S.R.R., *Monasterien., Matrimonii,* 5 dec. 1696, *coram Caprara,* dec. CCCXIX—*Sacrae Rotae Romanae Decisiones coram Alexandro Caprara* (2 vols., Romae, 1758-1763), I, p. 508, n. 10 (hereafter cited *Decisiones*). The local custom described here was the toast and kiss offered the woman by the man after promising to marry her.

[114] Cf. S.R.R., *Baren., Sponsalium,* and *Melevitana., Matrimonii* cited above in footnotes 110 and 111.

[115] S.R.R., *post Coscium,* dec. XXIII—Cosci, *De Sponsalibus,* p. 353, n. 11. For references to other cases, cf. Pallottini, XVI (1892), p. 398, nn. 64-65.

command credence. The priest particularly, as a witness to the fact of betrothals, was cited as one whose "testimony enjoyed the fullest value and probatory force."[116] Relatives and friends were regarded as incompetent witnesses before the law when they had employed constraint in order to induce espoused couples to contract marriage. Affection for kin or friend prejudiced truth.[117] Also, when the espousals had taken place at night or secretly, the testimony of kinsmen was unacceptable to the court, since, often enough, these kin were interested parties to the clandestine affair.

Several Rota decisions held out for the principle that in doubt liberty was to be favored to the exclusion of any contracted bond of betrothal.[118]

C. Parental Consent and Dissolution of Betrothals

Parental consent to the plighting of troth was reckoned unnecessary in the eyes of the Church's Tribunal, i.e., the Roman Rota. Parental objection, when unreasonable and unfounded, was regarded also as unjust.[119] Yet, as seen in a previous ruling of the Sacred Congregation of the Council,[120] when disobedience to parents was tantamount to serious harm or evil, then, once the forbidden espousals had taken place, the Rota judged it wiser to dissolve the pledge.[121] Contrariwise, when no just cause existed, the

---

[116] S.R.R., *Romana, Pecuniara,* 4 apr. 1629, *coram Pirovano* dec. CCLXVI —*Sacrae Rotae Romanae Decisionum Recentiorum Tomi XIX* (19 vols. in 25, Romae, 1623-1703), I (1642), pars V, p. 509, n. 8 (hereafter cited *Decisiones Recentiores*); S.R.R., *Romana, Pecuniaria,* 3 dec., 1653, *coram Melite,* dec. CI—*Decisiones Recentiores,* XII (1670), pars XII, p. 211, n. 6; S.R.R., *Legionen, Puritatis Sanguinis,* 16 maii 1631, *coram Queipo,* dec. DCCXXXIX—*Decisiones Recentiores,* III (1646), pars IV, p. 426, n. 5.

[117] S.R.R., *Coimbrien, Sponsalium,* 14 dec. 1609, dec. CCVII—*Decisiones Recentiores,* I (1623), I, pars I, p. 251, n. 4.

[118] S.R.R., *Maioricen, Sponsalium,* 10 iun. 1735, *coram Crescentio,* dec. CCCXXXI—*Decisiones Sacrae Rotae Romanae coram Marcello Crescentio* (4 vols., Romae, 1725), II, 171-173. For other references cf. Pallottini, XVI, p. 403, n. 79.

[119] Cf. Pallottini, XVI, p. 408, n. 98, for the reference.

[120] S.C.C., *Tudertina, Sponsalium,* 22 apr. 1719—*Thesaurus,* I (1739), 182.

[121] S.R.R., *post Coscium,* votum I—Cosci, *De Sponsalibus,* p. 23, n. 171.

Rota declined to set aside the *sponsalia,* but insisted on their termination in marriage, unless other factors intervened.[122]

D. Other Causes for Dissolution

Subsequent abhorrence between the betrothed parties was deemed a sufficient cause for the dissolving of the *sponsalia,* even though these had been confirmed by oath. The marriage could hardly be a happy one, and most likely evil could ensue.[123]

Regarding espousals between a Catholic and a baptized non-Catholic, it was in earlier times held both by theologians and canonists that such contracts were null because based on a promise of a *"res turpis."* According to these authors, such attempted betrothals were also sinful, although the subsequent marriage could stand valid. Consequently, no juridic effects could flow from a betrothment between a Catholic and a baptized non-Catholic, for the compact was void before the law.[124]

The Rota decided a case in point and declared the espousals invalid.[125] However, there were many others who wished to mitigate this view and to allow for exceptions in those regions where non-Catholics freely and amicably lived side by side with the faithful.[126] Accordingly, when a case with this attendant circumstance was presented to the Rota, it adjudged the betrothment

---

[122] S.R.R., *Calaguritana, Praetensi Matrimonii,* 11 febr. 1647, coram *Melito,* dec. XIX—*Decisiones Recentiores,* VI (1666), pars X, p. 55, n. 30.

[123] "Qua de re in his circumstantiis, pia Mater Ecclesia ad avertenda scandala, ac mala probabiliter contingibilia, abstinet a coactione, quantumvis indubitata intercesserint sponsalia, primitivamque sponsis libertatem restituit." —S.R.R., *post Coscium,* votum VII—Cosci, *De Sponsalibus,* pp. 138-139, n. 110; votum IV, *ibid.,* p. 181, n. 141. Cf. also S.R.R., *Comen., Sponsalium,* 10 iun 1705, *coram Molines,* dec. CMLXXIX—*Decisiones,* VI, p. 125, n. 5. For decretal law in this regard, cf. c. 25, X, *de iureiurando,* II, 24.

[124] Thus, v.g., Sanchez, *De Matrimonii Sacramento,* lib. VII, disp. LXXII, n. 3: "Sponsalia vero inita inter personam Catholicam et hereticam, vel apostatam, sunt irrita, quia promissio illa est de re turpi, et omnino illicita, ac proinde nullam sponsalium obligationem inducere potest." Cf. also Petra (*Commentaria ad Constitutiones Apostolicas* [5 vols., Romae, 1705-1711], IV, p. 74, n. 6), who substantially stated the same teaching.

[125] Cf. Pallottini, XVI, p. 401, n. 96.

[126] Cf. Petra, *op. cit.,* IV, p. 75, n. 11.

valid on the grounds that peaceful conjugal life was possible where Catholics and non-Catholics lived in harmony.[127]

Other decisions by this and other bodies acting for the Holy See concerned matters already treated or points of little importance to the purpose of this work. For mission territories, practically the same decisions were made that have been delineated above.[128]

Article 5: Papal Decrees

Two papal decrees of note must be treated here. The first is that of Pope Benedict XIV, issued in letter form in 1747,[129] and the second is that of Pope Leo XIII, enacted in 1892.[130]

A. The Decree of Benedict XIV

Benedict XIV dealt at great length in his famous letter *Postremo mense* on the question of Jewish converts and their subsequent baptism in the Catholic Church. Toward the end of his document

---

[127] ". . . nec ex eo quod Lambertus [actor in causa] haeresim profiteatur, liberatur a coactione ad matrimonium cum Catholica, quam sub hac spe defloravit; quia quicquid fit in genere, et in abstracto, hodie agitur de matrimonio in Regionibus, in quibus Catholici permistim cum haereticis vivunt, sibique invicem non infestantur, sed familiariter agunt, et pacifice, coniugaliterque cohabitare consueverunt, ideo haec matrimonia ad instar aliorum contractuum civilium ob amicitiae leges, et communem pacem, et tranquillitatem conservandam tolerantur ab Ecclesia iure consuetudinario, quod moribus utentium communiter receptum habet vim legis et canonum rigorem temperat."—S.R.R., *Monasterien, Matrimonii,* 5 dec. 1696, *coram Caprara,* dec. CCCXIX—*Decisiones,* I (1725), p. 508, n. 14. The Rota also cited S. Thomas, lib. 4, dist. XXXIX, q. un.—*Commentaria,* II, 575-583.

[128] Cf. *Collectanea Sacrae Congregationis de Propaganda Fide* (2 vols., Romae: Typographia Polyglotta de Propaganda Fide, 1907), II, 563, where the *Index Rerum* (s.v. *Sponsalia*) points to the various replies, decisions, instructions, etc.

[129] Benedictus XIV, ep. *Postremo mense,* 28 febr. 1747—*Codicis Iuris Canonici Foutes,* cura Em̃i Petri Card. Gasparri editi, 9 vols., Romae: Typis Polyglottis Vaticanis, 1923-1939 (Vols. VII-IX ed. et cura Em̃i Card. Serédi), II, n. 377 (hereafter cited *Foutes*). Cf. also §§ 59-71 of this document.

[130] Leo XIII, decr. *Consensus mutuus,* 15 febr. 1892—*Fontes,* III, n. 613.

he spoke of those Jewish converts who had presented their children, wives and even *betrothed* for conversion and baptsim on the strength of their dominative power over these persons.[131]

In reference, however, to the betrothed woman, when presented for baptism by her converted Jewish lover and then instructed for forty days in a house for catechumens,[132] the Holy Father called attention to the occasional evils that ensued when doubts arose about the validity of the espousals subsequent to the conversion, and sometimes even prior thereto.[133] Wherefore, the Pontiff decreed that all the Hebraic prescriptions governing espousals needed to be observed by the Jewish couple prior to the conversion, i.e., before the woman could be presented for her conversion. The theory was that the couple was bound by that law before they came under the jurisdiction of the Church. Further, the Pope declared that the four following conditions had to be observed. First, the espousals had to be entered into between the man and the parents or guardians of the girl, and not by the maiden herself, for this was indecorous in Jewish eyes. Later her consent was to be given formally and publicly at the solemn ceremony of *Kiddushim.*[134]

Secondly, betrothment contracted in this way bound both of the parties. However, if the betrothed damsel had refused to ratify the compact entered into by her parents or guardians, she was not to be forced into marriage. Since it was not she, but her parents who made the contract, she could not be held to the contract, so the Pontiff declared, in the event that she dissented. She did not

---

[131] "Igitur, quemadmodum cum ad fidem accedunt [i.e. Iudaei], qui potestatem in filios, aut filias habent, eorum oblationem [i.e. ad Baptismum] Ecclesiae libere, ac iure faciunt; ita vir, aut sponsus Christi legem amplexus iure optimo oblationem facit suae vel uxoris, aut sponsae, in quam ius a legibus, et auctoritatem sibi concessam habet."—Benedictus XIV, *ibid.,* § 59.

[132] ". . . suam offert Ecclesiae sponsam, quod haec illico evocatur, domumque Cathechumenorum transfertur, ubi quadraginta dierum spatio detinetur."—*Ibid.,* § 60.

[133] "Clamant in casu eiusmodi nimiam Christianos incertis vocibus habere fidem, et imprudenter agere, priusquam ullis probationibus demonstratum fuerit, sponsalia rite ac valide contracta fuisse. Hinc dictitant damna, turbationesque oriri plurimas. . . ."—*Loc cit.*

[134] *Ibid.,* §§ 61 ff. Cf. also pp. 18-20 of this dissertation.

by dissenting break the contract; nonetheless, according to Hebrew law the maiden sinned grievously against parental obedience.[135]

Thirdly, the betrothal contract was to be regarded *obligatory* and *absolute* when thus entered into by the couple through the above-mentioned intermediaries together with two or more witnesses. This contract, so Pope Benedict XIV stated, was in Rome customarily drawn up by a public notary, elsewhere by any Jew delegated by the interested parties.[136]

Fourthly, the supreme legislator added that an espousal agreement was also to be considered *absolute* when confirmed by an oath given by both parties in the presence of a Rabbi or other witnesses. If the oath was mutually exchanged in private, a written document was necessary to make the contract *absolute*. All other forms of plighting one's troth, if they lacked these formalities, did not fall under the definition of a betrothal contract, and hence could not induce an obligation before the law. The parties were free to recede at any time from a mere promise thus given.[137]

Furthermore, the pope declared that both could mutually recede from an espousal agreement made even before witnesses, provided that an absolution for the violation of the pledge was first sought from the Rabbi.[138]

Thus Benedict XIV acknowledged the Hebrew law and custom as governing their espousals, and held Jewish couples to the Hebraic form, as long as they were subject to Hebraic law. Otherwise there would be serious doubt about the intent of the parties in regard to their engagement.

B. The Decree of Leo XIII

The second papal decree considered here, namely that of Pope Leo XIII, dealt with the traditional question regarding the presumptive marriage as considered in this and in a previous chapter.[139]

---

135 ". . . sed peccare graviter iuxta Hebraeos, debitam nempe obedientiam parentibus, aut maioribus denegando."—*Ibid.*, § 64.

136 *Ibid.*, § 65.

137 *Ibid.*, § 66.

138 ". . . at si de sponsione constet, et de iuramento per testes, tunc recedere licet utrique parti, dummodo praeviam a Rabbino impetrent absolutionem a iuramento."—*Loc. cit.*

139 Cf. pp. 37-47; 93-98.

Pope Leo acknowledged that his illustrious predecessors,[140] Alexander III, Innocent III and Gregory IX, well decreed that *carnalis copula* consequent upon *sponsalia de futuro* was presumed at law as constituting marriage.[141]

In the light of modern thought, however, and at the request of many bishops, the great Pope Leo stated that such carnal union should no longer enjoy the status of presumptive marriage by favor of the law even in places where the decree *Tametsi* was not fully operative. To many people the *copula carnalis* on the part of the espoused couples connoted an act of fornication rather than an act of marital intimacy in counter-distinction to the presumption of law, which in the past was ready to regard such an action as an act performed with marital interest and affection.[142] Consequently, the Holy Father deemed it necessary to abrogate the old presumption and thus to put an end to the scandal that many saw in these presumptive marriages.[143]

It remains now to glance at particular conciliar legislation, in order to measure the trend of legislation toward an essential canonical form for espousals. We will then conclude the consideration of the historical development of espousals with a study of the decree *Ne temere,* the forerunner of the present law of the Code relative to the law on betrothal.

---

[140] Leo XIII, decr. *Consensus mutuus,* 15 febr. 1892—*Fontes,* III, n. 613.

[141] Cc. 15, 26, 30, X, *de sponsalibus et matrimoniis,* IV, 1.

[142] "Plures enim Episcopi exiis regionibus, in quibus matrimonia clandestina contra fas quidem inita, sed tamen valida iudicantur, haud ita pridem rogati quid populus ea de re sentire videretur, plane retulerunt, canonicam de coniugiis presumptis disciplinam passim exolevisse desuetudine atque oblivione deletam: propterea vix aut ne vix quidem contingere ut copula inter sponsos affectu maritali nec fornicario habeatur: eamque non matrimonii legitimi usum sed fornicationis peccatum communi hominum opinione existimari: imo vix persuaderi populo posse, sponsalia de futuro per coniunctionem carnalem in matrimonium transire."—*Fontes,* III, n. 613.

[143] "Simul per has litteras Nostras decernimus ac mandamus, ut deinceps illis in locis in quibus coniugia clandestina pro validis habentur, a quibusvis iudicibus ecclesiasticis, in quorum foro causas eiusmodi matrimoniales agitari et iudicari contigerit, copula carnalis sponsalibus superveniens non amplius ex iuris praesumptione coniugalis contractus censeatur, nec pro legitimo matrimonio agnoscatur seu declaretur."—*Loc. cit.*

SECTION II. LOCAL CONCILIAR ACTIVITY

Article 1: Western Legislation

The first council to legislate on betrothals after the Council of Trent was that of Cambrai. It was convoked for that province by Archbishop Maximilian a Bergis in 1565, in the pontificate of Pope Pius IV (1559-1565). The Council demanded that betrothals take place within a reasonable time (*tempore commodo*) before the celebrating of the marriage. The espousals were not to take place in an inn or tavern, nor was dissolute drinking to occur on the occasion of the agreement. The future bride and groom were to be sober and sound in mind when plighting their troth.[144]

Eleven years later, betrothals received mention at the IV Provincial Council of Milan. Cardinal St. Charles Borromeo (1538-1584) had begun his famous reforms. In one of his constitutions he enunciated the need of investigating the parties' freedom from impediments when they intended to wed or to become betrothed.[145]

In 1585 the Provincial Council of Aix in southern France, under the presidency of Archbishop Canigianus, considered espousals under but one aspect. The sin of fornication committed by espoused couples was regarded so serious that it was declared reserved to the bishop. Each bishop within the province was also advised to impose a heavy penance for the immoral deed. The words *sponsalia de futuro* and *matrimonium per verba de praesenti* were used in the description of the two institutions of betrothals and marriage.[146]

In the New World for the *first time* legislation (albeit brief) was enacted on espousals in the Provincial Council convoked in Mexico, also in 1585. The body of laws enacted by this convocation was voluminous. Betrothals were treated in the fourth book of the code drawn up by that Council. The language employed by the legislator was replete with unction and zeal for carrying out reforms even in the new land of Mexico. Multiple references were made to the Council of Trent, the decrees of which were almost verbatim incorporated in the conciliar acts. Betrothment was men-

---

[144] Can. 6—Mansi, XXXIII, 1414.

[145] Pars III, n. IX—Mansi, XXXIII B, 316.

[146] Mansi, XXXIV B, 958.

tioned only once, possibly because it existed as something new to the natives, or perhaps because no abuse was noted among the Spaniards occupying the new land. The legislator made the contracting of the *sponsalia* dependent on episcopal permission. If a couple plighted their troth without the ordinary's authority, he was to punish them according to the gravity of the guilt.[147]

With the dawn of the eighteenth century further legislation was enacted in the New World. In 1717 the Archbishop of Bahia, Brazil, gathered for the first time the clergy of his diocese to enact statutes necessary for the uplifting of morality among his people. A commentary on the acts of this synod, as found in the *Collectio Lacensis,* shows that the legislation prescribed the age of seven years as the minimum for valid espousals. Breach of the betrothal pledge if accompanied with an act of betrothment to another, or with an act of carnal copulation, merited money fines and even incarceration. Parents and episcopal visitators were to be vigilant lest cohabitation occur prior to marriage. No further particulars appear in the legislation.[148]

Nearly a century and a half afterward the Provincial Council of Ravenna (1855) also passed statutes against premarital cohabitation. Pastors were exhorted to instruct the espoused in Christian doctrine and to inquire into their intentions, not only prior to the marriage, but even before the proclamation of the banns.[149]

At the provincial council held in Venice four years later (1859), the Cardinal Patriarch together with the bishops of the province vigorously upheld the Church's attempts at stamping out clandestine unions. *Sponsalia* were to precede marriage. Witnesses were required for the betrothal ceremony. Mature deliberation on the part of the contractants, and vigilance on the part of the pastors against hasty and secret espousals, were exhorted. Parental consent was to be obtained for the betrothals in view of the Church's "abhorrence" of nuptials contracted contrary to the wishes of the parents, inas-

---

[147] Lib. IV, tit. I, C. VII—Mansi, XXXIV B, 1145.

[148] Cf. *Acta et Decreta Conciliorum, Collectio Lacensis* (7 vols., Friburgi Brisgoviae, 1870-1892), I, col. 851-852. Cf. also the introduction in I col. 847-849 (hereafter cited *Collectio Lacensis*).

[149] Cap. VII, n. III—*Collectio Lacensis,* VI, col. 167.

much as much wrangling, many quarrels and serious scandal as a rule ensued from such compacts.[150]

In 1860 the Council for the Province of Cologne adverted to the practicality and utility of betrothals as a preparation for marriage. It decreed that, although clandestine espousals were valid, the rite was to be celebrated *coram ecclesia.* The reason given was that the absence of solemnity, the presence of levity and the frequent failure of the parties to consult their parents and to seek their approval and blessing made for occasions of sin and often furnished a pretext for seduction. What was light-heartedly joined, became light-heartedly disjoined, the Council warned. The advantages accruing from solemn espousals were then noted, viz., the Church's blessing, the opportunity to prepare for the obligations of married life, etc.[151]

In accordance with the Tridentine regulations, affianced couples were also warned by this Council not to cohabit, but to prepare prayerfully for the coming nuptials.[152]

In the same year the bishops of the Province of Prague met to deliberate and enact statutory law. Clandestine espousals were roundly scored, and the consent of parents and the presence of two or three witnesses, or a written document in attestation of the contracted betrothment, became mandatory.[153] The betrothed were reminded of the impediment of *public propriety* arising out of espousals, and pastors were obligated to instruct the future spouses in Christian doctrine and in the gravity of the obligations attending the married state.[154]

Although the Council of the Vatican (1869-1870) largely promulgated dogmatic decrees, it had planned to pass disciplinary measures as well. The outbreak of the Franco-Prussian War prevented the Council from so doing. Nevertheless, in one of the preliminary deliberations it was proposed that legislation be passed in

---

[150] Cap. XXII, § 8—*Collectio Lacensis,* VI, col. 337.
[151] Pars II, cap. XVI—*Collectio Lacensis,* V, col. 353.
[152] *Loc. cit.*
[153] Tit. IV, cap. XI—*Collectio Lacensis,* V, col. 517.
[154] *Loc. cit.*

prohibition of clandestine espousals, just as legislation was enacted at the Council of Trent in respect to clandestine marriages.[155]

On February 19, 1870, the Bishop of Concordia, in the province of Venice, requested the Church's twentieth General Council to demand a canonical *form* for the validity of the espousals. His reason was that family feuds and various misunderstandings would thereby be eliminated.[156]

The proposals were not enacted into law until 1907, as will be seen in the last section of this chapter.[156a]

Article 2: Eastern Legislation

With the return of some of the oriental churches into the fold of Peter, history records the emanating of conciliar activities from these re-united bodies. Thus, in 1736, there was held the Synod of Mount Lebanon, celebrated by the Maronite Catholics. In the fortieth chapter the assembly enacted that, although *sponsalia* are not required for a valid marriage, nonetheless they should precede it. Since *sponsalia* were of long standing through customary use, and served as a proper preparation and anticipation of the sacramental grace conferred by the sacrament of matrimony, the Council considered it wise to legislate on this matter in a detailed manner.[157]

The Council also pointed out the difference between espousals

---

[155] *Concilium Vaticanum,* appendix, n. 3, *Postulata Episcoporum Neapolitarum,* Pars I, cap. II, § V; "Sponsalium instabilitas postulat, ut aliquod ineatur consilium, quo malis occursetur, quae originem ducunt a sponsionum facilitate, quae vel incaute, vel callide fiunt ab adolescentioribus, qui postea stare promissae fidei nolunt. Hinc feratur lex, iuxta quam valida non sint, nisi nonnullis appositis conditionibus."—*Collectio Lacensis,* VII (1), col. 784.

[156] *Concilium Vaticanum,* appendix, n. 17, *Postulata Episcopi Concordiensis,* n. 3: "Ut ad vitandas contentiones, rixas, inimicitias, quae facile oriuntur ex sponsalibus temere et clam celebratis, constituatur, dehinc sponsalia, quae facta non fuerint cum aliquibus solemnitatibus, ex. gr. coram duobus testibus, ac monitis parentibus, esse invalida, atque cum solemnitatibus inita fieri invalida, si, quin renoventur, annus integer ex quo facta sunt transeat."—*Collectio Lacensis,* VII (1) col. 882.

[156a] Pp. 142-152.

[157] *Synodus Montis Libani,* Pars II, cap. XL, n. 3—*Collectio Lacensis,* II col. 160.

and nuptials through its use of the terms *promissio per verba de futuro* and *de praesenti.* Further, the juridic capacity for the contracting of betrothals was acknowledged even for such persons as were still under the age of puberty, provided they had completed their seventh year and had the use of reason. Parents were allowed to contract in behalf of their children, but with the proviso that the child concurred with at least an implicit consent or at a later date supplied such consent.[158]

The impediment of public propriety was decreed to exist as a result of the betrothal, but to be applicable only within the first degree of relationship, in accord with the Tridentine legislation. Dissolution of the espousals was possible, the statute continued, even when the promise was confirmed by oath, in the following eight instances: 1. through mutual consent; 2. through a prolonged absence (two or three years); 3. through entry into religion; 4. through the reception of Holy Orders in the Oriental Church (in which marriage prior to the subdiaconate was valid, but not after); 5. through a subsequent act of fornication (in favor of the innocent party, but not vice versa); 6. through affinity arising out of fornication with relatives of the affianced in the first degree; 7. through serious infirmity or deformity occurring after the espousals, such as leprosy, paralysis, loss of an eye or of the nose; and, lastly, 8. through a serious disagreement and abhorrence arising after the contracted espousals.[159]

The disciplinary measures as enacted forbade the cohabitation of the espoused men and women as well as all undue familiarity. Only the bishop could absolve from the sin, if it occurred. Pastors, on the other hand, were given the responsibility of keeping a betrothment *register,* in which detailed information on the time and place of the betrothals, the names of the contractants and of their parents, as also of the official before whom the pact was concluded, and a listing of the reasons for the dissolution were to be carefully noted. Documents based on the information contained in such registers were to enjoy full credence.[160]

---

[158] *Loc. cit.*

[159] *Loc. cit.*

[160] *Loc. cit.*

In the following century, a patriarchical synod for the Graeco-Melchite Catholics was held in May of the year 1812. This Council decreed in the seventh canon of its constitutions that betrothment as well as marriage was not to take place between a Catholic and a non-Catholic. Inter-ritual espousals, however, were expressly declared *licit.* The dispensation from the impediment of consanguinity and affinity, necessary for the validity of the contract, was to be obtained from him who had power to dispense, after complete freedom from coercion was duly certified by competent witnesses. (The number of witnesses was not specified.) The age requisite for the contracting of espousals was fixed at *thirteen* years for boys and *eleven* for girls. Not more than one year was to elapse between the promise and its fulfillment, unless the ordinary of the locale granted a dispensation for a prolongation of the betrothal pact.[161]

With the appearance of the nineteenth century there is found legislation from far-off China on the subject of *sponsalia.* Scene of the legislating was the Vicariate of Szechwan. A synod was convened there on the 2nd, 5th and 9th day of September, 1803, under the Apostolic Vicar, Bishop Gabriel Taurinus. The diocesan constitutions, approved by the prelate during the sessions, forbade parents to betroth their daughters to pagans without first obtaining a dispensation.

Furthermore, it was declared that the betrothal contract between an infant and one in his majority was null and void, and that no impediment of *public propriety* could arise out of such attempted betrothals. However, once the child came of age, consent could be expressed. The party who was over the age of puberty did not need to wait for the other party to reach the age of puberty before withdrawing from or denouncing the pact. This he could do at any time.

When helping to draw up the betrothal pact, missionaries were to append a clause to the effect that espousals, when made by parents in behalf of their offspring not yet seven years of age, were invalid unless later ratified by the children. Conversely, parents were to abstain from violating the pledges ratified by the son or the

---

[161] *Canones Concilii Patriarchalis Graeco-Melchitici Catholici,* can. 7—*Collectio Lacencis,* II, col. 583.

daughter until the child attained the age of puberty. When this age was attained by the child, the parents could cancel the contract, but only with the concurrent consent of the son or the daughter.

Betrothals entered into by the parents or the parties in infidelity were, according to the desire of the council, to be terminated wherever possible. Marriage was not to be insisted on unless the affianced pair desired it, and the necessary dispensation had been obtained.[162]

Prenuptial cohabitation, as in other lands, was also made the object of reform in China. But in so heathen a land an immemorial pagan custom needed to be extirpated by Christian law. It was customary for Chinese maidens to dwell with the future in-laws sometimes for years before proceeding to the nuptials. The Synod ruled that this practice was to cease.[163]

Lastly, the Synod announced that, inasmuch as by the general law of the Church, in places where the Tridentine legislation had not been promulgated, the *copula carnalis* consequent upon *sponsalia* had the presumptive effect of marriage, missionaries were to be careful not to grant a dispensation or a permission for new espousals. The presumption was to be retained, namely, that at law such betrothed parties were validly married. Even threats by the party or parties to apostatize were not to sway the missionary from observing this decree. When apostasy did occur, the missionary priest was granted faculties to permit a separation *a mensa et thoro* to the innocent party.[164]

SECTION III. PROVISIONS OF THE DECREE *Ne temere*

Article 1: The Decree NE TEMERE

Just as many evils followed in the wake of clandestine marriages, so too with clandestine espousals. Seduction, particularly, family feuds and civil suits were a frequent occurrence.[165] It

[162] *Synodus Vicariatus Suchensis,* sess. III, cap. IX—*Collectio Lacensis,* VI, col. 620-621.

[163] *Loc. cit.*

[164] *Collectio Lacensis,* VI, col. 622.

[165] "Docuit enim experientia satis, quae secum pericula ferant euismodi sponsalia: primum quidem incitamenta peccandi causamque cur inexpertae puellae decipiantur; postea dissidia ac lites inextricabiles."—S.C.C., decr. *Ne temere,* 2 aug. 1907, *Fontes,* VI, n. 4340.

was time for legislation to appear that would make a substantial form obligatory for the validity of the contract, as in the case of clandestine marriages at the time of the Council of Trent.[166] Many petitions had reached the Holy See from various bishops to this effect.[167]

Consequently, when Pope Pius X (1903-1914) authorized the Sacred Congregation of the Council on May 20, 1905, to consider new marriage legislation, the question regarding espousals was included in the proposed legislation. On March 23, 1907, canons concerning *sponsalia* were added to the already corrected and amended schema on marriage. For the next two years the whole decree was carefully discussed, debated, and recast by the Cardinals of the Sacred Congregation of the Council, of the Pontifical Commission for the Codification of Canon Law (organized in 1904), as well as by the Church's leading canonists consulted at the time.[168] The decree received papal approbation and was published on August 2, 1907.[169] It went into effect the following Easter, April 19, 1908.[170]

The new law on betrothals read as follows:

I. Only those betrothals are considered valid and have their canonical effects, that have been contacted by means of a written document signed by both parties and by either the parish-priest, or the local Ordinary, or at least by two witnesses.

In case one or both of the parties be unable to write, this fact is to be noted in the document and an additional witness must sign it, together with the parish-priest, or the local Ordinary, or two witnesses as mentioned above.

---

[166] Conc. Trident., sess. XXIV, *de ref. matrim.*, c. 1.

[167] S.C.C., decr. *Ne temere*: "Flagitatum simul est ab Episcopis, tum Europae plerisque, tum aliarum regionum, ut incommodis occurreretur, quae ex sponsalibus, idest mutuis promissionibus futuri matrimonii, privatim initis, derivantur."—*Fontes,* n. 4340.

[168] Cf. *Acta Sanctae Sedis* (41 vols., Romae, 1865-1908), XL (1907), 531 sq.; XXXVIII (1905-1906), 208 sq. (hereafter cited *ASS*). Cf. also Cronin, *The New Matrimonial Legislation* (New York, 1908), pp. 19-25.

[169] S.C.C., decr. *Ne temere—Fontes,* n. 4340.

[170] *Loc. cit.*

II. Here and in the following articles by the term *parish-priest* is to be understood not only the lawful pastor of a canonically erected parish, but also, in those parts where churches are not canonically erected, the priest to whom the cure of souls has been legitimately entrusted in any specified district, and who is equivalent to a parish-priest; and in missions, where as yet there are no clearly defined territorial divisions, all priests who are appointed by the Superior of the mission to the universal cure of souls in any station.[171]

Article 2: Interpretation and Explanation of the New Law

A. Canonical Form

With the appearance of the new legislation all private espousal compacts were abrogated. The form, as specified in the decree, was essential. Hence, almost immediately after the promulgation of the decree, the Sacred Congregation of the Council was called upon to clarify doubts concerning the form, the instrument, and witnesses.

To the question whether for validity the betrothed needed to affix their signature to the document in each other's presence together with the required witnesses, or whether, when signed by one in the presence of the aforesaid witnesses, the document might be sent to the other party for signature before his or her witnesses,[172] the reply was affirmative to the first part of the question, negative to the second part, i.e., both parties had to affix their signatures to the agreement, as it was drawn up, in each other's presence. There was to be added, then, the signature of the ordinary, or of the pastor or of two witnesses.

To a second query, viz., whether for a valid contract the day, the month and the year had to be noted in the document, the Congregation responded that these specifications were necessary

---

[171] Translation by Cronin, *op. cit.,* pp. 12-13.

[172] "Utrum ad valida ineunda sponsalia partes teneantur subsignare scripturam unico textu cum parocho seu Ordinario aut cum duobus testibus; an potius sufficiat, ut scriptura, ab una parte cum parocho vel cum duobus testibus subsignata, remittatur ad alteram partem quae vicissim cum parocho vel cum duobus testibus subscribat."—S.C.C., *Romana et aliarum,* 27 iul. 1908, ad I—*Fontes,* n. 4350.

for validity.[173] Finally, to the petition that an exemption from the form as set for espousals be granted to the ordinaries in China because of the peculiar and prevalent customs of child-betrothals, the Congregation responded in the negative. The general law of the Church was to prevail.[174]

B. Assistance at Espousals

Earlier, the Congregation had been asked to settle a controversy among canonists concerning the second paragraph of the new decree on espousals. The authors wished to know whether the local ordinary or the pastor of the place where the couple had their domicile, or where they had been residing for at least a month, or whether *any* local ordinary or pastor constituted the official witness as demanded by the new law. The Congregation of the Sacred Council replied that espousals could be contracted before *any* local ordinary or pastor, provided that they functioned within their respective territorial limits.[175] But, to the question whether a delegate of either the local Ordinary or the pastor could act as signatory, the same Congregation gave a negative reply. Delegation was not possible.[176]

C. Abrogation of the Notion of Presumed Espousals

With the new legislation was swept away the notion and legal recognition of *sponsalia praesumpta* as found in the law of the Decretals. Thus the legislation of Boniface VIII,[177] which had

---

[173] *Ibid.*, ad II.

[174] *Ibid.*, ad VII.

[175] S.C.C., *Romana at aliarum,* 27 mart. 1908, ad VII: "Posse celebrari coram quolibet Ordinario aut parocho, dummodo intra limites territorii eiusdem Ordinarii vel parochi."—*Fontes,* n. 4349.

[176] *Ibid.*, ad VI. Ojetti, *Synopsis Rerum Moralium et Iuris Pontificii alphabetico ordine digesta* (3 vols. et Index, Romae, 1909-1914), s.v. *Sponsalia,* III, n. 3793 (hereafter cited Ojetti) gives the reason for the Congregation's reply: "Parochus autem ad subscribendum sponsalibus non potest sibi alterum substituere seu suum privilegium ex eo proveniens quod ipse sit testis qualificatus alteri delegare."

[177] C. unic., *de sponsatione impuberum,* IV, 2, in VI°.

regarded as valid such betrothals as were made by parents in behalf of their children, provided a ratification at least by way of tacit consent was present, no longer obtained. The reason, obviously, was the lack of the essential form. Ojetti (1862-1932) states in this regard that a minimum age for the contracting of betrothals seemed established. The decree *Ne temere* postulated the signatures of the contracting parties, which seven year olds in ordinary circumstances were not able to give. Of course, the second provision of the decree still stood available. The parties' inability to write could be noted in the document, and an additional witness could be procured. However, Ojetti objected to this last consideration. He declared that it was the mind of the legislator to require express consent of those who wished to plight their troth. This seemed scarcely verifiable in the case of children under seven years of age, he opined.[178]

Discussion on this matter, as applied to Code law, will be found in the next chapter.

The second type of *presumed* betrothals abrogated by the new law enacted in 1907 was that which arose after the Council of Trent, namely, that in which the presence of *sponsalia* was to be presumed when the marriage itself was invalid, not indeed for lack of form, but because of the impediment of nonage. The attempted marriage by fiction of law was construed as betrothment in the old law.[179] The law on the canonical form as passed by the decree *Ne temere* made the old law obsolete and no longer binding.

D. Canonical Effects of Betrothals

As to the *canonical effects* of betrothal, as mentioned in the decree, these were, first, the moral obligation to fulfill the terms

---

[178] "Haec iuris praesumtio (i.e., Bonfatii VIII) non amplius procedere potest iure novo, quum requiratur subscriptio ipsarum partium. Quod procedit etiam in casu, quo filii scribere nesciant, quia nimis clara ex decreti contextu legislatoris mens est, ut ad sponsalia requiratur expressa voluntas ipsorum contrahentium, nec sufficiat tantummodo scientia promissionis ab aliis factae et taciturnitas aut ignorantia et superveniens ratihabitio."—Ojetti, s.v. *Sponsalia,* III, n. 3789.

[179] Cf. pp. 51-52 of this dissertation.

of the betrothal contract; secondly, the contracting of the diriment impediment of *public propriety* in the first degree in both the direct and indirect lines; and, thirdly, the contracting of the *impedient impediment* in respect to marriage with anyone other than the betrothed. The old law remained in force in this regard.[180]

Detailed and further commentary on this topic will be given in the doctrinal portion of this dissertation, for the law of the decree *Ne temere* was substantially that which was to be later incorporated in the Code of Canon Law. The object here has been merely to present the historical development of this topic up to the time of the enactment of the present Code.

SECTION IV. THE APPEARANCE OF THE CODE OF CANON LAW

Article 1: Historical Antecedents

From the Decretals of Gregory IX, promulgated in 1234, until the appearance of the present Code of Canon Law in April of 1917, 683 years, i.e., nearly seven centuries, had elapsed. Of necessity, then, the vast number of laws accumulating over the centuries clamored for re-organization and codification. At the Council of the Vatican in 1870 the assembled prelates urged revision and re-arrangement of ecclesiastical legislation.[181]

Hence, at long last, Pope Pius X on March 19, 1904, issued his *Motu proprio* in which he declared that the "laws of the universal Church be brought together and arranged in lucid order."[182]

Article 2: The Work of Codifying the Law

Pius X appointed a Pontifical Commission of Cardinals (Cardinal Codifiers), to which he added a body of skilled consultants (*coetus consultorum*), to begin the tremendous task of condification.[183] The secretary of the commission was the renowned

---

[180] Cf. Cronin, *op. cit.*, p. 33.

[181] *Acta et Decreta SS. Concilii Vaticani Appendix—Collectio Lacensis,* VII, tom. I, coll. 825-826, 840, 874, 879, 882, 889.

[182] Pius X, Motu propr, *Arduum sane munus,* 19 mart. 1904—*ASS,* XXXVI (1903-1904), 549-551.

[183] Pius X, *loc. cit.*

Peter Gasparri (then Secretary of the Sacred Congregation for Extraordinary Ecclesiastical Affairs) who also alternated as President of the body of consultors, thereby becoming a modern Tribonian, another Raymond of Pennafort. Other consultors, bishops, universities, canonists, and theologians of great repute were likewise invited to collaborate in the immense work. As a matter of fact, the entire episcopate the world over was enjoined to assist in the codification or re-organization process. All metropolitans were requested on March 25, 1904, to set forth what new laws and modifications of existent legislation they deemed necessary or desirable. They were to confer with their suffragans in this regard. Suggested legislation was to be sent to the Holy See within four months.[184] The Commission of Cardinals constituted itself into two committees, one sitting on Sundays, the other on Thursdays. Every bishop had a right to keep a representative at Rome to attend the meetings.[185]

When a tentative draft had been prepared it was submitted not only to expert canonists, who acted as consultors, but, moreover, all the bishops, and those superiors of religious Orders who by law are invited to attend a general council, were asked to express their views. The replies were collected by the Secretary and were discussed and considered by the Commission. Every canon of the Code was thus scrutinized from four to twelve times.[186]

Finally, despite the outbreak of World War I and the untimely, lamentable death of Pius X, the new law was ready. Benedict XV, completing the work of his illustrious predecessor, promulgated the new, codified legislation on May 27th (Pentecost Sunday), 1917. It became legally binding (except for a few canons which became effective at once) the following year, i.e., on May 19, 1918.[187]

---

[184] *Praefatio—Codex Iuris Canonici Pii X Pontificis Maximi iussu digestus, Benedicti Papae XV auctoritate promulgatus* (Typis Polyglottis Vaticanis, 1917. Reimpressio, 1933), p. XXXIII.

[185] *Ibid.*, p. XXXV.

[186] *Ibid.*, p. XXXVI.

[187] Benedictus XV, const., *Providentissima*, 27 maii, 1917—*Acta Apostolicae Sedis, Commentarium Officiale* (Romae: Civitate Vaticana, 1909—), IX, tom. II (1917), 5-8 (hereafter cited *AAS*).

Within the framework of the new law, after much debate and deliberation as to its inclusion and after careful revision, legislation on espousals was assigned to the section on the preliminaries of marriage and fitted into canon 1017.

This canon will be the subject of discussion and commentary throughout the next chapter.

PART TWO

Commentary

CHAPTER IV

Legislation in the Code of Canon Law

SECTION I. NATURE OF BETROTHALS ACCORDING TO CANON 1017

Article 1: Canonical Concept of Espousals

Unlike pre-existing legislation, the Code of Canon Law considers betrothals as a bilateral promise, or contract (*sponsalia* properly so-called), and as a unilateral promise, i.e., a pledge made by only one of the parties.[1] Although the technical term "bilateral contract" hitherto had been seldom used to describe betrothments, decretal law, as well as the decree *Ne temere* of 1908, saw in betrothals a *mutual* pact, a promise by one party with a reciprocal promise expressed in some way by the other party.[2]

The Decretals had followed faithfully the celebrated definition of Pope Nicholas I, scil.: "Espousals are pacts of promise [*promissa foedera*] of future marriage."[3] The definition did not differ essentially from that of Florentinus of Roman Law fame who defined betrothals as "the mention and promise (*mentio et repromissio*) of future marriage."[4] The terms "foedera" and "repromissio" indicate the mutuality and reciprocity of consent.

Likewise the legislator of the *Ne temere* did not deviate from his predecessor in this regard—the difference then introduced being the solemnity of canonical form which he made juridically mandatory so as to preclude further clandestinity.[5]

Since, therefore, *sponsalia* are construed in the Code as both bilateral and unilateral contracts, or promises, it will be advisable

---

[1] Can. 1017, § 1: "Matrimonii promissio sive unilateralis, sive bilateralis, seu sponsalitia. . . ."

[2] Cf. the entire Sec. II, Chap. II, of this dissertation for decretal law, and Sec. III of the same chapter on the legislation of the decree *Ne temere*.

[3] Nicholaus I, *Responsa ad Consulta Bulgarorum*, c. III—Mansi, XV, 402. Cf. also pp. 26-30 of this work.

[4] D. (23.1) 1. Cf. p. 4 of this dissertation.

[5] S.C.C., decr. *Ne temere—Fontes*, n. 4340.

to elucidate at least briefly the notion and divisions of contracts in general. To effect this it is necessary to hark back once more to Roman law.

Labeo, a jurist living in the last half of the first century B. C., and the beginning of the first century, A.D., succinctly stated that a contract is a "mutual obligation."[6] Canonists and moralists have enlarged on this basic concept (considered here causally (*causaliter*) by Labeo).[7] Thus, De Lugo (1583-1660) for instance defined a contract as an "agreement and consent of two or more parties in one and the same resolve."[8] This was the definition originally furnished by Ulpian.[9]

More accurately, however, a contract as known at law today is an agreement whereby one or more of the parties acquire a right, *in rem* or *in personam,* in relation to some person, thing, act or forbearance.[10] It is the result of the concurrence of agreement and obligation, i.e., an agreement enforceable at law made between two or more persons by which rights are acquired by one or more of the parties to acts or forbearances, i.e., abstentions from acts, on the part of one or other of the contractants.[11]

An *agreement,* in the sense in which the term is used in the law of contracts, means an expression on the part of two or more persons, either by words or by conduct, of a common intention. In legal contemplation, at least, there must be a meeting of two minds in one and the same intention, as De Lugo and all legalists aver. An *obligation,* on the other hand, as understood in the law of contracts, is a legal bond whereby constraint is laid upon a

[6] ". . . ultro citroque obligationem . . ."—D. (50.16) 19.

[7] "Accipitur enim causaliter, non enim est contractus ipsa obligatio, sed causa obligationis."—De Lugo, *De Iustitia et Iure* (4 vols. in 2, Venetiis, 1718), II, disp. XXII, Sec. I, n. 1 (hereafter cited *De Iustitia*).

[8] "Est autem [contractus] pactum duorum vel plurium in idem placitum atque consensus."—De Lugo, *loc. cit.* Cf. also Molina, *De Iustitia et Iure, Opera Omnia Tractatibus Quinque Tomisque Totidem Comprehensa* (5 vols. in 4, Coloniae, 1759), II, disp. CCLII, n. 3 (hereafter cited *De Iustitia*).

[9] D. (2.16) 1.

[10] Cf. Smith, *Handbook of Elementary Law* (2. ed. by Archie W. Gray, Hornbook Series, St. Paul: West Publ. Co., 1939), p. 260 (hereafter cited *Elementary Law*).

[11] Smith, *loc. cit.*

person or a group of persons to act or to forbear on behalf of another person or group of persons. Hence, an agreement which results in a contract is an agreement which directly contemplates an obligation, and a contractual obligation is that form of obligation which springs directly from an agreement. Thus, to establish a contractual relation there must be a distinct communication by the parties to one another of their intention, a.v., an offer and an acceptance.[12] Hence, De Lugo comments, a contract, in the strict sense engenders an obligation in both parties.[13] Today this type of contract is known as bilateral or synallagmatic.[14]

On the other hand, contracts in the broad sense beget an obligation only in one of the parties, scil., in the promisor. This type of contract is called unilateral.[15] However, it is commonly called a promise. The Code employs the generic term "promise" when referring to both types of espousal contracts, as mentioned previously.[16] Careful reference, nonetheless, is made in the Code to the fact that espousals in the proper sense belong to the bilateral class, i.e., give rise to an obligation in both contractants.[17]

A unilateral contract is one in which a promise is given by one party in exchange for actual performance by the other party, v.g., an offer of a reward. In this type of contract the promisee is not bound to perform the requested act or forbearance, but if he does, the contract comes into being and the promisor is bound to fulfill his pledge. A bilateral contract, obviously, is one in which mutual promises are given and exchanged, as just explained.[18]

---

[12] Cf. Smith, *ibid.*, pp. 260-261.

[13] ". . . contractus stricte acceptus exigit obligationem utriusque mutuam quae in omni proprio et stricto contractu invenitur."—De Lugo, *De Iustitia*, II, disp. XXII, sec. I, n. 1.

[14] Smith, *op. cit.*, p. 261. Cf. also Noldin-Schmidt, *Summa Theologiae Moralis* (3 vols., 1940-1941, Vol. I, De Principiis, 17. ed., 1940, Vol. II, *De Praeceptis*, 17. ed., 1941, Vol. III, *De Sacramentis*, 16. ed., 1940, Oenipotente), II, n. 524; Davis, *Moral and Pastoral Theology* (4 vols., Vol. II, 5. ed., 1946, New York: Sheed and Ward), II, 353. Cf. also D. (50.16) 19.

[15] De Lugo, *ibid.*, n. 2; Smith, Davis, *loc. citatis.*

[16] Can. 1017, § 1: "Matrimonii promissio sive unilateralis, sive bilateralis seu sponsalitia. . . ."

[17] *Loc. cit.*

[18] Cf. Smith, *Elementary Law*, p. 261.

Another classification of contracts of some moment is the one involving nomenclature. From Roman Law days onward contracts have been divided into nominate and innominate.[19] Nominate contracts are those which are specified by name, v.g., sale, barter, exchange, etc.[20] Innominate contracts, as the term clearly implies, have no proper appellation.[21] They are reducible to four categories, viz.: *Do ut des; Do ut facias; Facio ut des; Facio ut facias.*[22] Espousals fall under the nominate class.[23]

Another important classification is that which divides contracts into real, verbal, literal and consensual. When a contract is concluded by the delivery of the object agreed upon, it is styled a real contract; if by a set form of words alone, then a verbal contract is had; when writing is employed, a literal contract comes into being; when by consent alone, a consensual contract is born.[24] The contract of solemn affiancement, as legally recognized by the Church today and which alone enjoys canonical effects, is a *literal* contract.

Still another and very momentous consideration involves contractual obligation. This problem will be treated at great length in Article 7 of the following Section V of this work.

Lastly, a distinction is made between *onerous* and *gratuitous* contracts. The first is a bilateral agreement because a mutual obligation is engendered. The second is the unilateral promise for the reason that only one party contracts an obligation, namely he who promises something, a.v., the promisor.[25] Espousals properly so called, i.e., as bilateral compacts, are onerous contracts.

---

[19] D. (19.5) 1-5. Cf. also De Lugo, *op. cit.*, sec. II, n. 1; Molina, *op. cit.*, disp. CCLIII, n. 1.

[20] De Lugo, Molina, *loc. citatis.*

[21] *Loc. cit.* The term is no longer used in Anglo American Law. Cf. Sherman, *Roman Law in the Modern World*, II, n. 760.

[22] De Lugo, *De Iustitia*, II, disp. XXII, sec. II, n. 1; Molina, *De Iustitia*, tract. II, disp. CCLIII, n. 1.

[23] "Eiusdem generis [contracti nominati] sunt, locatio, societas, commodatum, mutuum, et alii similes, in quibus computa sponsalia et matrimonium."—Molina, *loc. cit.*

[24] G. (3. 89-90); (3.13) 2, (3.14), (3.15); Molina, *op. cit.*, disp. CCLIV; De Lugo, *op. cit.*, sec. III

[25] Thus, v.g., De Lugo, *De Iustitia*, II, disp. XXII, sec. IV, nn. 29 sqq.

Under the aspect of a unilateral promise, betrothals are gratuitous contracts.

Article 2: Subject Matter of the Betrothal Contract

Upon examination of the contractual aspect of betrothment, it becomes necessary to speak of its constituent element, namely, the promise of future marriage itself. This promise, so all canonists agree, differs from a *mere* proposal or desire to enter into espousals. De Lugo, for instance, drew an excellent distinction between a promise and a proposal. The latter, he explained, even when externally manifested, is an intention, a resolution of performing some act in the future without, however, imposing upon oneself a new obligation. An example of such an intention is had in the penitent who resolves not to sin again. This sort of proposal does not beget a new obligation to avoid sin—for the reason that the contrite sinner does not intend to commit new sins by failing to live up to his resolve. On the other hand, one who sincerely and seriously makes a promise not only gives expression to his resolve but also manifests his intent to oblige himself, to come under some obligation, so that on failure to fulfill he will be acting contrary to some virtue, be it fidelity or justice.[26]

Desire, i.e., mere velleity, as previously seen in the preceding chapter,[27] also differs greatly from a betrothment pact. The Sacred Congregation of the Council decided this question in several cases brought before it at various times.[28] The Roman Rota decided in like fashion when confronted with this problem.[29] The basic difference between the two concepts is that a promise as such carries with it an obligation, has juridic effects in respect to betrothals, whereas mere desire or simple velleity to contract

---

[26] De Lugo, *De Iustitia,* II, disp. XXIII, sec. I, n. 1.

[27] Cf. pp. 59-60 of this thesis.

[28] Thus, v.g., S.C.C. *Tarentina., Sponsalium,* 13 mart. 1852—Pallottini, XVI, p. 384, n. 11

[29] S.R.R., *Baren., Sponsalium,* 26 iun. 1711, *coram Lancetta,* dec. DCLXXXII—*Decisiones,* III, 112, n. 4. Cf. also pp. 69-70 of this work.

espousals carries no such obligation, as is the case with a mere proposal.[80]

SECTION II. QUALITIES OF THE BETROTHAL CONTRACT

Article 1: Genuineness or Sincerity of the Betrothal Promise

To meet canonical requirements the betrothment promise must be internal, i.e., true, mutual (except in its unilateral form), deliberate, freely exchanged (freely given by one party and freely accepted by the other in unilateral espousals), literal and, lastly, specific, i.e., determinate.

The first four of these requisites will be treated in this article, the last two in the section (dealing with juridic form) to follow. The bilateral and unilateral species of contracts will be treated simultaneously, a notation being made of the differences wherever they occur.

The first qualification characterizing a canonical promise of future marriage is *truth* or sincerity. Fictitious or feigned promises of themselves do not bind the conscience, but they would be upheld in the external form till proven fictitious, as will be shortly explained. Now, fiction may be had, first, when the promisor indeed entertains the notion of obligating himself, but, at the same time, does not have the intention of fulfilling that obligation, and, secondly, when he entertains no notion even of obligating himself, but simply pronounces the words and at the same time positively bars all intention of assuming any obligation.[81]

The first type of fiction in the unanimous verdict of canonists

---

[80] *Loc. cit.* Cf. also Sanchez, *De Martimonii Sacramento,* lib. I, disp. 5, n. 12 sq.; Schmalzgrueber, *Ius Ecclesiasticum,* lib. IV, tit, I, n. 49; Gasparri, *De Matrimonio,* I, n. 53; Wernz-Vidal, *Ius Canonicum,* V, n. 79; De Smet, *De Sponsalibus et Matrimonio,* n. 45; Coronata, *Institutiones Iuris Canonici de Sacramentis* (3 vols., Taurini: Marietti, 1943-1946), III, 47-48 (hereafter cited *De Sacramentis;* Cappello, *De Sacramentis,* V, n. 82.

[81] "Potest fictio in promissione sponsalitia contingere dupliciter. 1. Quando promittens habet quidem animum promittendi, non tamen animum eam implendi. 2. Quando etiam non habet animum promittendi, sed verba solum pronuntiat, positive excludens animum se obligandi."—Schmalzgrueber, *Ius Ecclesiasticum,* lib. IV, tit. I, n. 25.

actually engenders an obligation, although the promisor by so doing commits sin, since a promise implies fidelity as to its fulfillment.[32]

There is doubt among writers, however, as to the existence of an obligation in the second species of fiction. A few of the older moralists[33] contended that the promisor *was bound* both in fidelity and in justice to keep his promise. He was obligated out of fidelity, since he gave his pledge to marry in the future; in justice, since the other party accepted the offer as genuine and sincere.[34]

Greater authority, however, was had for the opposite view. Sanchez (1550-1610), Lessius (1554-1623), Laymann (1574-1635), Pirhing (1606-1679), Schmalzgrueber (1663-1735) and others argued that the very substratum of a promise is based on the notion of obligation. Hence, if no obligation was intended by the deceitful promisor, no espousal promise could result.[35]

Schmalzgrueber specifically answered his opponents by insisting that the deceiver is *not bound* to fulfill his false promise out of fidelity, because fidelity arises only out of a true and sincere promise. Nor is he bound to fulfill his pledge out of justice, because justice arises only when a right has been transferred to the promisee, whereby the said promisee acquires grounds to seek its fulfillment. Hence, this type of fiction invalidates the betrothal contract.[36]

Among modern commentators, Cappello sides with all the old authors as to the validity of the first type of fictitious promise. He acknowledges betrothment as binding when the intention of

---

[32] *Loc. cit.*

[33] Cf. Schmulzgrueber, *loc. cit.*, for a list of these authors.

[34] Thus, v.g. Vazquez, *Opera Omnia* (8 vols. in 7, Lugduni, 1531), VII, Disp. IV, *De Matrimonii Sacramento,* cap. III, n. 27 (hereafter reference will be made only to the section *De Matrimonii Sacramento* as found in Vol. VII of the *Opera Omnia*).

[35] Sanchez, *De Matrimonii Sacramento,* lib. I, disp. IX, n. 5; Lessius, *De Iustitia et Iure* (3. ed., 4 vols. in 1, Antverpiae, 1612), lib. 2, cap. 18, dub. 5 (hereafter cited *De Iustitia*); Laymann, *Theologia Moralis,* lib. V, tract. X, pars I, cap. I, n. 10; Pirhing, *Ius Canonicum,* lib. IV, tit. I, sec. 1, n. IV; Schmalzgrueber, *Ius Ecclesiasticum,* lib. I, tit. I, n. 29.

[36] Schmalzgrueber, *loc. cit.*

obligation is present, though the intention of fulfilling that obligation is lacking, on the principle that simulation and fiction in the *strict sense* are present only where the intent to assume the obligation does not concur.[37] Cappello does not consider the second category of specious promises. Nonetheless, as can be gathered from the answer which he gives to the first problem above, no obligation can arise out of this type of promise if the will positively excludes all obligation. Consequently, the inference is that this sort of promise does not bind.[38] Hence, instead of treating this problem theoretically, this canonist observes that in practice the law in the *external* forum presumes a promise to be valid and true till the contrary is proved. In the *internal* forum, on the other hand, a *fictitious* promise does not give rise to any obligation.[39]

Coronata also disposes of the problem by stating that consent is presumed true when the proper canonical form as prescribed by the Code is observed.[40]

Summarizing and concluding the consideration of this controversy, one may state that all canonists unanimously agree that espousals are valid and the promise to marry binds in both *fora* when the promisor entertains the notion of obligating himself to a specific performance, scil., to a future marriage, but does not intend to execute that promise. All authors, *including* those opposed to Vazquez (1549-1604), also concur in the view that when total simulation occurs the promise is regarded valid in the external forum till the fraud is proved. Lastly, all authors, *except* Vazquez and his few followers, affirm that no obligation is effected in the *internal* forum when total simulation has taken place. Hence, the common opinion is against the Spanish canonist. This common

---

[37] "Qui matrimonium promittit cum animo se obligandi, at sine voluntate susceptam obligationem adimplendi, sponsalia valide init, nam simulatio seu fictio proprie dicta, in ordine ad contractus, tunc solum habetur, cum deest intentio sese obligandi."—Cappello, *De Sacramentis,* V, n. 83.

[38] *Loc. cit.*

[39] "In foro externo donec contrarium probetur, promissio semper habetur ut vera et valida; in foro interno ficta promissio nullam parit obligationem." —Cappello, *loc. cit.*

[40] Coronata, *De Sacramentis,* III, n. 45.

opinion the writer regards more probable than that of Vazquez, since the very substance of a promise lies in the intention to bind oneself. This intention is not found in the case contemplated. Therefore, no obligation ensues in conscience.

Article 2: Acceptance of the Betrothal Promise

A second quality imperative in a promise of betrothment is its acceptance and, in the case of a bilateral espousal contract, also its *mutual exchange*.

All authors are in agreement concerning the need of accepting the betrothal promise. The very nature of a promise presupposes its acceptance, otherwise no obligation can ensue so as to bind the promisor to his pledge. The promise is worthless unless accepted.[41]

Prior to the Code, when only the bilateral type of betrothal contract was recognized by the law, it was debated whether on the part of the second party the mere acceptance of a promise of marriage without the reciprocal promise to marry in the future by the same second party sufficed for validity. Vazquez and a few others[42] believed that valid espousals were had in such a case, because the acceptance carried with it a *virtual reciprocal promise*. In other words, the reciprocal promise was *already contained* in the acceptance of the promisor's word to marry at some future date. Acceptance *implicitly* conveyed the notion that the accepting party promised in turn to marry the promisor, so Vazquez declared.[43]

Schmalzgrueber refuted the reasoning of the Spanish canonist by observing that the betrothment contract cannot be gratuitous

---

[41] Thus, v.g., Gasparri (*De Matrimonio*, n. 53) states: "In definitione [sponsalium] dicitur promissio, sine qua sponsalia non intelliguntur. Promissio, inquam, ab una parte facta alteri et acceptata, quia promissio non acceptata nil prodest." Cf. also Schmalzgrueber, *Ius Ecclesiasticum*, lib. IV, tit. I, n. 40, where he says: "Matrimonium autem, et sponsalia, habent rationem contractus: ergo nec promissio futuri matrimonii obligat, nisi eidem accedat acceptatio promissarii." Thus, too, De Lugo, *De Iustitia*, I, disp. XXII, nn. 26-32.

[42] Cf. Schmalzgrueber, *loc. cit.*, for the list of these authors.

[43] Vazquez, *Opera Omnia*, VII, disp. IV, cap. II, nn. 1-19.

nor can it bind only one party, since it is defined as the *"mentio, et repromissio futurarum nuptiarum."* Hence, it does not suffice, he concluded, that one party merely accept the other party's promise. It is necessary, he concluded, for the party to reply to the promisor and promise him marriage in turn.[44]

Sanchez, Laymann, Engel, Reiffenstuel and many others were of the same opinion.[45] It was conceded, however, that *under certain circumstances,* peculiar to the old law, the reciprocal promise could be construed from "mere" acceptance of the promise given by the promisor, as when marriage or carnal intercourse with the espoused, who was ordinarily a virtuous and moral woman, followed very soon, if not immediately, in the wake of the espousal promise.[46] A reciprocal promise could also be construed, these authors added, when the acceptance by the promisee was taken by the onlookers to mean an actual return of the promise, i.e., when common estimation saw a mutuality of promise in the acceptance.[47]

The controversy is of no practical consequence today. Present legislation acknowledges the existence of a unilateral promise of betrothment in addition to the traditional bilateral type. Furthermore, a specific instrument is demanded by law, if canonical effects are to follow, in which the mutual promises are set forth in writing when the contract is bilateral, or promise and acceptance are written out when the unilateral form is employed, followed by the signatures of the parties and the witnesses, as will be later explained.[48]

---

[44] Schmalzgrueber, *Ius Ecclesiasticum,* lib. IV, tit. I, n. 42.

[45] Cf. Sanchez, *De Matrimonii Sacramento,* lib. I, disp. V, n. 12; Laymann, *Theologia Moralis,* lib. V, tract. X, cap. I, n. 2; Engel, *Collegium Iuris Canonici,* lib. IV, tit. II, nn. 2, 3, 8; Reiffenstuel, *Ius Canonicum,* lib. IV, tit. 1, § 1, n. 15.

[46] In the territory where the decree *Tametsi* was not binding, sexual intercourse constituted marriage by a presumption of law when it followed on espousals, until Pope Leo in 1892 abrogated whatever legal force had attached to that presumption. Cf. also pp. 75-76 of this thesis.

[47] Thus, v.g. Engel, *op. cit.,* § 2, n. 8; Schmalzgrueber, *ibid.,* n. 45.

[48] Cf. canon 1017, § 1, 2. Discussion on the juridic form of betrothals is found in Section IV of this chapter (pp. 130-149).

Article 3: Freedom in Contracting Espousals

A third requirement for a valid espousal promise is *freedom* of choice and consent. Now, marshalled against a free betrothal promise are force and fear—as they are arrayed also against the free marital consent. However, before proceeding with the matter more deeply, the writer deems it advisable to review briefly the notion and the divisions of these two obstructions to liberty.

A. The Notion of Force

Force is violence whose impetus is too great to be resisted. This is the general definition given by all canonists and moralists.[49] It consists in an impulse from without, compelling the object against which it is directed to do or suffer something against its natural inclination. In legal and moral matters violence is always understood as the use of force by an external agent to compel another to do what is opposed to his will.[50] Force, greater than can be resisted, is applied by an external agent, through compulsion of the passive subject without concurrence on his part to perform or to refrain from performing some action. In a word, the fact of violence is verified when a person is forced by another to act in such a way that he cannot do the contrary.[51]

Violence may be either absolute (called also: physical) or relative (called also: moral, conditional and even causative). Absolute violence or force, is that which is to be understood in the strict sense, scil., that which cannot be resisted in any way whatsoever. Three elements enter into this notion. First, the force must originate from an extrinsic principle, i.e., from an external agent to the passive subject.[52] Secondly, the will must in no way give its approval or consent, as is obvious. Thirdly, the passive subject

---

[49] Cf., v.g., Schmalzgrueber, *Ius Ecclesiasticum,* lib. IV, tit. I, n. 384. The definition is also found in Roman law in D. (4.2) 1, 2.

[50] Cf. Callan-McHugh, *Moral Theology* (2 vols., New York, 1929), I, 20. In Anglo-American law a person who suffers such violence is said to be "under duress."—Cf. Smith, *Elementary Law,* p. 267.

[51] Cf. St. Thomas, *Summa Theologica,* Ia-IIae, q. 82, a. 1.

[52] St. Thomas, *Summa Theologica,* Ia-IIae, q. 6, a. 6 ad 1.

must hold himself not negatively or indifferently, but actually, virtually or at least constructively (*interpretative*) opposed to the force. Hence, whenever force is exercised against a person who both interiorly dissents and exteriorly resists, the fact of violence is established.

Relative or *moral* force is accepted in a twofold sense. According to some, it is had when the passive subject can resist or at least is able to diminish the impetus or onset of the force but *de facto* fails to do so. Others term violence relative when the person cannot indeed resist it, but at the same time does not altogether dissent interiorly or suffer it unwillingly.[53] It is this latter species of violence, moral compulsion, which excites fear in the subject who suffers it. Hence, conditional or moral force is commonly identified with and used synonymously for fear.[54]

B. The Notion of Fear

Fear, therefore, is something interior in a person, a subjective state intimately affecting the individual in contradistinction to violence as something external. Canonists and theologians have adopted the definition of fear from Roman law[55] and explain it as a perturbation of the mind caused by the apprehension of an imminent or future danger.[56]

The evil or danger exciting the fear may be of the physical or the moral order, such as death, bodily injury, financial loss, damaged reputation, etc. It is also distinguished according to its origin or cause, mode or manner, and degree of intensity. From the standpoint of origin fear may be supernatural or natural according as it is inspired by belief in God's omnipotence, by an

---

[53] Cf. St. Thomas, *Commentaria,* dist. XXII, q. 1, a. 1; Schmalzgrueber, *loc. cit.;* St. Alphonsus, *Theologia Moralis* (2 vols., Augustae Taurinorum, 1879), lib. VI, n. 1045.

[54] "Haec posterior [vis conditionalis] et metus, pro synonymis, vel saltem connexis, accipiuntur."—Schmalzgrueber, *Ius Ecclesiasticum,* lib. IV, tit. I, n. 384.

[55] Cf. D. (4.2) 1.

[56] Cf. St. Alphonsus, *Theologia Moralis,* lib. VI, n. 1046.

evil privative of supernatural good, as eternal punishment, by qualms of conscience or by some natural evil or danger, whether from within or from without.[57] Fear from within (*ab intrinsico*) results from a necessary or natural event whether internal or external to the individual, the existence of which does not depend on the free agent, e.g., death, virulent disease, fire, etc. Fear from without (*ab extrinsico*) is that which is caused by a free human agent, e.g., by an individual who threatens evil to obtain some purpose.[58] According to another distinction, fear is termed extrinsic when it results from an external cause whether necessary, natural or free, while intrinsic fear is that which results from a cause internal to the individual. Thus, v.g., Cappello.[59] Either distinction may be accepted, as both are practically of the same importance in matters pertaining to morals.[60]

As to its mode or manner of infliction, fear from an extrinsic free cause is just or unjust. It is just when for a really merited reason it is inflicted by a competent person and in a lawful manner. Thus, v.g., an authorized judge who threatens a delinquent taxpayer with the penalty provided by law for such offenses induces a just fear. If fear is inflicted for no adequate reason, or for a cause not connected with the evil threatened, or if the one inspiring the fear has no right or authority to threaten an evil, the fear is unjust. Should the above-mentioned taxpayer, for instance, be free from guilt, or should the judge be incompetent or threaten a penalty exceeding that determined by law, the inflicted fear would be unjust.[61]

Concerning quality, intensity or degree, fear is grave or slight. Grave fear arises from a serious evil that is certainly or very

---

[57] Cf., v.g., Gasparri, *De Matrimonio,* II, n. 946.

[58] Cf. Sanchez, *De Matrimonii Sacramento,* lib. IV, disp. XII, n. 2; St. Alphonsus, *Theologia Moralis,* lib. VI, n. 1046; Laymann, *Theologia Moralis,* lib. I, tract. II, cap. VI, n. 2.

[59] *De Sacramentis,* V, n. 605.

[60] Cf. Genicot-Salsmans, *Institutiones Theologiae Moralis* (8. ed., 2 vols., Bruxellis, 1919), I, n. 28 (hereafter cited *Institutiones*).

[61] Genicot-Salsmans, *loc. cit.;* Augustine, *A Commentary on the New Code of Canon Law* (8 vols., 2 ed., Vol. V, 1920, St. Louis: Herder, 1918-1924), V, 246.

probably imminent. Slight fear is induced by a trifling evil or by the fact that there is little danger that the evil or harm will ensue. Grave fear may be absolutely or relatively grave. It is absolutely grave when the evil or danger is objectively serious and will intimidate any one of ordinary prudence and courage, even though in some extraordinary case it might not disturb an exceptionally courageous person. Relatively grave fear is caused by an evil which might not affect the average person but which in relation to certain individuals, in view of the circumstances of sex, age, health, disposition, etc., becomes serious.[62]

In this connection mention must be made of reverential fear. This usually has its origin in the desire not to offend one's parents or superiors so as to avoid incurring their wrath, displeasure or indignation. In itself, reverential fear is slight, but under certain circumstances it can become grave.[63]

Fear is also antecedent or concomitant according as the act is performed out of fear (*ex metu*) or with fear (*cum metu*). Fear is concomitant when it is not the cause of an act but is merely the occasion of it. Fear is antecedent when it is the cause, inasmuch as it is anterior to the action and moves the will to act. Were the fear not present, the action would not be done.[64]

C. Force as Exerted in Espousals

Hence, in the light of the distinctions just made, it is possible now to state the principles which govern betrothals in reference to force and fear. First, absolute violence obviously invalidates espousals, as all voluntariness of the act is destroyed and consequently consent is excluded.[65] An act performed under such con-

---

[62] Cf. St. Alphonsus, *Theologia Moralis,* lib. VI, n. 1045.

[63] Cf. Cappello, *De Sacramentis,* V, n. 605.

[64] Cf. Sangmeister, *Force and Fear as Precluding Matrimonial Consent,* The Catholic University of America Canon Law Studies, n. 80 (Washington, D. C.: The Catholic University of America, 1932), p. 10.

[65] Cf. De Smet, *De Sponsalibus et Matrimonio,* n. 5; Vlaming, *Praelectiones Iuris Canonici* (3. ed., 2 vols., Bussum in Hollandia, 1919-1921), I, n. 80 (hereafter cited *Praelectiones*); Wernz-Vidal, *Ius Canonicum,* V, n. 85; Coronata, *De Sacramentis,* III, n. 51.

ditions clearly has no juridic value, for the principle of law operative here is thus enunciated in the Code: "Actions which are performed either by a physical or by a moral person through extrinsic compulsion that could not be resisted are considered as though they were not done."[66]

Relatively grave violence does not invalidate betrothment of itself, because the voluntariness of an act is not thereby destroyed —hence it admits consent.[67]

D. The Influence of Fear on Betrothals

As for fear affecting betrothals, the first principle applicable is this: Fear that destroys voluntariness and consequently excludes consent nullifies engagements. Secondly, if fear leaves reason intact, then even grave fear when it arises from intrinsic causes or is justly induced by some external agent, not, however, to extort consent, does not invalidate espousals. The reason is, of course, that voluntariness is present, although it be diminished to some extent.[68]

Unjust grave fear induced by an external agency to extort the promise *probably* does *not* invalidate the espousal contract. The qualifying term "probably" is employed here, for some of the older authors, writing after the Council of Trent, *denied* that betrothals were valid when unjustly extorted through grave fear exerted from an outside agency.[69] Other older as well as recent authorities maintain that such affiancements are *valid*, but insist on their rescindibility at law. Neither natural nor positive legislation urges invalidity, they point out.[70]

---

[66] Canon 103, § 1.

[67] Cf. Ballerini-Palmieri, *Opus Theologicum Morale* (3. ed., 7 vols., Prati, 1898-1901), I, tract. I, nn. 119-122, Schmalzgrueber, *Ius Ecclesiasticum*, lib. IV, tit. I, n. 384.

[68] Cf. Cappello, *De Sacramentis*, V, n. 98.

[69] Thus Sanchez, *De Matrimonii Sacramento*, lib. IV, disp. XIX, n. 3; Barbosa, *Collectanea Doctorum*, lib. IV, tit. II, cap. *Ex litteris*, X, n. 4; Covarruvias, *Opera Omnia*, pars 2, cap. III, § V, n. 27.

[70] Thus Lessius, *De Iustitia*, lib. 2, cap. 17, dub. 37; Pirhing, *Ius Canonicum*, lib. IV, tit. I, sec. 1, n. 21; Schmalzgrueber, *Ius Ecclesiasticum*, lib. IV, tit. I, n. 427; De Smet, *De Sponsalibus et Matrimonio*, n. 5; Wernz-Vidal, *Ius Canonicum*, V, n. 85, Vlaming, *Praelectiones*, I, n. 80.

Current legislation in the Code of Canon Law clearly formulates the general rule: "Actions based on great fear unjustly created or on deceit are valid unless the law rules otherwise; they can, however, be rescinded by means of a judicial sentence, according to the norms of canons 1684-1689, at the instance of the injured party or *ex officio* [by the judge].[71]

Cappello regards the opinion of Sanchez and his followers as the *more probable* one.[72] He subscribes to it, adducing canon 1087, § 1, as support for his view. This canon declares that marriage is null not only when contracted under the influence of main force, as previously seen, but also when entered into under the influence of grave fear, which an outside agent, unjustly exercises over a person, so that the individual is forced to choose marriage as a means of extricating himself from the predicament.[73] Cappello, therefore, argues by analogy in defense of his position that, since it follows from canon 1087, § 1, that the party experiencing the fear, as described, cannot be obligated to a marriage which under the circumstances is null, hence, espousals entered into under similar conditions, cannot be valid nor can they engender an obligation.[74] By the very fact, he also adds, that the law explicitly declares marriages null when contracted because of the fear as described, it seems, at least, to declare *implicitly* that betrothals similarly contracted also lack validity.[75]

However, Cappello's conclusions and those of Sanchez and others do not seem acceptable to this writer. Although the parallel

---

[71] Can. 103, § 2. Cf. canons 1684-1689 for further details on the judicial process involved. Procedural practice in reference to the dissolution of betrothment compacts will be treated in Section VII of this chapter.

[72] Cappello, *De Sacramentis,* V, n. 98.

[73] Canon 1087, § 1: "Invalidum quoque est matrimonium initum ob vim vel metum gravem ab extrinsico et iniuste incussum, a quo, ut quis se liberet, eligere cogatur matrimonium."

[74] ". . . sequitur, partem quae metum sit passa, ad eiusmodi matrimonium, utpote nullum, sese obligare non posse, ideoque sponsalia in eo rerum statu inita, esse invalida."—Cappello, *De Sacramentis* V, n. 98.

[75] "Eo ipso quod lex nullum explicite declarat matrimonium ob metum initum, saltem implicite declarare videtur nulla etiam sponsalia sub tali metu contracta."—Cappello, *loc. cit.*

they draw between espousals and marriage and the close relationship they see in these two juridic entities is acceptable to some, it does not follow necessarily that what the law prescribes for marriage it also prescribes for betrothment. On the contrary, Canon 103, § 2, declares that, generally, actions based on great fear unjustly created are *valid,* unless the law states the contrary. Now, the law does state the contrary in canon 1087, § 1, declaring that marriage is canonically ineffectual because of the fear just described. Nowhere, however, does the law state this in reference to espousals. Canon 1017 does not speak of it. One cannot presume that the legislator was thoughtless or forgetful in this regard. Had he desired to declare espousals null on the grounds of grave fear unjustly caused, he would have added a paragraph to this effect. As a matter of fact he did not; he left the principles governing contracts intact and thus, seemingly, made the norm of canon 103, § 2, operative in this regard.

Furthermore, as canon 1087, § 1, speaks of an invalidating effect, it is not permitted to extend the law to other cases. Canon 19 demands a strict interpretation of laws which establish penalties, restrict rights or contain an exception to the law. Hence canon 1087, § 1, must be interpreted in the light of canon 19, since an exception to the law is involved.

Lastly, since canon 11 ordains that only those laws are to be considered invalidating which explicitly or equivalently state an action to be null and void, invalidity for espousals entered into because of grave fear exerted from without cannot be urged. The law neither explicitly nor equivalently has ever decided that betrothment under such circumstances is invalid.

That the presence of such a fear readily admits grounds for a dissolution of the betrothal, i.e., makes for rescindibility, as mentioned above, is quite evident. In a later section of this chapter[76] rescissibility and dissolution of betrothals will be treated in detail.

As for slight fear influencing engagements, some writers, as St. Alphonsus (1696-1787) and Lehmkuhl (1834-1918), insisted that even such compacts were null on the grounds of violation of

---

[76] Pp. 159-175.

freedom.[77] The more common and more probable opinion, however, merely admits that such contracts are rescissible at law. Thus Sanchez, De Lugo, etc.[78] Cappello's conclusion on this matter is that fundamentally betrothals entered into because of light fear are valid in view of the legislation enunciated in canons 103, § 2, and 1087, § 2.[79] Cappello also grants that such espousals may be rescinded at law. As a matter of fact, he states that if the fear gave cause for the contract, the injured party is even bound (*tenetur*) to rescind it.[80]

In keeping with the principles employed in the previous controversy on grave fear, the writer here also holds the opinion which favors validity, and concedes that rescindibility is available when light fear precipitated the betrothment promise. Canon 103, § 2, is the foundation for this position, as it was in the controversy on grave fear. If grave fear unjustly inflicted by an outside agency does not invalidate an act, *a fortiori* neither does light fear in itself. The voluntariness of the act is not destroyed by slight fear nor is consent excluded. Hence espousals remain valid, but they may be dissolved, v.g., on the grounds of a probably unhappy marriage.

E. Abduction and Espousals

A discussion of force and fear naturally brings up the problem of abduction. Does violent seizure or forcible detention of a woman by a man in view of betrothal with her invalidate such an unusual engagement? This question is thorny, as was the preceding one, because of the dispute among canonical commentators as to whether or not liberty is so impaired as to void espousals

---

[77] St. Alphonsus, *Theologia Moralis,* lib. VI, n. 844; Lehmkuhl, *Theologia Moralis* (12. ed., 2 vols., Friburgi, Brisgoviae, 1914), n. 838.

[78] Sanchez, *De Matrimonii Sacramento,* lib. I, disp. XIX, n. 6; De Lugo, *De Iustitia,* I, disp. XXII, n. 134.

[79] "Attento iure novo, scl., praescripto canonis 1087, § 2, ob rationem illatam in praecedenti quaestione, et praesertim attento can. 103, § 2, dubitandum non est quin per se valida sint sponsalia."—Cappello, *De Sacramentis,* V, n. 98.

[80] *Loc. cit.*

contracted by the abducted with her abductor. The Council of Trent declared all marriages null when the impediment of abduction was present.[81] The Code of Canon Law today legislates in the same vein.[82]

Nothing, however, was mentioned in Tridentine law in regard to abduction perpetrated for the purpose of *betrothment*. Code legislation has no express statutes either which refer directly to betrothals. Some of the older authors before the Code affirmed outright that the impediment was to be extended to espousals. Others insisted on the contrary view. Sanchez represented the first group. Pichler led the second.

Sanchez (1550-1610) was of the period immediately following the great Council of Trent; Pichler (1670-1736), a little later. Sanchez mentioned the doubts on this matter as already extant in his time, and stated his own position in the problem then current.[83] His reason was that a *corrective* and *penal* law was to be extended to those cases where the same reasons applied. Since the Council of Trent, he argued, demanded full liberty and freedom from coercion in matters pertaining to marriage, it likewise intended similar freedom in espousals—which of their nature demand an unimpaired consent.[84]

Pichler, on the other hand, with many others pointed to three facts. First, the Council of Trent did not mention betrothment in its decree; secondly, less freedom is required for affiancement than marriage and, thirdly, corrective law, if, moreover it be penal in its nature, cannot exceed the limits assigned it. Hence, the view

---

[81] Conc. Trident., sess. XXIV, *de ref. matrim.*, c. VI—Schroeder, *Canons and Decrees of the Council of Trent*, p. 458.

[82] Can. 1074. For the penalties inflicted, cf. canon 2353.

[83] "Tandem dubitatus an, sicut praedictum Tridentini decretum irritat matrimonium inter raptorem et raptam, quamdiu in eius potestate manserit, ita irritet quoque sponsalia tunc inita. . . . Sed dicendum est sponsalia quoque non valere."—Sanchez, *De Matrimonii Sacramento*, lib. VII, disp. XIII, n. 17.

[84] "Quia lex etiam correctoria et penalis extendi debet, ubi omnino eadem ratio militat. . . . Quia Tridentinum irritavit pro eo tempore matrimonium, consulens plenae libertati ad id requisitae, quae non omnino plena est dum rapta manet in raptoris potestate. Quae ratio in sponsalibus militat, ad quae iura quoque plenam libertatem postulant."—Sanchez, *loc. cit.*

of Sanchez, he said, could not be upheld.[85] St. Alphonsus Liguori called this last opinion the *more probable* one.[86] Pichler called the opinion of his opponents the *more common* one.[87]

Among more recent authors, Cappello adheres to the school of Sanchez, since the opposite view in his judgment does not seem to rest on satisfactory arguments. Particularly now that the Code of Canon Law is in eistence, he asserts, *sponsalia* are invalid, as is marriage, whenever abduction intervenes.[88]

To the writer of this thesis it seems that a distinction should be made. If abduction was such that the abducted party could not escape except through feigned and fictitious consent to the espousals, the act is obviously null from the very nature of the case. A simulated consent but not any genuine desire to become engaged was present, thus voiding the contract in its very beginning. If, on the other hand, a true consent was given and all the formalities of law were duly observed when the parties entered the betrothment, the espousals appear valid. Mere abduction, i.e., an abduction taken in and by itself, does not, in the opinion of the present writer, by that very fact invalidate an engagement, as it does marriage.

Since the impediment of abduction is mentioned by the Code only in reference to marriage, it does not appear plausible to the writer that the legislator intended it also as invalidating espousals. Had the latter been of this frame of mind he would have made himself explicit on this point, for an *invalidating* factor is involved—a serious matter. Canon 19 states too that a strict interpretation is to be accorded to those laws which deal with exceptions, which restrict the exercise of a right and which lay down penalties, as was previously stated in reference to the effect of fear. Moreover, canon 11 can also be invoked, since it enjoins that no law is to be

[85] Pichler, *Ius Canonicum secundum quinque Decretalium titulos Gregorii Papae IX practice explicatum* (2 vols., Ravennae, 1741), lib. IV, tit. I, n. 122.

[86] S. Alphonsus, *Theologia Moralis,* lib. VI, tract. VI, n. 110.

[87] Pichler, *loc. cit.*

[88] "Haec ratio [Pichleri et aliorum] nostro iudicio sat efficax non videtur ideoque, praesertim iure novo attento, sponsalia in casu nulla esse opinamur." —*De Sacramentis,* V, n. 84.

regarded as invalidating or disqualifying unless it expressly or equivalently so declares.[89]

Article 4: Proper Deliberation

A. The Nature of the Deliberation Needed

A fourth requisite essential to the espousal promise is *deliberation.* Full knowledge and mature consideration must precede the promise, i.e., the intellect must be clear in its perception before the will can responsibly operate, as in all human acts. Authors commonly appeal to the analogy of the deliberation necessary before one can be said to commit a mortal sin. They state that for the validity of the betrothal contract it is necessary but also sufficient that one have the same advertence and attention requisite before one be considered guilty of sinning seriously.[90]

Cappello, acknowledging with due respect the weight of the authorities just mentioned, disagrees with the common viewpoint. That advertence, *at least* such as must intervene before there can be a question of the commission of mortal sin, is necessary for a valid betrothment agreement, he readily concedes. That it *suffices,* he doubts.[91] His reason is that *more* maturity of thought and deliberation are mandatory in an espousal promise than in the perpetration of sin. The import of affiancement is that the contractants understand the meaning of marriage envisioned in the betrothal contract.[92] In addition, experience teaches that not *any sort* of

[89] For a more lengthy explanation of the problem, cf. Fair, *The Impediment of Abduction,* The Catholic University of America Canon Law Studies, n. 194 (Washington, D. C.: The Catholic University of America Press, 1944), pp. 67-70.

[90] "Ea [advertentia] requiritur et sufficit quae requiritur, et sufficit, ad mortaliter peccandum."—Schmalzgrueber, *Ius Ecclesiasticum,* lib. IV, tit. I, n. 18. So also Molina, *De Iustitia,* tract II, disp. CCLXVII, n. 7; Pirhing, *Ius Canonicum,* lib. IV, tit. I, n. IV; Sanchez, *De Matrimonii Sacramento,* lib. I, disp. VIII, n. 5; St. Alphonsus, *Theologia Moralis,* lib. VI, n. 831.

[91] "Quod requiratur saltem ea deliberatio et advertentia, quae necessaria est ad culpam lethalem constituendam, certissimum est; quod autem eiusmodi deliberatio et advertentia sufficiat, valde dubitamus."—Cappello, *De Sacramentis,* V, n. 83.

[92] "Sane ad validitatem sponsalium necesse omnino est, vir ac mulier cognoscant *quid importet promissio sponsalitia, et ideo quid sit matrimonium.*" —Cappello, *loc. cit.* (Italics inserted.)

mental reflection meets the requirements for so serious a step as future marriage, he continues, but there is required one that is endowed with a fuller and more mature contemplation of the obligations to be assumed. What child, he argues from another analogy, approaching the Holy Table for the first time, can in general be regarded as possessing sufficient insight into the nature of espousals or to have the knowledge that matrimony is a permanent society constituted by a man and woman, the primary purpose of which is the procreation of offspring? Yet, children at this age are capable of sinning mortally.[93]

Cappello's contemporaries, as Coronata, De Smet and Gasparri incline toward this view, stating that the obligations of the intended marriage must be perceived *at least in a confused way.*[94]

The modern view held by Cappello and others basically appears unwarranted. It does not seem correct to say that *any sort* of deliberation and reflection suffices for the commission of a mortal sin. A child of seven years realizes that the sin that confronts him is serious and in a confused way he is aware of its terrifying consequences. In like manner, theoretically considered, a child at seven years can be made conscious of the gravity of espousals and be given the realization in a confused way at least of their serious consequences. Certainly, the authority of the superior instructing him on the matter carries sufficient weight to make the youngster in question conclude for himself that the action that he is about to perform is a sober and serious matter. Were this not a fact of experience, the old decretal law would not have provided seven years as the minimum age for valid betrothment. Since that age was required, surely it also sufficed, otherwise one who had not passed beyond that age could not be deemed juridically capable of contracting espousals under the old discipline.

---

[93] Cappello—*loc. cit.*

[94] "Requiratur praeterea in eisdem personis sufficiens usus rationis et discretio necessaria ad percipienda saltem in confuso iura et officia ipsius ineundi matrimonii."—Coronata, *De Sacramentis,* III, n. 45. So too De Smet, *De Sponsalibus et Matrimonio,* n. 15; Gasparri, *De Matrimonio,* I, n. 62.

This discipline, as will be later explained, has not been abrogated, so that the seventh year of life still remains as the minimum age today determining juridical capacity in this regard.[95]

B. Emotional Disturbances and Espousals

Now, what of such emotional disturbances as love, hate, anger, and so on? Do they militate against the validity of the betrothal contract? Sanchez and Molina, among the older writers, and Cappello, Coronata and Vlaming (+ 1935) among the modern writers, clearly indicate that these disturbances as a rule do not destroy or take away the use of reason. There remains, in spite of them, sufficient liberty and deliberation to safeguard the espousal promise from possible nullity.[96]

When doubts do arise as to whether or not such an impetus or impulse deprived the contractant of the use of reason at the time of the making of the contract, the *Glossa ordinaria* maintained that the party alleging defective consent was to be favored and that the agreement was to be regarded as not binding. The source is the gloss to one of Gratian's *decreta*.[97] Sanchez contradicted this view, adjudging the contract valid on the grounds that *rarely* does it happen that anger, for instance, is so violent as to impede reason in matters of this nature.[98] Schmalzgrueber added that the *contract rather than the individual enjoys favor of law,* since it is *"in possession,"* that is, the agreement once entered upon is presumed to have been executed with due deliberation and sufficient thought.[99] With this view the present writer also agrees, since

[95] Cf. pp. 117-126 of this thesis.

[96] Sanchez, *De Matrimonii Sacramento,* lib. I, disp. VIII, n. 4; Molina, *De Iustitia,* II, disp. CCLXVII, n. 1; Cappello, *loc. cit.;* Coronata, *De Sacramentis,* III, n. 45; Vlaming, *Praelectiones,* I, n. 80.

[97] "Ira rescindit contractum."—*Glossa Ordinaria* s.v. *iratus,* c. 5, C. II, q. 3. Cf. Schmalzgrueber, *Ius Ecclesiasticum,* lib. IV, tit. I, nn. 21-23, for similar Roman Law sources.

[98] Sanchez, *loc. cit.*

[99] ". . . in nostro casu sponsalia sunt in possessione; quia certum est ea fuisse contracta, et tantum dubitatur, an contracta sint cum sufficienti rationis usu, qui tamen, uti dixi, praesumitur." Schmalzgrueber, *ibid.,* n. 23.

the reasons adduced by Sanchez and Schmalzgrueber accord with the general principles underlying legal presumptions.

C. Intoxication and the Betrothal Contract

A final consideration to be accorded attention here relates to the defect of consent because of intoxication. All canonists are agreed that if one is drunk in the theological sense, i.e., bereft of reason at the moment of betrothment, no obligation is assumed. The compact is void both at law and by nature, since it fails to qualify as a human act.[100]

A more subtle question, however, is asked about the validity of consent when the intent to enter espousals or marriage was manifested *prior* to the actual giving of it in a state of intoxication. Schmalzgrueber replied that such a resolve does not suffice. Nor does it help to appeal to the analogy of validity of baptism, when administered to one having a virtual intention, since for marriage, as this eminent scholar retorted, an *actual* intention must intervene, as the parties themselves are the ministers of the sacrament. Hence, the parity with baptism must be denied.[101]

What Schmalzgrueber intended to say is this: Espousals and marriage demand an *actual* intention for the contracting of the obligation. In this regard marriage and espousals are closely allied. On the other hand, the analogy between baptism and marriage, as well as betrothal, does not apply. In contracting matrimony the parties act as ministers; in contracting a betrothal the parties act in an analogous manner by exchanging promises. But in baptism an outside agency effects the action. Consequently, in Schmalzgrueber's opinion, which the present writer also espouses for the above-indicated reasons, marriage and engagement lack the requisite consent when they are contracted by one who is intoxicated, his previous intent to become espoused notwithstanding.

---

[100] Thus, v.g. Schmalzgrueber, *ibid.*, n. 15.

[101] "Sed dicendum, non sufficere eam voluntatem . . . negatur paritas: ad baptismum enim sufficit intentio habitualis in suscipiente; non autem in matrimonio, ubi suscipientes sunt ministri eius sacramenti, cuius actus debet esse humanus."—*Loc. cit.*

SECTION III. JURIDIC CAPACITY TO CONTRACT BETROTHALS

Article 1: Physical Age

A. Ancient Discipline in Brief

In the Decretals of Popes Gregory IX (1227-1241) and Boniface VIII (1294-1303) the canonical age that was required and that in and of itself legally sufficed for valid betrothals was seven years.[102] This norm was already established in Roman law[103] and in the *Decretum* of Gratian.[104]

However, two exceptions to the law were commonly admitted. First, espousals were regarded *valid* even when the contractants lacked the requisite age but enjoyed the intellectual substitute, scil., *precocity* (*malitia*), i.e., the use of reason and sufficient deliberation.[105] Secondly, espousals were considered *invalid* when the principals to the contract had indeed reached their seventh year but lacked the proper discretion and deliberation.[106] These two exceptions had to be proved, of course, as the law presumed that the requisite use of reason was not enjoyed before the age of seven but that it was had at the seventh year of life. The latter presumption was a *presumptio iuris et de iure*.[107]

The law remained unaltered through the centuries. In the decree *Ne temere*[108] Pope Pius X did not legislate on this particular point of law. The Code also made no express provisions. Hence, the immediate pre-Code and Code authors must be consulted when one seeks to determine the status of the question as it exists today.

---

[102] Cc. 4, 5, 13, X, *de desponsatione impuberum,* IV, 2; IL, nn. 13847, 13887; Potthast, n. 535; cap. un., *de desponsatione impuberum,* IV, 2, in VI°; cf. also pp. 31-37 of this thesis.

[103] D. (23.1) 14. Cf. pp. 7-8 of this dissertation.

[104] C. un., C. XXX, q. 2. Cf. pp. 35-37 of this thesis.

[105] Cf. Sanchez, *De Matrimonii Sacramento,* lib. I, disp. XVI, nn. 9, 16; Schmalzgrueber, *Ius Ecclesiasticum,* lib. IV, tit. I, n. 19.

[106] Sanchez, *ibid.,* nn. 10-11; Schmalzgrueber, *ibid.,* nn. 20-21.

[107] Cf. De Smet, *De Sponsalibus et Matrimonio,* n. 16, nota 1.

[108] S.C.C., decr. *Ne temere,* 2 aug., 1907—*Fontes,* n. 4340

B. Views of Pre-Code and Code Commentators

De Smet (1868-1927), one of the commentators on the *Ne temere* provisions, upheld the traditional ruling on canonical age in the 1909 edition of his work on espousals and marriage,[109] only to modify his position when the Code of Canon Law appeared in 1917. In the 1927 edition of his work he averred that *discretion* is frequently *wanting* at the age of seven, *even though use of reason is had*. Hence, according to De Smet, the seventh year age limit does not *suffice*.[110]

Gasparri (1852-1934), who also was both a pre-Code and a post-Code writer, opposed the common teaching before as well as after the promulgation of the present law on espousals. In the 1892 edition of his work,[111] he paid due deference to the formidable line of authorities of the past arrayed against him. He also acknowledged that the decision of the Sacred Congregation of the Holy Office, given in 1779 to the Prefect Apostolic of Szechwan, militated against his views. This decision[112] had reiterated that betrothals of children who are not yet *puberes* are valid until repudiated by these same children when they reach the age of puberty.[113]

Notwithstanding all this, Gasparri observed that the common opinion still contained many serious difficulties.[114] These difficulties, he explained, concern the sufficiency of knowledge and maturity of deliberation necessary for those who contemplate future marriage in the betrothment compact. Now, all the pre-Code authors, who agreed that the age of seven sufficed for a

---

[109] De Smet, *De Sponsalibus et Matrimonio* (Brugis, 1909), n. 10: "Ad sponsalia ineunda requiritur . . . aetas septennalis."

[110] ". . . non sufficit septennium: illo quidem completo, supponitur usus rationis, sed non raro adhuc desideratur necessaria discretio."—De Smet, *De Sponsalibus et Matrimonio*, n. 15.

[111] Gasparri, *Tractatus Canonicus De Matrimonio* (2 vols., Parisiis, 1892), I, n. 17. (Hereafter, whenever reference to this edition will be made, the year 1892 will also appear.)

[112] S.C.S. Off., *Sutchuen.*, 15 febr. 1779—*Collectanea*, I, n. 532.

[113] *Loc. cit.*

[114] "Salva reverentia erga communem sententiam DD. et praesertim S.C.S. Officii, liceat animadvertere hanc doctrinam non leves pati difficultates."—Gasparri, *De Matrimonio* (1892 ed.), n. 17.

valid contract, provided that the use of reason was had or that the factor of precocity supplied for the want of age, taught that requisite knowledge and discretion comes only with *puberty*. This Gasparri considered an "inconsistency" in the thinking process of the decretalist school.[115]

Further, as the great Cardinal pressed his point, the older authors commonly granted that "impuberal" children, i.e., those approximating infancy, in general, cannot contract an obligation either in civil law or by the natural law when entering into any sort of contract, precisely because of the lack of a proper discretion.[116] Why, he inquired, make an exception for espousals? "Why is knowledge and deliberation presumed at the seventh year in this contract [betrothals], while presumed only at the age *verging* on puberty [i.e., just before puberty] in other contracts?"[117]

Referring to the ancient practice of betrothments concluded by parents in behalf of their children,[118] Gasparri pointed to another "illogical" conclusion of his predecessors. He recalled that such child espousals could not be dissolved by children before the age of puberty. The age of discretion, i.e., puberty, was required. The "inconsistency" lies in the opponents' maintaining the sufficiency of seven years for the contracting of betrothals and yet insisting on twelve and fourteen years for the girl and the boy respectively for a ratification or a repudiation.[119] Nowhere does the law, he continued, state that betrothment of *impuberes* begets an obligation in conscience. Yet canonists maintain this obligation, basing their views on the old Roman and early Christian

[115] "Atqui mentis discretionem matrimonialem, i.e., sufficientem et necessariam ad matrimonium valide contradendum praesumitur ex communi DD. sententia (n. 678) advenire cum pubertate."—*Loc. cit.*

[116] "Praeterea DD. communiter admittunt impuberes infantiae proximos contractibus in genere *nec civiliter nec naturaliter obligari praecise ob defectum debitae mentis discretionis.*"—*Loc. cit.* Italics inserted.

[117] "Eccurnam, quaeso, exceptio pro contractu sponsalitio? Curnam pro hoc contractu intelligentia et consensus sufficiens praesumitur post septennium, dum pro aliis contractibus praesumitur post aetatem infantiae proximam?" —*Loc. cit.*

[118] Cf. pp. 42-51 of this thesis.

[119] Gasparri, *De Matrimonio,* I, n. 63.

discipline—which no longer obtains, viz., the father's consent sufficed even for a son who had attained the use of reason.[120] The fact that the Church legislated positively that the impediment of public propriety was contracted, even when children under the age of puberty were principals to espousals, does not undermine his argument, Gasparri claimed, since the impediment in question was an ecclesiastical one—which the Church could impose if it saw fit even in the case of invalid espousals.[121]

The eminent canonist concluded that for valid affiancement the *same* knowledge, consent and discretion are *mandatory* as are required for marriage. This knowledge and discretion comes only with puberty. Hence, espousals are to be considered null when contracted before puberty without due deliberation, unless it is proved that knowledge or prudent circumspection (even though ability for copulation is wanting) preceded the requisite age. The possession of such knowledge and circumspection is, as a general rule, not difficult to verify when one is near the age of puberty.[122]

In his later work, which was edited in 1932, Gasparri briefly enumerated three important factors. First, he noted, the Code lays down the ages of fourteen and sixteen as the minimum for valid marriage in the case of the female and male respectively.[123] Yet, pastors are directed to dissuade young people, even though they are of canonical age, from marriage at an age earlier than that which is commonly recognized as acceptable according to the established custom and usage.[124] Secondly, the Code demands for marriage the knowledge that the married state is a permanent society consisting of a man and a woman for the purpose of the

---

[120] *Loc. cit.* Cf. also pp. 7-8 and pp. 26-30 of this dissertation.

[121] Gasparri, *loc. cit.*

[122] "Ob has rationes quis non immerito fortasse putaret pro sponsalium validitate ex ipso naturae iure revera requiri eandem mentis discretionem, quae pro matrimonio quaeque, ut diximus, praesumitur advenire cum pubertate; hinc sponsalia ante pubertatem esse nulla defectu debitae discretionis, nisi probetur prudentiam etiam sine potentia coeundi praevenisse aetatem quod in proximis pubertati non difficile potest verificari. . . ."—*Loc. cit.*

[123] Can. 1067, § 1.

[124] Can. 1067, § 1.

procreation of new life.[125] This knowledge is presumed after puberty.[126] This knowledge is more mature at the ages of fourteen and sixteen. Consequently, Gasparri concluded, if such more mature knowledge which follows upon the attainment of the "puberal" age is demanded for the contracting of marriage, it should likewise intervene as something necessary and requisite in promises of marriage.[127]

However, as to the third consideration, an ordinary *cannot* declare espousals null when contracted before this age, since the Code does not legislate on the juridic capacity of age for the contracting of espousals. Canon 1067 treats of marriage, not betrothals. Nonetheless, Gasparri asserted, the ordinary could pass a statute *forbidding* betrothals to be contracted before the canonical ages established for valid matrimony on the grounds of lack of discretion in the parties. This statute, Gasparri judged, would be sustained—as it conforms to the mind of the Code.[128]

Cappello also departed from the pre-Code view for three reasons. First, he asserted, the texts of the decretal law as supported by the pre-Code canonists can no longer be urged under the new legislation. Secondly, the Code considers *impuberes* destitute of due discretion as required for the performance of juridic acts.[129] Thirdly, the legislator today expressly declares that the pastor must refer to his ordinary the question of publishing the banns of marriage whenever the parties concerned lived in another place for a period of six months after attaining the age of puberty.[130] According to this requirement of law, Cappello con-

[125] Can. 1082, § 1.

[126] Can. 1082, § 2.

[127] "Atqui illa melior cognitio iurium et officiorum matrimonialium, sicut expedit ad matrimonium contrahendum, ita et ad matrimonium promittendum."—Gasparri, *De Matrimonio,* I, n. 63.

[128] "Hinc Ordinarius non potest quidem sponsalia inita ante hanc aestatem invalida declarare, quia cit. can. 1067, § 2, de aetate ad sponsalia valide ineunda non agit; sed eius statutum quo vetaret iuvenes, qui praedictam aetatem nondum attigerunt, admitti ad scripturam signandam qua promissio matrimonii valida redditur, putamus sustineri, quia esset conforme menti Codicis. . . ."—Gasparri, *De Matrimonio,* I, n. 63.

[129] Cf. can. 167, § 1, 1°; can. 1224, 1°; can. 1757, § 1; can. 2230.

[130] Can. 1022, § 2.

cluded, those who have not attained the age of puberty are to be considered as children, i.e., as incapable of contracting espousals.[131]

Vlaming also adopted the same position. He confessed that it always appeared "strange" to him that the sufficiency of the seventh year of age should have survived as a legal standard from laws that flourished in a medieval age, whose customs and social concepts differed so diametrically from those extant in modern times.[132] He does admit, however, that a perfect parity between the contract of marriage and its promise by betrothment is lacking. Nevertheless, by virtue of canon 88, § 2, and the above-cited canons, he concluded, the seventh year is unacceptable as a juridic minimum today, except perhaps in certain mission lands.[133]

Vidal (1867-1938) dismissed the pre-Code problems relating to juridic capacity as valueless today. To espousals, he wrote, the general principles governing contracts are to be applied. There is no need to descend into particulars.[134] Vidal's predecessor, Wernz (1842-1914), whose work Vidal edited anew, had adhered to the old school concerning the requisite age for the contracting of betrothals.[135]

Woywod (1880-1941)-Smith do not mention the question. In passing, they merely cite the decision of the Holy Office sent to the Prefect Apostolic of Szechwan concerning the freedom of children to repudiate their espousals obligations contracted by them under the age of puberty.[136] Chelodi (1880-1922)-Ciprotti also by-pass the problem. They speak in a very general vein, mentioning the insane, the intoxicated and *children* lacking sufficient discretion as excluded *ex natura rei* from the rank of those who

---

[131] Cappello, *De Sacramentis,* V, n. 86.

[132] Vlaming, *Praelectiones,* I, n. 88.

[133] *Loc. cit.*

[134] Wernz-Vidal, *Ius Canonicum,* V, n. 83.

[135] Wernz, *Ius Decretalium,* IV, n. 93.

[136] Woywod-Smith, *A Practical Commentary On the Code of Canon Law* (2 vols., revised and enlarged edition, New York: Joseph F. Wagner, 1948), I, n. 988 (hereafter cited *Commentary*).

enjoy capacity to contract betrothals.[137] Ayrinhac (1867-1930)-Lydon and Petrovits, recent American canonists (as are Woywod-Smith), likewise fail to mention the age requisite for espousals.[138]

Coronata does not commit himself directly on this question. He informs his readers that infants who have attained the use of reason are by common opinion regarded as in and of themselves (*per se*) capable of contracting espousals.[139] He admits too that a lack of discretion is presumed before the age of seven and its presence is presumed after that age. Yet he states that the modern opinion sees such a simple use of reason as *insufficient* for a valid betrothal. More is required, scil., that kind of reasoning which is needed when marriage itself is contemplated.[140] But Coronata does not indicate in any way that he approves or disapproves of this viewpoint.

Dissenters to the modern opinion seem few. One such rare dissenter is Regatillo.[141] He adheres to the decretal law, citing the well-known decree of Pope Boniface VIII as his principal proof.[142] He grants that individuals may rescind their betrothals, when they have arrived at the canonical age of puberty, within three days after learning of their rights.[143] Regatillo waives Cappello's objections as of little weight.[144]

---

[137] "Ex natura rei excluduntur, proinde, amentes, ebrii, pueri qui carent sufficienti maturitate iudicii, fatui."—Chelodi-Ciprotti, *Ius Canonicum de Matrimonio* (Vicenza: Società Anonima Tipografica Editrice, 1947), 16b (hereafter this work will be cited *De Matrimonio*).

[138] Ayrinhac-Lydon, *Marriage Legislation in The New Code of Canon Law* (New revised ed., New York: Benziger, 1941), 14-22 (hereafter cited *Marriage Legislation*); Petrovits, *The New Church Law on Matrimony* (Philadelphia, 1919), nn. 70-81 (hereafter cited *New Church Law*).

[139] "Infantes usum rationis assecuti ex communi doctrina per se habiles sunt ad sponsalia contrahenda."—Coronata, *De Sacramentis*, III, n. 45.

[140] *Loc. cit.*

[141] *Ius Sacramentarium* (2 vols., Santandar: Sal Terrae, 1945-1946, II, n. 238.

[142] C. un., *de desponsatione impuberum*, IV, 2, in VI°.

[143] "Quae capaces sunt, qui consensum naturalem praestare possunt. Hinc: (a) Impuberes septennio maiores usum rationis habentes. Hi pubertatem adepti poterant sponsalia retractare intra triduum ex quo ius suum cognoverant."—Regatillo, *loc. cit.*

[144] "Rationes hae . . . [a Cappello adhibitae] parum movent."—*Loc. cit.*

C. Conclusions on the Controversy Concerning the Requisite Age

Theoretically considered, Regatillo's views seem more probable, despite the number of canonists opposed to him. The basic argument, as given by Regatillo's lone reference to Boniface VIII, is the *pre-existing law.* Although the Code of Canon Law is the new law, nevertheless the Code in canon 6 explicitly states that much of the old law has been retained in the present legislation of the Code.[145] No express mention is made in the Code of a minimum age for valid betrothment. From the above-mentioned canon 6 it can be inferred that the former law, therefore, is still operative and applicable. Certainly, it has not been, explicitly at least, abrogated. Therefore, in this respect the pre-Code law is to be retained as canon 6, § 3, directs, viz.: "Those canons which agree only in part with the former law must be interpreted according to the old law in the part in which they agree with the former law; in the parts which differ from the old law, the canons must be interpreted according to the meaning of the words employed."[146]

This is the first argument offered in defense of the pre-Code law. The second is founded on the provisions of number four of the same canon 6. This number ordains that in cases of doubt as to whether or not some provision of the canons differs from the old law, one *must adhere to the old legislation.*[147] Since, therefore, a doubt of law has been engendered by the conflicting opinions, that doubt is to be resolved in favor of the previous law.[148]

Thirdly, had the legislator so desired he could have enacted in his new legislation a statute on the requisite age for engagements. He did provide explicitly for juridic capacity as to age in the case

---

[145] Canon 6: "Codex vigentem huc usque disciplinam plerumque retinet, licet opportunas immutationes afferat."

[146] "Canones qui ex parte tantum cum veteri iure congruunt, qua congruunt, ex iure antiquo aestimandi sunt, qua discrepant, sunt ex ipsorum sententia diiudicandi."—Canon 6, 3°. (Writer's translation.)

[147] Canon 6, 4°: "In dubio num aliquod canonum praescriptum cum veteri iure discrepet, a veteri iure non est recedendum."

[148] *Loc. cit.*

of a contract of marriage.[149] He did not act thus in reference to betrothal.

Fourthly, since affiancement has been included in the Code as a time-honored custom and as a traditional, legal entity, all its time-honored and traditional adjuncts are presumed retained, unless expressly rejected or changed. The Code has added only a few canonical mutations. Age is not expressly found among these mutations. Therefore, the age of seven years seems sufficient for valid espousals in the present legislation until the contrary rule is established.

It is conceded that *in practice* children who have just completed their seventh year of life hardly, if ever, enter betrothment. The question here, however, is a juridic one; a question of the law is the issue, not its application in practice. Consequently, there is no validity in the argument based on present custom and social observance, unless, of course, these have the force of law in some locality, where a definite age is a requisite for espousals.

D. Disparity as to the Age of Puberty

As a consequence of the defended opinion, it is obvious that betrothals, if valid when contracted by parties who are one or both below the age of puberty, are *a fortiori* valid when one of the parties is of age whereas the other is not. Prior to the decree *Ne temere* and the Code, when marriage was attempted between parties of whom only one had reached puberty, by a fiction of law espousals resulted rather than matrimony, i.e., the act took on the character and status of betrothment, not marriage.[150] In other words, the lawgiver at that time attributed only the juridic effect of a betrothal, and not that of marriage, to such contracts.[151]

---

[149] Canon 1067.

[150] Cf. pp. 37-43 and 53-67 of this dissertation.

[151] C. 14, X, *de desponsatione impuberum*, Iv, 2; Sanchez, *De Matrimonii Sacramento,* lib. I, dist. XXI, n. 2; Laymann, *Theologia Moralis,* lib. V, tract. X, pars I, cap. I, n. 17; Barbosa, *Collectanea Doctorum,* lib. IV, tit. II, cap. 1, n. 1, 8; Gonzales-Tellez, *Commentaria,* lib. IV, tit. II, n. 4; Covarruvias, *Opera Omnia,* pars I, cap. I, para III, n. 3; Fagnanus, *Com-*

This presumption of law in favor of espousals no longer obtains, since a substantial form, specifically a written form, is alone recognized as lending validity to espousals, i.e., outside the normal requirements of nature.[152] This state of affairs, however, is not to be construed to mean that affiancement cannot be concluded between principals who labor under disparity as to the age of puberty. As mentioned above and explained in the opinion submitted, such betrothals, when the due canonical form has been employed and all juridic requirements have been met, are valid.

E. The Physically Defective

Upon a discussion of the engagements of children, the next question concerns the espousals of the physically defective, i.e., of the deaf, of the dumb and of the blind. Obviously, one who is bereft of hearing, speech and sight, even from birth, is capable at law of contracting betrothals, as long as all other requisites are met.[153]

At one time, however, it was debated whether or not one who is deaf, dumb and blind *from birth* was able to be affianced validly. Sanchez, for instance, came to a negative conclusion[154] on the assumption that such persons could not be sufficiently instructed or could not express adequately their intentions as to the choice of a partner, etc.[155] This incapacity Sanchez extended even to those who suffered loss of hearing, speech and sight *accidentally after birth.*[156] Schmalzgrueber, on the other hand, did not commit himself either way. He stated simply that Sanchez's argu-

---

mentaria, lib. IV, *De Despons. Impub.* in Cap. *Tua,* n. 1; Reiffenstuel, *Ius Canonicum,* lib. IV, tit. II, n. 18, Schmalzgrueber, *Ius Ecclesiasticum,* lib. IV, tit. II, n. 61; Gasparri, *De Matrimonio,* I, n. 504; Wernz-Vidal, *Ius Canonicum,* I, n. 326.

[152] Canon 1017, § 1.

[153] Cf. Cappello, *De Sacramentis,* V, n. 87, Schmalzgrueber, *Ius Ecclesiasticum,* lib. IV, tit. I, n. 16, etc.

[154] Sanchez, *De Matrimonii Sacramento,* lib. I, dist. VIII, n. 13.

[155] *Loc. cit.*

[156] *Loc. cit.*

ments were of themselves insufficient to prove incapability in this regard.[157]

Today no canonist adheres to the view of Sanchez. Modern medicine, pedagogics and other means of rehabilitation have to a great extent conquered these physical handicaps. Even congenital disabilities, as here described, have not barred some of these unfortunate persons from leading almost normal lives. Hence, if the use of reason and volitional freedom are enjoyed by them, in the canonical sense, the betrothals of the congenitally deaf, dumb and blind persons are valid till the contrary appears.[158]

Article 2: Mental Requisites

In the preceding section of this work it was said that a betrothment promise must be true or sincere, reciprocal (in the bilateral contract), freely made and accepted. In this article consideration will be given to that psychological state, namely insanity, which interferes with these fundamental qualities.

A. Insanity as Precluding Consent

Since it is required that for valid betrothals there be present *at least* that use of discretion and deliberation which is postulated for subjective guilt in the commission of a mortal sin, it is apparent that insane persons cannot validly contract espousals. As they are incapable of sinning seriously, so too they are psychologically powerless to assume a contractual obligation. Obviously, canonists are unanimously agreed concerning this point of natural and positive law.[159] The former law stressed this doctrine frequently, particularly in reference to marriage.[160]

---

[157] Schmalzgrueber, *Ius Ecclesiasticum,* lib. IV, tit. I, n. 16.

[158] Cf. Cappello, *De Sacramentis,* V, n. 87.

[159] Cf., v.g., Schmalzgrueber, *Ius Ecclesiasticum,* lib. IV, tit. I, n. 14.

[160] Cf., v.g., Gratian, c. 26, c. XXXII, q. 7; JK, n. 97; c. 24, X, *de sponsalibus et matrimoniis,* IV, 1; Potthast, n. 22656.

B. Lucid Intervals

What is to be said, however, of those insane persons who enjoy lucid intervals? Are espousals valid when contracted at such a time? St. Thomas, Covarruvias, Sanchez, Schmalzgrueber and others judged betrothments of this nature *valid*. The reason was that understanding and volition are present at this lucid period when the person enters the contract.[161] Schmalzgrueber called attention to the fact that it is precisely the question of validity that is the problem under discussion. All authors agree that espousals, as well as marriage, contracted under these circumstances is *illicit*.[162] The reason for the incontestable illicitness is the incapability of the insane person to discharge his obligations, once the lucid moment passes.[163]

What of doubtful lucidity?

When doubts arise as to the quality of the lucid state, i.e., when it is not clear whether the contractant at the time is in full possession of his mental powers, the presumption in the estimation of canonists is against the party's sanity and his act is to be adjudged null until sanity has been demonstrated.[164]

Cappello, on the other hand, again departs from the traditional view and regards engagements contemplating marriage as *invalid* when entered into even in lucid intervals by persons ordinarily bereft of reason. He draws his arguments from analogous situations, v.g., from cases evincing parental dissent, from factors involving scandal or loss of reputation, from circumstances attended with social disparity, etc. Since such factors in the opinion of many authors, he argues, occasion invalidity, therefore this circumstance should have the same result.[165] He readily concedes that such betrothals are illicit.[166]

---

[161] St. Thomas, *Commentaria,* IV, dist. 34, q. un., art. 4; Covarruvias, *Opera Omnia,* pars II, cap. II, n. s; Sanchez, *De Matrimonii Sacramento,* lib. I, disp. VIII, n. 16.

[162] Schmalzgrueber, *Ius Ecclesiasticum,* lib. IV, tit. I, n. 14.

[163] Schmalzgrueber, *loc. cit.*

[164] Molina, *De Iustitia,* tract II, disp. CXXXVI, n. 3; Sanchez, *De Matrimonii Sacramento,* lib. I, disp. VII, n. 16, Pirhing, *Ius Canonicum,* lib. IV, tit. I, n. X; Schmalzgrueber, *loc. cit.*

[165] Cappello, *De Sacramentis,* V, n. 87.

[166] *Loc. cit.*

However, Cappello's argumentation seems very vulnerable. First, it contravenes the common notion that betrothals once entered are acts that presumably stand as human acts, hence as valid until proven otherwise. Secondly, not all canonists declare that such factors as parental objection (even when reasonable), fear of subsequent discord, possible scandal, etc., necessarily beget invalid compacts, as Cappello would have it.[167] Vlaming, for example, regards all these elements as militating against licitness, not validity.[168]

Therefore, it must be maintained that there is no reason why espousals concluded during a lucid period, i.e., at a time when sanity obtained, should be considered invalid. This consideration, again, is a juridic one. In practice a case of this nature would hardly occur.

C. Espousals of Demented Persons

As for *demented* people, i.e., those who are sane in all respects except one or another, it is likewise disputed whether or not these persons are capable of contracting espousals validly.

Sanchez, after explaining both sides of the question, decided in favor of validity, so long as the operations of the mind and will were not so impaired at the time of the making of the contract that the party was unaware of the significance of the act which he or she placed.[169] This opinion seems reasonable. It also appears preferable to the opposing one which, according to the explanation furnished by Sanchez, is based on the broad philosophical principle that the intellect cannot judge correctly when the imaginative faculty is vitiated in its potential operation.[170] This principle does not demonstrate satisfactorily that due deliberation and proper discretion are in such an event absent at the time of the espousals.

---

[167] *Loc. cit.*

[168] Vlaming, *Praelectiones,* I, n. 90. These factors will again be discussed when the dissolution of the contract is treated in pp. 204-233.

[169] Sanchez, *De Matrimonii Sacramento,* lib. I, disp. VIII, n. 22.

[170] ". . . ergo vitiata sensuum principe imaginativa, intellectus non poterit recte ratiocinari, quod ad libertatem desideratur."—Sanchez, *loc. cit.*

Hence, the opinion of Sanchez appears more acceptable. Cappello does not agree with Sanchez, but he offers no proof for his own view.[171]

More about the complex psychological state of the demented need not be said. In practice the juridic form, requiring as it does a written document, signatures and witnesses, serves as a safeguard against such mental aberrations and prevents them from destroying the value of the act.[172]

SECTION IV. JURIDIC FORM OF THE BETROTHAL CONTRACT

Article 1: Historical Background in Brief

The need of a canonical form for the espousals is something relatively new in the general legislation of the Church. In a previous chapter,[173] it was shown how the Holy See opposed any solemnity of form as a requisite for the validity of the betrothment.[174] This policy over the years was gradually mitigated in Spain. In fact, by 1880 the observance of a specific form became obligatory under pain of nullity in that realm.[175] By 1900 espousal form was required for validity by force of law in South America.[176] On August 2, 1907, the decree *Ne temere* made a canonical form for espousals obligatory for the universal Church under pain of nullity.[177]

Ten years later the Code appeared, re-stating the *Ne temere* provision in the first paragraph of canon 1017 and adding the

[171] Cappello, *De Sacramentis,* V, n. 87.

[172] For a fuller explanation of the nature of the demented state, cf., v.g., D'Annibale, *Summula Theologiae Moralis* (5. ed., 4 vols., Romae, 1908), III, n. 30 (hereafter this work will be cited *Summula*).

[173] Pp. 53-67.

[174] *Loc. cit.* Cf. also S.C.C., *Bracaren., Sponsalium,* 26 ian. 1715—Pallottini, XVI, 384, n. 8; Feije, *De Impedimentis,* n. 558, footnote 6; Wernz-Vidal, *Ius Canonicum,* V, n. 36; pp. 53-68.

[175] S.C.C., *Placentina, Sponsalium;* 31 ian. 1880—*Thesaurus,* CXXXIX (1881), 33-41. Cf. also p. 58 of this work.

[176] S. C. Neg. Eccl. Extra., 1 iul. 1900—*Analecta Ecclesiastica,* VIII, 167-169. Cf. pp. 53-67 of this thesis.

[177] S.C.C., decr. *Ne temere,* 2 aug. 1907—*Fontes,* n. 4340. Cf. pp. 83-86 of this dissertation.

notion of *unilaterality* to the hitherto bilateral concept of espousals. Invalidity was made effective in both fora, so as to preclude the doubts that had arisen in 1901 and which the Holy See had solved that year.[178] In the second paragraph, canon 1017 repeated the *Ne temere* provision concerning the need for a *third* witness in the event one or both parties are unable to write, and the necessity of noting in the contract the person's inability to write. The Code made it explicit that invalidity results if these two elements are lacking. The Sacred Congregation of the Council did not state whether licitness or invalidity was involved when it issued the *Ne temere* law.[179]

Article 2: The Provisions of the Code on the Canonical Form for Espousals

The new legislation on the juridic form for betrothment, as found in the first two paragraphs of canon 1017, reads as follows:

1. "A promise of marriage, whether unilateral or bilateral, that is, in the nature of a mutual espousal, is null in both fora unless it is made in writing, signed by both parties and by either the pastor or the ordinary of the place, or at least by two witnesses."
2. "If both parties, or either of them, do not know how to write, or are unable to do so, then for validity of the act mention must be made of this fact in the contract and another witness must sign the document, together with the parish priest or the ordinary of the place, or the two witnesses spoken of in § 1."[180]

---

[178] Cf. S. C. pro *Neg. Eccl. Extr.*, 5 nov. 1901—*ASS*, XXXIV (1901-1902), 398.

[179] S.C.C., decr. *Ne temere—Fontes*, n. 4340.

[180] Writer's translation.

Can. 1017, § 1: "Matrimonii promissio sive unilateralis, sive bilateralis seu sponsalitia, irrita est pro utroque foro, nisi facta fuerit per scripturam subsignatam a partibus et vel a parocho aut loci Ordinario, vel a duobus saltem testibus.

§ 2: Si utraque vel alterutra pars scribere nesciat vel nequeat, ad validitatem id in ipsa scriptura adnotetur et alius testis addatur qui cum parocho aut loci Ordinario vel duobus testibus, de quibus in § 1 scripturam subsignet."

Three principal types of espousal form are, therefore, recognized as canonically valid by the Code today. First, espousals contracted in the presence of either the ordinary of the place or before the pastor; secondly, before two or more law witnesses; thirdly, before three witnesses when one or both contractants are unable to write. The first two species of form, as contemplated by the Code, comprise the *ordinary* solemnity. The third may be styled the *extraordinary* form.[181]

Careful consideration of the nature of the betrothal contract reveals that three conditions are necessary for validity if the espousals are to be made in due canonical form. These are: first, the promise must be made in writing; secondly, the date, that is, the day, month and year must be indicated; thirdly, the document must be subscribed simultaneously by both the principals as well as by the witnesses. Each of these conditions will now be explained in detail.

Article 3: The Nature of the Written Instrument

A. Manner of Drawing up the Instrument

First, the promise itself: It must be written—whether by the parties themselves or by others, whether by hand, on the typewriter or on the press, is immaterial.[182] If any conditions should be appended (about which more will be said in the section to follow)[183] or a stipulated time for the fulfillment of the obligation added, then a mention of these limitations must be included, for otherwise no canonical effects can follow.[184]

B. Indication of Date and Place

Secondly, the date must be indicated. This specification is not found in canon 1017. Certainly, it would not be safe to omit the

[181] Coronata, *De Sacramentis,* III, n. 47. Cf. the various formularies given at the end of this section (pp. 150-154).

[182] "Redactio actus a qualibet persona fieri potest et quovis modo, nempe vel impressione typographica vel machina dactilographica vel currenti calamo." —Coronata, *De Sacramentis,* III, n. 47. Cf. also Cappello, *De Sacramentis,* V, n. 89.

[183] Pp. 161-174.

[184] Cf. the formularies at the end of this section, pp. 150-154.

day, month and year in the format.[185] The *Ne temere* law required the date for validity, as is evidenced by the reply given by the Holy See in 1908 to a question on this matter.[186] Hence, although the Code is silent in this respect, there must not be any departure from the previous law in a case of doubt, as canon 6, 2° and 4°, as well as canons 22 and 23, declare. The pre-Code law retains its full vigor in this regard.[187]

It is permissible to indicate the month and day equivalently, v.g., the Feast of the Assumption, Wednesday in Holy Week, etc. The year must appear absolutely.[188] However, it is suggested by this writer that, if the equivalent month and day are written (which is also approved Christian practice), the *unequivocal* statement of date should also be added. This would expedite matters were a suit for damages, arising from the breach of contract, to be later filed in civil court.

A *false* date, all Code commentators acknowledge, *voids* an espousal pact.[189] If the error was committed inadvertently, i.e., without intent at fraud, and from the context the date is ascertainable with centainty, i.e., recognized in its equivalent form, the instrument is to be regarded as valid.[190]

What of the annotation of the *place* of contract? Neither the Code nor the Pontifical Commission for the Authentic Interpretation of the Code has declared for or against validity when the mention of place has been omitted. Both Wouters (1864-1933) and Vlaming (+ 1935) maintained that failure to insert the nota-

---

[185] Ayrinhac, *Marriage Legislation*, n. 22.

[186] S.C.C., *Romana et aliarum*, 27 iul. 1908, ad II—*Fontes*, n. 4350.

[187] Cf. Cappello, *De Sacramentis*, V, n. 90; Wouters, *Manuale Theologiae Moralis* (2 vols., Brugis: Beyaert, 1932-1933), I, 665, footnote 1 (hereafter this work will be cited *Manuale*); Wernz-Vidal, *Ius Canonicum*, V, n. 89; Coronata, *De Sacramentis*, III, n. 47, footnote 6; Gasparri, *De Matrimonio*, I, n. 72; Ayrinhac, *loc. cit.*, Woywod-Smith, *Commentary*, I, n. 984.

[188] *Loc. cit.*

[189] Thus, v.g., Cappello, Wouters, Wernz-Vidal, Coronata, Gasparri, *loc. citatis.*

[190] "At si appositio falsae datae errori involuntario sit adscribenda, et vera data ex contextu erui *certo* possit, dubitandum, non est de valore sponsalium." —Cappello, *De Sacramentis*, V, n. 90. Cf. also Wouters, *Manuale*, I, n. 665; Vlaming, *Praelectiones*, I, n. 94.

tion of the place of the making of the contract in the betrothment document renders it invalid. They argued that the necessity of mentioning the place where the engagement is effected is to be adjudged from the customary practice of inscribing the date on all legal documents and important papers. Furthermore, whenever it happens that the ordinary or the pastor attests the prenuptial alliance, the need to inscribe the name of the diocese or the parish seems to be derived from the nature of the contract. That the ordinary or the pastor validly subscribe to the legal fact of affiancement, it is required that they do so in their respective territory, presumably indicated by name and place in the document.[191] The customary practice in the view of Wouters has foundation in canon 1884, 4°, where the Code legislates that a judicial sentence labors under remediable nullity when the year, month, day and place are not indicated.[192]

Cappello admits that this argumentation is in part valid, but he does *not* regard it peremptory. Indicating the place of contract, he avers, is indeed customarily deemed necessary in documentation, *but never interpreted as essential for validity*. Further, even though the annotation of the place is useful for determining whether the ordinary or the pastor were acting within their respective jurisdiction, that fact is *not the only means of determining jurisdiction*. Lastly, Cappello adverts, the argument from analogy taken from canon 1884, 4°, is not valid, as it does not apply.[193]

---

[191] Dubitatur utrum necne etiam appositio *loci, in quo promissio fit,* ad valorem requiratur. Pro sententia affirmante militat *primum*, quod consuetudo subscriptionem datae ita interpretatur, ut etiam locus apponatur. Deinde ubi agitur de sponsalibus subsignatis a parocho vel ab Ordinario, appositio loci summopere conducit ad documentum, quod valorem sponsalium possit firmiter probare; siquidem ut praedicti valide subsignent, requiritur ut id peragant in loco territorii sui. Quod S.C. Conc. quum datam addendam esse respondit, de appositione loci tacuit, id forte explicatur ex eo, quod de ea interrogata non fuit. Quum res dubia sit, appositio loci practice non omittatur." —Wouters, *loc. cit.* Cf. also Vlaming, *loc. cit.* Cf. also Theodori, *"De Promissionis Matrimonialis forma" apollinaris* (Romae, 1928-), VII (1934), 242.

[192] "Sententia vitio sanabilis nullitatis laborat quando . . . 4° non refert indicationem anni, mensis, diei et loci quo prolata fuit."—Canon 1884, 4°.

[193] Cappello, *De Sacramentis,* V, n. 90.

Whereupon, until it has been otherwise authoritatively decided, the indication of the place of the espousal contract is to be deemed not essential for validity. Thus Cappello's conclusion. In practice, however, he concludes, it must not be omitted.[194]

Since a doubt of law here exists, it is the opinion of the present writer that invalidity cannot be urged under the circumstances here described. Canon 15 states that invalidating and disqualifying laws lose their binding force when a doubt is involved in the law.[195] Further, canon 11 indicates that only those laws are to be construed as invalidating and disqualifying which state *explicitly or equivalently* that an action is null or that a person is incapacitated from acting.[196]

Consequently, the view of Cappello in favor of validity of betrothment contracts, even though the place of contract is not mentioned, seems more acceptable than the opposing one of Wouters and Vlaming.

C. The Signature of the Parties

Thirdly, the betrothal document must be attested by means of the simultaneously affixed signatures of the parties themselves.

The attestation must be set down in the parties' own hand. A rubber stamp, a typewritten signature, an engraving or an imprint of any sort will not be legally sufficient. In the common estimation of prudent men these devices do not properly constitute or serve as a genuine signature.[197]

---

[194] "Quare tenendum appositionem loci, donec aliud authentice declaratum fuerit, ad validitatem non requiri. At practice ea numquam omittatur."—*Loc. cit.*

[195] Canon 15: "Leges, etiam irritantes et inhabilitantes, in dubio iuris non urgent. . . ."

[196] Canon 11: "Irritantes aut inhabilitantes eae tantum leges habendae sunt, quibus aut actum esse nullum aut inhabilem esse personam expresse vel aequivalenter statuitur." These same canons served for refuting Cappello's view on the subject of the insufficiency of the seventh year of life relative to capacity for entering espousals. Cf. pp. 117-125 of this thesis.

[197] "Invalide subsignat, qui utitur instrumento, quod nomen ad similitudinem characteris insculptum refert, aut qui utitur machina scribendi; haec sane ratio subsignandi omni signo authenticitatis destituitur, nec est vera ac proprie dicta subsignatio iuxta communem usum atque aestimationem hominum."—Cappello, *De Sacramentis,* V, n. 91 f.

Absence of the parties' signatures is excusable only on two grounds, illiteracy and physical incapability. This fact must be noted in the document, should it occur, and the defect must be supplied by means of an additional signature of a new witness. Only one such extra witness is needed, even though both parties are unable to sign the instrument.[198]

To preclude all possible suspicion of fraud, it is perhaps advisable to state the *reason* for the inability to write. Ignorance of the art of writing or physical disability, proceeding from loss of a hand or fingers, as well as from a passing injury or a current illness, when noted in the betrothal document will help dissipate any doubts that may later arise as to the validity of the attestation. However, writing the letter "X" or any equivalent sign taken to mean inability to write is not necessary in the betrothment formulary. Especially would this sign not suffice, if the additional witness failed to add his signature and the mention regarding the illiteracy or the inability to attest the proceedings were omitted from the text of the agreement.[199]

It is controverted, however, whether it is necessary for the party *capable* of writing to affix his signature to the document when his espoused cannot write. Does the signature of the added witness substitute adequately for the signature of both parties, or does it merely supply for the one absent? It seems that it serves as a legal remedy for only the legitimately missing signature. It hardly appears logical for the legislator to relieve the capable party from attesting his espousal-form when the deficiency to perform the same is found only in the other contractant. Yet, the second paragraph of Canon 1017 can be understood as relieving the capable contractant, since in that paragraph no specific mention is made of the need for this capable party to subscribe the act. In practice, however, it would not be safe to neglect the formality of adding the capable party's signature.[200]

Helping the party to sign his or her name is licit, so long as

[198] Canon 1017, § 2.

[199] Cappello, *loc. cit.;* Davis, *Moral and Pastoral Theology*, IV, 82.

[200] Cf. Cappello, *loc. cit.;* Ayrinhac, *Marriage Legislation*, n. 22.

that party remains the *principal cause* of the writing; otherwise it would be not only illicit but invalid as well.[201]

A final consideration to be accorded here concerns the prescription of the Sacred Congregation of the Council apropos of the necessity for the principals to attest their espousal agreement simultaneously, i.e., in each other's presence. The affirmative decision to this effect was given by the said Congregation in 1908 in answer to a question submitted after the appearance of the *Ne temere* legislation.[202] In the opinion of present day commentators on the Code, this decision still binds and is applicable to the law of the Code, as the legislation in question here is identical with that of the decree *Ne temere.*[203]

D. The Use of Proxies and Letters

Would *proxies,* substituting for the principals, act invalidly in the light of the foregoing? Pighi (1847-1926) thought that they would, since no mention is made of them in canon 1017.[204] The common opinion is contrary to Pighi's view.[205] Proxies, therefore, may be employed by the contracting parties in virtue of a special mandate. This fact, however, would have to be noted in the document. Subscription would have to be simultaneous, since the proxies represent the principals.[206]

Hence, it follows that betrothals *by letter,* for instance, would not meet with canonical approval, as simultaneity in signature is

---

[201] Cappello, Ayrinhac, *loc. citatis;* Coronata, *De Sacramentis,* III, n. 46.

[202] S.C.C. *Romana et aliarum,* 27 iul. 1908, ad I—*Fontes,* n. 4350. Cf. pp. 85-87 of this dissertation.

[203] Cappello, *loc. cit.,* Coronata, *ibid.,* n. 46, footnote 2; De Smet, *De Sponsalibus et Matrimonio,* n. 10; Wernz-Vidal, *Ius Canonicum,* V, n. 89; Vlaming, *Praelectiones,* I, n. 94.

[204] Pighi, *De Sacramento Matrimonii* (ed. altera, Veronae, 1921), n. 12.

[205] Cf. Cappello, *De Sacramentis,* V, n. 96.

[206] Cappello, Coronata, *loc. citatis;* Gasparri, *De Matrimonio,* I, n. 76; Davis, *Moral and Pastoral Theology,* IV, 82. The rules governing lawful representation of the parties in the person of the proxy are found in canon 1089.

lacking when letters are employed.[207] Cappello states that a mere *unilateral promise* of marriage can be effected through the instrumentality of epistolary correspondence or a similar communication, since a letter or a note of its very nature is a one-sided act. However, the letter would have to be drafted in legal form, he admits, bearing particularly the notice of each party's consent, before it could enjoy a legal status.[208]

Article 4: The Provision as to Witnesses

Consideration may now be given to the juridic requirements as they apply to the *witnesses* attesting compacts of engagement.

The Code recognizes three types of witnesses as meeting the requisites for attestation. First, the local ordinary is mentioned, then the pastor, and finally the two ordinary or private witnesses.

A. The Local Ordinary

The term "local ordinary," as used here, is to be taken in the meaning assigned it in canon 198, § 1, scil., besides the Roman Pontiff, the residential bishop, the abbot or prelate *nullius*, their vicar general, the administrator of a diocese (i.e., an apostolic administrator), the vicar and prefect apostolic, and in their default, any one who *de iure* or constitutionally succeeds to their administration.[209]

Since the term "local ordinary" is used, it is *not* necessary for validity that the prelate witnessing the espousals be the party's *proper* ordinary.[210] What is required is that this act take place *within* his territory.[211] Should be perform the duty of a witness

---

[207] Cappello, Coronata, Davis, *loc. citatis;* Wernz-Vidal, *Ius Canonicum*, V, n. 89.

[208] "Epistola enim est natura sua actus unilateralis, et quamvis ex parte seu viri seu mulieris habeatur eiusmodi promissio unilateralis per epistolam facta, tamen verus contractus sponsalitius nondum est, nisi accedat scriptura, legali forma subsignata, quae utriusque partis consensum referat."—Cappello, *loc. cit.*

[209] Canon 198.

[210] Cf. Cappello, *De Sacramentis,* V, n. 91.

[211] *Loc. cit.*

outside his jurisdictional limits, he ceases to be an authorized or official witness in the sense of canon 1017, § 1, and becomes merely one of the two private witnesses mentioned in that canon. In other words, another witness would be necessary for a valid affiancement were the ordinary to attest the deed in a place other than that subject to him.[212] Moreover, he could not delegate any other cleric to act in his stead, v.g., his secretary or the chancellor, as an official or *authorized* witness. The *faculties to designate* another to witness betrothals are *not* granted the ordinary as is the case with reference to matrimony. The Congregation of the Council also decided this point in 1908, when the *Ne temere* provisions came into legal existence.[213] Nonetheless, the ordinary and the pastor, when outside their territory, can act as a private witness in the absence of authority proper to either, but always in conjunction with another witness.

B. The Pastor and the Lawful Substitutes

As for the second kind of witness, namely the pastor, the Code under this term includes all those who can rightfully act in that capacity. Accordingly, the word is to be understood, first, in the strict sense of canon 451, § 1, namely, with reference to the priest to whom a parish has been given in juridic possession (*in titulum*) with the care of souls to be exercised under the authority of the ordinary of the place. Secondly, it is also taken in the sense of quasi-pastor, i.e., with reference to the priest who is in charge of a quasi-parish, as in vicariates and prefectures apostolic.[214] Thirdly, the vicar in charge is also comprehended within the meaning of pastor, i.e., that cleric who has full responsibility for a parish held in the name of a moral person, as a religious order.[215] Fourthly, an *administrator* of a parish can validly attest engagements of marriage, since he falls within the meaning of pastor.[216] Fifthly, a *substitute vicar,* who assumes parochial duties with the permission of the ordinary, when the pastor is to be absent for

---

[212] *Loc. cit.*

[213] S.C.C., *Romana et aliarum,* 28 mart. 1908, ad VI—*Fontes,* n. 4349.

[214] Cf. Canon 451, § 2, 1°.

[215] Canon 471, § 4.

[216] Cf. canon 472.

over a week,[217] or even without that permission in urgent cases, according to the Pontifical Commission for the Authentic Interpretation of the Code,[218] is also comprehended as pastor, and hence is able to witness espousals validly, pending the actual pastor's return. Sixthly, the *substitute vicar* who is appointed by the ordinary to manage a parish when its pastor has been removed by way of judicial sentence and the case is being appealed is likewise to be regarded as coming within the law's category of pastors.[219]

In reference to the substitute's powers, the ordinary could limit the substitute's power of witnessing espousals and marriages, should he so choose. If the pastor were only administratively removed,[220] then the one whom the bishop has appointed in the erstwhile pastor's place enjoys parochial privileges in the same manner as the priest who substitutes for the pastor whose appeal from a penal removal is pending. The powers of this vicar cease once the Holy See appoints a new pastor in place of the one administratively removed.[221]

Lastly, the *vicar assistant,* or the *neighboring pastor,* or the *superior* of a religious house falls into the category of pastor, prior to the appointment by the ordinary of a canonical administrator, when assuming the parochial administration according to law.[222] Hence, while in that office, such a cleric could validly subscribe a betrothal pact in the capacity of an authorized or official witness.[223] Whether a vicar adjutant, in the sense of canon 475, can also attest betrothment documents authoritatively, i.e., as pastor, depends on his letter of appointment. If his appointment carries with it all parochial powers and duties (except those of offering the official Mass for the faithful), he may subscribe en-

---

[217] Canons 465, § 5; 474.

[218] *Pontificia Commissio ad Codicis Canones Authentice Interpretandos,* 13 mart. 1921, ad II—*AAS,* XIV (1922), 527 (hereafter the Commission will be cited *PCI*).

[219] Canons 474; 1923, § 2.

[220] Cf. canons 2147-2156.

[221] Cf. canon 2156, § 2.

[222] Canon 472, 2°.

[223] Cappello, *De Sacramentis,* V, n. 92, 8°.

gagement contracts as an authorized witness, otherwise not, unless from his letter of deputation the complete care of souls in matters pertaining to marriage is actually entrusted to him.[224] Parish assistants,[225] even though they may enjoy delegated powers to act as official witnesses for marriages, are not empowered by that fact to act as official witnesses for espousals. Delegation to attest espousal agreements is not admissible, as was explained above.[226]

Military chaplains are not capable at law to act as official witnesses, unless by Apostolic provision they enjoy full parochial powers as described in canon 451, § 2 and § 3. Other chaplains are also incapable of this act unless they are completely entrusted with the care of souls and consequently with correlative matrimonial matters. However, their subjects *alone* to the exclusion of all non-subjects could benefit from this authorization, as the Sacred Congregation of the Council took pains to explain in 1908.[227]

Rectors would also be incapacitated, unless full parochial rights and prerogatives were accorded them. Their powers would then be exclusive—if the place where they are to be exercised is exempt; cumulative with those of the local pastor—when the latter place is non-exempt.[228]

Like the ordinary, the pastor must subscribe the espousal instrument *within his territory*. On the other hand, the couple promising each other to marry does not have to appear before its proper pastor. A national or personal pastor who has charge of souls not only within the limits of some territorial parish but also outside of it may validly attest betrothals outside of the smaller limits so long as the betrothed are actually his own subjects and not those of the local pastor. In other words, he has cumulative rights with the local pastor. This is especially true when the pastor administers a national parish in a place where there are several parishes, as, v.g., in a city.[229]

---

[224] Cf. Cappello, *loc. cit.*

[225] Canon 476.

[226] Cappello, *loc. cit.*, Gasparri, *De Matrimonio,* I, n. 74.

[227] S.C.C., *Romana et aliarum,* 1 febr. 1908, ad X—*Fontes,* n. 4344.

[228] Cf. canon 464, § 2.

[229] Cf. Cappello, *De Sacramentis,* V, n. 93; Wouters, *Manuale,* II, n. 665.

A *putative pastor,* i.e., one who is commonly regarded as a duly constituted pastor, Cappello claims, can act as an authorized witness when subscribing a betrothment agreement. The espousals are valid, he argues, since the Church in virtue of canon 209 supplies for the defect.[230] But Cappello is mistaken here, since witnessing betrothals is an act of parochial administration, in no wise an act of jurisdiction. Hence, the suppletory principle does not apply.

What of the pastor or the ordinary who has not yet taken canonical possession of his parish or of his diocese? Can he validly witness engagement contracts? There is disagreement among authors. Wouters affirmed that there seems no need for canonical possession, since the law does not mention this condition. The only requisite, Wouters argued, is that he be pastor.[231] Cappello, Coronata, Chelodi-Ciprotti and Wernz-Vidal, deny that a pastor or an ordinary can act as an official witness, unless he has already entered upon the government of his parish or the diocese according to the conditions prescribed in canons 461, 1443-1445 and 334, § 3. The latter lacks administrative power (as well as jurisdiction) prior to his taking canonical possession.[232]

Wouters' argumentation appears unsustainable. Canon 1472 attributes canonical rights to a holder of an ecclesiastical benefice *only after canonical possession.*[233] Canon 461 legislates that a pastor assumes the care of souls in his parish *from the moment he takes possession.*[234] Hence, it would *not be safe* for a pastor to act as an authorized witness prior to the juridic entry upon his office

[230] Cappello, *loc. cit.*

[231] "Porro parochus videtur valide subsignare, etiamsi nondum adeptus sit possessionem beneficii; siquidem lex, ubi de promissione matrimonii dicit, de eiusmodi requisito sermonem non facit, atque solum requirit, ut quis sit parochus."—Wouters, *Manuale,* II, n. 665.

[232] Cappello, *De Sacramentis,* V, n. 93; Coronata, *De Sacramentis,* III, n. 47; Chelodi-Ciprotti, *De Matrimonio,* n. 17; Wernz-Vidal, *Ius Canonicum,* V, n. 89, n. 89.

[233] "Quilibet beneficiarius capta legitime beneficii possessione, omnibus iuribus fruitur tam temporalibus quam spiritualibus, quae beneficio adnexa sint."—Canon 1472.

[234] "Curam animarum parochus obtinet a momento captae possessionis. . . ." —Canon 461.

as described above. If he acted at all, another witness would have to be called in to fulfill the requirement as demanded in canon 1017, § 1. The enjoyment of the care of souls certainly authorizes the witnessing of betrothals. But the care of souls is not entrusted to the cleric until he is lawfully installed as pastor. Therefore, any act on the part of the priest prior to his canonical installation would, to all appearance, lack validity. Hence, assistance at espousals under such circumstances appears invalid, unless, as was indicated above, another witness were procured.

A similar question concerning the validity of attestation is presented in reference to the pastor who is by sentence excommunicated, interdicted or suspended from office or declared such. Wouters claimed that betrothals are valid when attested by a pastor in this condition; for which conclusion he advanced the same reason he adduced above, scil., that, since canon 1017 is silent on the question, nullity cannot be urged.[235]

Cappello distinguishes. *Prior* to the condemnatory or declaratory sentence, certainly an excommunicated, interdicted or suspended pastor acts *validly*. *After* the sentence has been passed, another distinction is made, namely, a pastor *suspended* from office would act *invalidly,* were he to attempt attesting espousals, whereas it is *not certain* whether or not an *excommunicated* and *interdicted* pastor even subsequent to the sentence would act validly.[236]

Concerning *suspension* from office, Cappello cites canon 2279, § 1, in defense of his position. Canon 2279, § 1, declares that suspension from office simply, i.e., without added limitation, forbids all acts involving the power of jurisdiction, of orders and even of mere administration to which a cleric is entitled by his office—with the exception of administering the goods of his own benefice. He also appeals to canon 2284. This canon forbids the administration of the sacraments and sacramentals when the priest has incurred the censure of a suspension which forbids such action, with the exception, of course, of urgency when the sacraments

---

[235] Wouters, *loc. cit.*

[236] Cappello, *De Sacramentis,* V, n. 93.

may be licitly given.[237] Furthermore, canon 2284, so Cappello claims, rules that, when there has been incurred a censure of suspension which forbids an act of jurisdiction in either the internal or the external forum, the act is invalid, if a condemnatory or declaratory sentence has been issued, or if the superior has explicitly declared that he has revoked the jurisdiction; otherwise it is merely illicit.

However, Cappello's arguments are not to the point. Canon 2279, § 1, which that author employs, states that suspension from office *forbids* acts of jurisdiction and administration. Nothing is said of *invalidity*—hence the canon deals with illicitness only. In virtue of the oft-cited canon 11 and canon 15, invalidity cannot be urged where the law merely declares for illicitness. Secondly, canon 2284, also cited by Cappello, concerns only *jurisdiction.* Attesting espousals is an act of parochial *administration,* hence canon 2284 is not apropos in this connection.

Consequently, Cappello's conclusion in this matter cannot be accepted. Wouters appears to be more correct, so that one may accept his opinion as the more probable. There is insufficient evidence to urge invalidity.

As for pastors, not suspended, but *excommunicated* or *interdicted* by court sentence, i.e., *subsequent* to a hearing and a trial, it is not certain whether or not such a pastor can be excluded from acting validly on the strength of canon 1095. This canon deals with *matrimony* and renders marriage invalid when witnessed by a priest laboring thus under excommunication or interdict. On this point Cappello inclines, therefore, to the negative side, and here we think rightly so, on the principle that in odious matters a strict interpretation of the law, in accordance with canon 19, prevails. He also admits that in the case a parity with marriage does not apply. Consequently, Cappello agrees with Wouters that excommunication and interdict, *after* the declaratory sentence has been passed, would not invalidate the attestation. Suspension from office, of course, would invalidate an engagement (as mentioned above, with Cappello agreeing but Wouters disagreeing).[238]

[237] Cf. canon 2261, §§ 1-2.

[238] Cf. Cappella, *loc. cit.;* Wouters, *Manuale,* II, n. 665.

In regard to another customary and legal procedure, the placing of a seal on the betrothal instrument, the pastor need not impress his parochial seal on the document for validity. It would be proper, however, to do so,[239] because of the official act that is being performed. The same can be said in reference to the ordinary, whenever he attests betrothals. A liturgical ceremony or sacred rite (*ritus sacer*) is not prescribed in the Latin Church on the occasion of the plighting of troth unless the ceremony be observed in compliance with a customary practice. No sacred rite, however, can be introduced without previous permission of the Holy See.[240] A liturgical ceremony is traditional among many of the Oriental Catholics.[241] The solemnities of *signing* may take place in the sacristy, in the parish rectory, or in any suitable office or dwelling.[242]

When the pastor or the ordinary witnesses the compact, parochial or diocesan stationery would serve best for the text of the covenant. The agreement, previous to its subscription, should also be read aloud so that all concerned may not be misled as to its import. Reading the document is customary when any legal transaction is reduced to writing.[243] A copy of the contract should be given to each of the parties and the original preserved in the parochial or diocesan archives, according as the pastor or the ordinary has witnessed the deed of affiancement.[244]

C. The Private Witnesses

Concerning the other competent but private witnesses, i.e., others than the local ordinary and the pastor, it suffices that these be of sound mind and adequate mental capacity to understand the nature of a contract and know what is taking place at the time

[239] Coronata, *De Sacramentis,* III, n. 49.

[240] Wernz-Vidal, *Ius Canonicum,* V, n. 90. Weller (*The Roman Ritual* (3 vols., Milwaukee: Bruce, 1946-1952), I, pp. 588-594) reproduces an ancient ritual which can be and is used even today. The *Religious Bulletin* (Notre Dame, Indiana, 1946-   ), V (1951), no. 20, in turn reproduces Weller's translation. It is also appended here (pp. 154-159).

[241] Cf. pp. 146-149 of this dissertation.

[242] Coronata, *De Sacramentis,* III, n. 49.

[243] Cappello, *De Sacramentis,* V, n. 93.

[244] Cappello, *loc. cit.* Cf. also Gasparri, *De Matrimonio,* I, n. 77.

of the making of the contract. The law does not lay down further specific qualifications. Consequently, men as well as women, minors, friends, relatives, apostates, schismatics, infidels and even those under censure may validly attest espousals, as all are juridically capable.[245]

Yet, apostates, heretics, schismatics and those under censure cannot licitly act as witnesses, unless such action is warranted for a just and serious cause. This the authors commonly aver.[246] The Holy Office declared in 1891 that the heterodox should not be employed as witnesses for *marriage,* but it said that this may be tolerated by permission of the ordinary in the absence of scandal.[247] However, nothing was said in that declaration about espousals. Cappello argues for the extension of the ruling to the contract of betrothment on an analogical basis.[248]

But it seems that not even illicitness can be urged, despite the close analogy that exists between marriage and the promise of marriage. The law does not distinguish as to the licitness of the use of the heterodox as witnesses to the contract of betrothal; it is silent, as a matter of fact, on this question. Hence no distinction should be made. Therefore, apostates, heretics, schismatics and those under censure can assist at the making of the contract of espousals in a licit manner.[249]

Article 5: The Obligation of Observing the Form for Espousals

A. Persons Subject to the Form

Fundamentally, no one is obliged to contract espousals before contracting a valid marriage. In that respect betrothment is optional.[250] However, to enjoy the canonical effects, as they are described in canon 1017, the formalities of the law must be ob-

---

[245] Coronata, *ibid.*, n. 48. Augustine, *A Commentary on Canon Law,* V, p. 42.

[246] Cf. Sanchez, *De Matrimonii Sacramento,* lib. III, disp. XLI, n.s.; Laymann, *Theologia Moralis,* lib. V, tract. X, pars II, cap. IV, n. 6; St. Alphonsus, *Theologia Moralis,* lib. VI, n. 1085, etc.

[247] S.C.S. Off., 19 aug. 1891—*Fontes,* n. 1144.

[248] *De Sacramentis,* V, n. 94.

[249] Cf. Coronata, *De Sacramentis,* III, n. 48.

[250] Cf. Vlaming, *Praelectiones,* I, n. 95.

served by those whom the law binds. Those certainly bound are Latin Catholics. Oriental Catholics are in virtue of canon 1 exempt from the general legislation of the Code. As of May 2, 1949, they are bound by their own marriage law, effective on that date. The Oriental Code dealing with espousals, prescribes a form, but not a written one, and requires a liturgical rite, wherever it is customary. Delegated assistance at espousals is permitted, i.e., ordinaries and pastors may appoint substitutes to attest the agreement. The fact of the making of the contract of espousals must be entered in a special register, as in the case of marriage. The new law under two canons, scil., canon 6 and canon 7 of the present Oriental Code,[251] reads as follows:

Canon 6

§ 1. The promise of marriage, even though bilateral, or in the nature of a mutual espousal, is null in both fora, unless made before the pastor or the local Hierarch, or before a priest to whom the faculty of assisting has been given by either of these.

§ 2, 1°. The same pastor or local Hierarch, or priest designated by either, validly assists at a promise of marriage, who, by the prescription of canons 86 and 87, validly assists at marriage;

2°. He who assists at a promise of marriage is by obligation bound to see to it that its celebration is entered in the book of espousals.

§ 3. However, from the promise of marriage no judicial action is made available for seeking the celebration of the marriage; but such action is granted for the repairing of damages if any be due.

Canon 7

The priest assisting at the promise of marriage must not

[251] Pius XII, motu propr., *De Disciplina Sacramenti Matrimonii pro Ecclesia Orientali,* 22 februarii, 1949—*AAS,* XLI (1949), 89-119.

> omit to impart to Catholic parties the blessing prescribed in the liturgical books, if particular law so provides.[252]

Secondly, baptized heretics and schismatics, it is generally admitted, are under obligation to observe the canonical form of betrothal for the enjoyment of its juridic effects. The Code does not indicate this fact expressly, but neither does it exempt these persons, as it does in reference to the canonical form prescribed for marriage (canon 1099) when they contract marriage among themselves. It is true that the decree *Ne temere* exempted non-Catholics from observing the necessary formalities on the occasion of affiancement,[253] but no such exemption can be found in the present legislation. Hence, baptized non-Catholics, whenever they desire to become espoused and to benefit juridically by that action are bound to the form, whether the betrothals be among themselves, with a Catholic or with any non-baptized non-Catholic.[254] Non-baptized persons are not subject to the espousal-form when contracting *among themselves*.[255]

The law governing the observance of formalities is in virtue of

---

[252] *Loc. cit.* (Writer's own translation.)

"Can. 6.

"§ 1. Matrimonii promissio, etsi bilateralis, seu sponsalitia, irrita est pro utroque foro, nisi facta fuerit coram parocho aut loci Hierarcha aut sacerdote cui ab alterutro facta sit facultas assistendi.

"§ 2, 1°. Matrimonii promissioni valide assistit idem parochus vel loci Hierarcha aut sacerdos ab alterutro designatus qui ex praescripto can. 86, 87, matrimonio valide assistit;

"2°. Ille qui matrimonii promissioni assistit obligatione tenetur curandi ut ejus celebratio in libro sponsalium adnotetur.

"§ 3. At ex matrimonii promissione non datur actio ad petendam matrimonii celebrationem; datur tamen ad reparationem damnorum, si qua debeatur.

"Can. 7.

"Sacerdos promissioni matrimonii assistens, sponsis catholicis benedictionem in libris liturgicis praescriptam impertire, si ius particulare id ferat, ne omittat."

[253] S.C.C. decr., *Ne temere,* 2 aug. 1907, XI, § 3—*Fontes,* n. 4340.

[254] Wouters, *Manuale,* II, n. 668.

[255] *Loc. cit.* Cf. also Romani, *Institutiones Iuris Canonici* (2 vols. in 3, Vol. II, Section II, 1945, Romae: Editrice Iustitia, 1941-1945), II, sec. 2, n. 671.

canon 10 not retroactive.[256] Hence, absence of the canonical form does not thereby invalidate espousals contracted prior to May 19, 1918, and still extant, i.e., not consummated, after that date. However, in regard to the *effects* flowing out of a contract that took place before the promulgation of the Code, no action other than a suit for damages was allowed after the Code-law went into effect. This was the decision of the Pontifical Commission for the Authentic Interpretation of the Code.[257]

B. Effects of Private Espousals

What of betrothals entered into privately, i.e., without the prescribed form? Are they illicit also by the very fact that the law declares them *invalid?*[258]

It does not seem so.

Commentators are generally agreed that the legislator succeeded in his purpose when declaring form-free espousals invalid. There was no need for him to add a prohibitory clause. Such a clause, they claim, would have provided opportunity for continuous and numerous transgressions of the law. This would hardly be conducive toward promoting the public good.[259]

Lastly, it is of interest to note that Vlaming was of the opinion that the unilateral promise of marriage does not admit of the form prescribed by the Code in canon 1017, § 1. The unilateral type of espousal, he contended, receives mention in canon 1017, § 1, simply to have any juridic effect denied to it. The words, "unless made in writing," as found in the first paragraph of canon 1017, so Vlaming stated, seem to refer not to the unilateral

---

[256] Coronata, *De Sacramentis,* III, n. 46.

[257] *PCI,* 2-3 iun. 1918, dub. IV—*AAS,* X (1918), 345.

[258] Cf. canon 1017, § 1.

[259] Thus, v.g., Wouters, *Manuale,* II, n. 666: "Quamvis promissio matrimonii informis invalida sit, tamen non videtur illicita. Etenim, finis legislatoris satis obtinetur sola irritatione promissionis informis, quin prohibitio accedat. Adde, legem, quae non solum irritaret, verum etiam prohiberet promissiones informes, innumeris atque continuis transgressionibus ansam praebituram, ideoque ad bonum commune non esse conducturam."

promise but only to the bilateral form of espousals.[260] The reason for his view, Vlaming wrote, was that the Church wishes to restrict as much as possible all court actions and damage suits arising out of mere, i.e., unilateral, promises of marriage, which hitherto were never acknowledged or recognized officially by the Church.[261]

However, hardly any canonist agrees with the view that unilateral promises are not subject to the canonical form. Vlaming's opinion does not seem conformable with the mind of the Code in this regard.[262]

Article 6: Formularies for Espousals

Formulary A

Bilateral Espousals Subscribed by the Principals and the Pastor.

We, the undersigned principals:

N.N., son of .... and ...., born on the ...... day of .... 19...... in the City of .... of the State of ...., a member of .... Parish in the Diocese of .... and currently residing at .... in ....;

And:

N.N., daughter of .... and ...., born on the ...... day of .... 19..... in the City of .... of the State of ...., a member of .... Parish in the Diocese of .... and currently residing at .... in ....:

---

[260] "Nostro vero judicio promissio huiusmodi [unilateralis] in canone [1017, § 1] non memoratur nisi ad quemlibet effectum ei abloquendum, quin ipsa deinde comprehendatur subsequenti hypothesi, nisi, etc."; "eandemque hypothesin ad solam promissionem bilateralem, seu sponsalitiam, referendam putamus."—Vlaming, *Praelectiones,* I, n. 84.

[261] *Loc. cit.*

[262] Cf. Coronata, *De Sacramentis,* III, n. 41, footnote 1; O'Neill, "The Obligation of An Informal Promise of Marriage," *The Irish Ecclesiastical Record* (Dublin, 1864-), LXIII (1934), 529.

In accordance with the prescriptions of Canon 1017, § 1, of the Code of Canon Law of the Roman Catholic Church:

Have mutually agreed, and do hereby mutually agree, with each other, in consideration of our present, mutual promise of future marriage with each other, to enter hereby absolutely into this engagement of future matrimony:

In witness whereof we have hereunto in each other's presence set our hands, this the .... day of ...., A.D. 19......, at ....

....

(Fiancé)

....

(Fiancée)

I, the undersigned, N. N., pastor of .... Parish, located at ...., in the Diocese of ...., do hereby attest, in accordance with the said prescription of canon 1017, § 1, of the Code of Canon Law of the Roman Catholic Church, that the foregoing instrument of betrothment was made and subscribed personally and in each other's presence by the above mentioned parties before me, the pastor of the above named parish at .... Rectory in ...., on this the .... day of ...., A.D. 19.......

In faith whereof I hereby set my hand and seal simultaneously with and in the presence of the above-named parties on the day and in the place last aforementioned.

....

(Pastor)

L. S.

Formulary B

Unilateral Promise of Marriage

I, the undersigned N. N., son of .... and ...., born at .... in the State of ...., on the .... day of .... 19........, a member of St. .... Parish in ...., in the Diocese of ...., and currently residing at .... Street, ...:

In accord with the prescriptions of canon 1017, § 1, of the Code of Canon Law of the Roman Catholic Church:

In view of marriage in the future with N. N., daughter of .... and ...., as her fiancé and/or as her consort in marriage, have agreed and covenanted and do hereby agree and covenant to be obligated absolutely on my part to her, the aforementioned, under the contract of engagement, to enter future marriage with her, the aforementioned N. N.

In faith whereof I do herewith in the presence of the aforementioned N. N., set my hand and seal, this the .... day of ...., A.D. 19......

....

(Fiancé)

Wherefore, I, N.N., the undersigned, daughter of .... and .... born on .... day of .... 19........ at .... in the State of ....,
a member at present of St. .... Parish in .... of the Diocese of ...., and currently dwelling at .... Street, City of .... in ....:

In view of the foregoing promise of future marriage now made to me the aforementioned by ...., the aforementioned, as my fiancé, do hereby accept the said promise of future matrimony as proposed herein to me by the aforementioned N. N.

In faith whereof I do herewith in the presence of the aforementioned N. N. set my hand and seal, this the .... day of ...., A. D. 19........

....

(N. N.)

I, the undersigned N. N., pastor of St. .... Parish of .... do hereby attest that the foregoing instrument of betrothment was made and subscribed personally by the above mentioned parties in the presence of each other before me the aforementioned pastor in my parish above mentioned at St. .... Rectory at .... Street of the City .... in .... on this the .... day of ...., A. D. 19......

In witness whereof I do hereby set my hand and seal simultaneously with and in the presence of the parties above mentioned and on the day and in the place aforementioned.

____
(Pastor)

Formulary C

Espousals Attested by Extra Witness

The undersigned N. N., son of ________ ________ and ________ ________ born at ________ in the State of ________ on the ____ day of ________ 19____, a member of St. ________ Parish in ________ of the State of ________ and at present residing at ________ ________ in the City of ________ in the State of ________:

and:

The undersigned N. N., daughter of ________ ________ and ________ ________, born in ________ of the State of ________ on the ________ day of ________ 19____, a member of ________ Parish in of the Diocese of ________________, and at present residing at ________ ________ of the City of ________ in the State of ________:

In accord with the prescriptions of canon 1017, § 1, of the Code of Canon Law of the Roman Catholic Church:

Hereby promise to contract marriage with each other on the ______ day of ____________ 19____: N. N. is unable to write because of ____________________

Given at ________ this ______ day of ________ 19____

____
(Fiancé)

____
(Fiancée)

____
(Witness)

____
(Witness)

I the undersigned, N. N., being personally present at the making of the above betrothment contract do hereby declare of my certain knowledge that the aforesaid N. N., party contractant in the aforementioned betrothment contract, is unable to write because ....

In faith whereof I hereunto set my hand on the date and at the place aforementioned.

....

(Added Witness)

Article 7: The Rite of Betrothal[202a]

"When a Christian man and woman intend to pledge themselves to marriage, it is praiseworthy and in accord with ancient ecclesiastical custom to have the engagement solemnized and blessed by the Church. For detailed discussion of a valid betrothal and its consequences it will be necessary to refer to Canon Law (canon 1017) and the added information of a commentary. May it suffice to state here that no action is admissible to compel the celebration of marriage, even after a formal engagement has taken place, although a damage suit would be permitted before a competent judge, either in ecclesiastical or civil court.

There is no prescribed ritual for betrothal. However, it is most fitting that the ceremony take place before the altar of God, and that it be followed by the offering of the Eucharistic Sacrifice, together with the reception of Holy Communion. The following prayers and ceremonies are suggested.

1. The priest (vested in surplice and white stole) with his assistants (vested in surplice) awaits the couple at the communion table. At hand are the stoup with holy water and the altar missal. As the man and woman come forward with the two witnesses they have chosen, the following antiphone and psalm are sung on the eight psalm tone:

Antiphon: To the Lord I will tender my promise: in the presence of all His people.

[202a] Reproduced with the permission of the author, Weller, *The Roman Ritual*, I, 588-593.

Psalm 126

Unless the house be of the Lord's building, in vain do the builders labor.

Unless the Lord be the guard of the city, 'tis in vain the guard keeps his sentry.

It is futile that you rise before daybreak, to be astir in the midst of darkness,

Ye that eat the bread of hard labor; for He deals bountifully to His beloved while they are sleeping.

Behold, offspring result from God's giving, a fruitful womb the regard of His blessing.

Like arrows in the hand of the warrior, are children begotten of a youthful father.

Happy the man who has filled therewith his quiver; they shall uphold him in contending at the gate with his rival.

Glory be to the Father and to the Son, and to the Holy Spirit.

As it was in the beginning, is now, and forever, through endless ages. Amen.

Antiphon: To the Lord I will tender my promise: in the presence of all His people.

2. The priest now addresses them:

ALLOCUTION

Beloved of Christ: It is in the dispensation of Divine Providence that you are called to the holy vocation of marriage. For this reason you present yourselves today before Christ and His Church, before His sacred minister and the devout people of God, to ratify in solemn manner the engagement bespoken between you. At the same time you entreat the blessing of the Church upon your proposal, as well as the earnest supplications of the faithful here present, since you fully realize that what has been inspired and guided by the will of your heavenly Father requires equally His grace to be brought to a happy fulfillment. We are confident that you have given serious and prayerful deliberation to your pledge of wedlock; moreover, that you have sought counsel from the superiors whom God has placed over you. In the time that intervenes, you will prepare for the sacrament of matrimony by a period of virtuous courtship, so that when the happy and blessed day arrives for you to give yourselves irrevocably to each other, you will have laid a sound spiritual foundation for long years of godly prosperity on earth and eventual blessedness together in the life to come. May the union you purpose one day to consummate as man and wife be found worthy to be in all truth a sacramental image and reality of the union of Christ and His beloved Bride, the Church. This grant, thou Who livest and reignest, God, forever and evermore. R. Amen.

3. The priest now bids the couple to join their right hands, the while they repeat after him the following:

The man:

In the name of our Lord, I, N.N., promise that I will one day take thee, N.N., as my wife, according to the ordinances of God and holy Church. I will love thee even as myself. I will keep faith and loyalty to thee, and so in thine necessities aid and comfort thee; which things and all that a man ought to do unto his espoused I promise to do unto thee and to keep by the faith that is in me.

The woman:

In the name of our Lord, I, N.N., in the form and manner wherein thou hast promised thyself unto me, do declare and affirm that I will one day bind and oblige myself unto thee, and will take thee, N.N., as my husband. And all that thou hast pledged unto me I promise to do and keep unto thee, by the faith that is in me.

4. Then the priest takes the two ends of his stole and in the form of a cross places them over the clasped hands of the couple. Holding the stole in place with his left hand, he says:

I bear witness of your solemn proposal and I declare you betrothed. In the name of the Father, and of the Son, and of the Holy Spirit. Amen. As he pronounces the last words, he sprinkles them with holy water in the form of a cross.

5. Thereupon he blesses the engagement ring:

V. Adjutorium nostrum in nomine Domini.	V. Our help is in the name of the Lord.
R. Qui fecit caelum et terram.	R. Who made heaven and earth.
V. Domine, exaudi orationem meam.	V. O Lord, hear my prayer.
R. Et clamor meus ad te veniat.	R. And let my cry come unto thee.
V. Dominus vobiscum.	V. The Lord be with you.
R. Et cum spiritu tuo.	R. And with thy spirit.
Oremus.	Let us pray.
Oratio	
Omnipotent Deus, creator et conservator humani generis, ac largitor aeternae salutis, permitte digneris Spiritum sanctum Paraclitum super hunc anulum. Per Dominum nostrum Jesum Christum, Filium tuum: Qui tecum vivit et regnat in unitate Spiritus Sancti Deus, per omnia saecula saeculorum. R. Amen. Et aspergatur aqua benedicta.	O God Almighty, Creator and preserver of the human race, and the Giver of everlasting salvation, deign to allow the Holy Spirit, the Consoler to come with His blessing upon this ring. Through our Lord, Jesus Christ, thy Son, who liveth and reigneth with thee in the unity of the Holy Spirit, God, for endless ages. R. Amen. The ring is sprinkled with holy water.

6. The man takes the ring and places it first on the index finger of the left hand of the woman, saying: In the name of the Father, then on the middle finger, adding: and of the Son, finally placing and leaving it on the ring finger, he concludes: and of the Holy Spirit.

7. The priest opens the missal at the beginning of the Canon, and presents the page imprinted with the crucifixion to be kissed first by the man and then by the woman.

8. If Mass does not follow (or even if Mass is to follow, if he

deems it opportune), the priest may read the following passages from Sacred Scripture:

Tobias 7:8

Tobias said: I will not eat nor drink here this day, unless thou first grant me my petition, and promise to give me Sara thy daughter. . . . The angel said to Raguel: Be not afraid to give her to this man, for to him who feareth God is thy daughter due to be his wife; therefore another could not have her. . . . And Raguel taking the right hand of his daughter, he gave it unto the right hand of Tobias, saying: The God of Abraham, and the God of Isaac, and the God of Jacob be with you, and may He join you together, and fulfil His blessing in you. And taking paper they made a writing of the marriage. And afterwards they made merry, blessing God. . . . Then Tobias exhorted the virgin, and said to her: Sara, arise, and let us pray to God today, and tomorrow, and the next day; because for these three nights we are joined to God; and when the third night is over, we will be in our own wedlock. For we are the children of saints, and we must not be joined together like heathens that know not God. So they both arose, and prayed earnestly both together that health might be given them. R. Thanks be to God.

John 15:4-12

At that time, Jesus said to His disciples: Abide in me, and I in you. As the branch cannot bear fruit of itself, unless it abide in the vine, so neither can you, unless you abide in me. I am the vine; you are the branches. He that abideth in me, and I in him, the same beareth much fruit; for without me you can do nothing. If any one abide not in me, he shall be cast forth as a branch, and shall wither, and they shall gather him up, and cast him into the fire, and he burneth. If you abide in me, and my words abide in you, you shall ask whatever you will, and it shall be done unto you. In this is my Father glorified; that you bring forth very much fruit, and become my disciples. As the Father hath loved me, I also have loved you. Abide in my love. If you keep my commandments, you shall abide in my love; as I also have kept my Father's commandments, and do abide in His love. These things I have spoken to you, that my joy be in you, and your joy may be filled. This is my commandment, that you love one another, as I have loved you. R. Praise be to thee, O Christ!

9. Lastly, the priest extends his hands over the heads of the couple, and says:

May God bless your bodies and your souls. May He shed His blessing upon you as He blessed Abraham, Isaac, and Jacob. May the hand of the Lord be upon you, may He send His holy Angel to guard you all the days of your life. Amen. Go in peace!"

SECTION V. ADJUNCTS TO THE BETROTHAL CONTRACT

Article 1: Error of Person in the Betrothal Contract

A final characteristic requisite in the espousal promise, namely, *specification* of the principals, will now be considered. The problem will first be approached positively, and then be considered from a negative point of view. In other words, first will be discussed the need of identifying the parties to a betrothment agreement and then the necessity of the absence of error as to person in the formation of this contract of future marriage.

Accordingly, for the proper formation of betrothals, since they follow the laws of contracts, it is essential that they be entered into by specifically determinate persons. Thus, in the unilateral type of engagement of marriage, the promise must be given to a definite party. The espoused must be sufficiently identified, for the purpose of precluding possible nullity and error. In the bilateral arrangement the promise of future nuptials must be mutually exchanged and it must refer to two certain and definite individuals who constitute the principals to the contract. Error, both as to the principals and as to the contract itself, must be guarded against, as it may invalidate the proceeding, as will be shown later.

Now, error is generally defined as a false apprehension of an object or a wrong judgment about some person or thing. It differs from ignorance which, in general, denotes a *lack* of knowledge.[263]

Error may relate to a *fact* or to a *right*. An error of *fact* is an error about the person with whom the contract is made or about his qualities. Error of *right* concerns the nature, property, character or validity of the contract in question.[264] In error of fact, a mistake concerning the person is known as *substantial* error; a mistake relating to his qualities is called *accidental* error.[265] However, an error concerning *quality* is said to redound to error regarding *person* when that quality serves to identify the person, i.e., it is so singular that it coincides with the individual himself.[266] Thus, for instance, John intends to enter espousals with the second eldest daughter of James. The maiden is not known to John. The *third* eldest is given to John for his espoused. He is under the impression that she is the second eldest. The quality, scil., circumstance of birth, is here identified with the person herself.

Error is also distinguished into *concomitant* and *antecedent*. The former has no real influence on consent or promise because, even if the error had not existed, the consent or promise would have been given. The latter, on the other hand, exercises such influence that, had the truth been made known or detected, the consent or promise would have been withheld. In this latter case the error is said to be one "giving cause to the contract."[267]

---

[263] Cf. St. Thomas, *Summa Theologica, Supplementum,* q. 51, a. 1; Sanchez, *De Matrimonii Sacramento,* lib. VII, disp. XVIII, n. 1 sqq.; Schmalzgrueber, *Ius Ecclesiasticum,* lib. IV, tit. I, nn. 433-434; Cappello, *De Sacramentis,* V, n. 584.

[264] Cf. Cappello, *loc. cit.,* and the *Decretum Gratiani,* C. XXIX, q. 1. In both these sources, however, the reference is to marriage. Nonetheless, as is obvious, the distinctions made here apply to espousals as well.

[265] Cf. Schmalzgrueber, *loc. cit.;* Cappello, *ibid.,* n. 98.

[266] Cf. Schmalzgrueber (*ibid.,* n. 435), where he states: "Praeterea error circa qualitatem aliquando redundat in substantiam, et individuum personae, aliquando non primum contingit, quando qualitas, circa quam ille versatur, est omnino singularis; et certum individuum denotans, e.g. quod is, cum quo matrimonium initur, sit certi regis filius aut primogenita filia . . ." etc.

[267] "Dicitur [error] antecedens seu dans causam contractui, si quis, in momento initi contractus, ita erat animo dispositus, ut veritate cognita, noluisset contrahere; concomitans, e contrario, si quis etiam errore detecto, contraxisset."—Cappello, *De Sacramentis,* V, n. 584.

Error will invalidate betrothals if it is a *substantial* one, i.e., if it relates to a person or to a quality identifying a person.[268] *Accidental* error, i.e., error concerning mere quality, whether concomitant or antecedent, does not invalidate espousals, as long as the mistake does not regard the freedom from *servile condition* on the part of the other party, or as long as the accidental quality was not appended to the contract as a condition *sine qua non.*[269] However, if the *accidental* error which gave rise to the betrothal contract was a *serious* error, it then renders the betrothment *voidable.* It is otherwise, if the error concerned some unimportant matter, or if the error was merely concomitant.[270] After the making of the contract, the disposition of a person who would have refused to enter the betrothal contract, if some defect or other had been known, is called an *interpretative will.* It is not an actual reality and does not affect the validity of the betrothal compact. What has to be econsidered is not what *would have been done,* if such a fact had been known, *but what has been done in reality.*[271]

Article 2: Conditional Betrothals

That *conditions* can be appended to espousal contracts is readily admitted by nearly all canonists,[272] if not by decretal law itself.[273]

---

[268] Cappello, *ibid.,* n. 98; Wernz-Vidal, *Ius Canonicum,* V, n. 85; Gasparri, *De Matrimonio,* II, n. 792; De Smet, *De Sponsalibus et Matrimonio,* n. 5.

[269] "Si error est accidentalis, nempe, versetur circa meram personae qualitatem sive concomitans sit sive det causam contractui, sponsalia valent, dummodo ne agatur de errore circa conditionem servilem alterius partis aut qualitatem accidentalem positam tamquam conditionem sine qua non."—Cappello, *loc. cit.*

[270] Cappello, *loc. cit.* Cf. also the decision to this effect in S.C.C., *Tarentina,* Sponsalium, 3 oct., 1705—*Canones et Decreta C. Tridentini a Pelella Edita,* pp. 222-223, n. 17.

[271] Cf. Ayrinhac, *Marriage Legislation,* n. 195.

[272] Cf. Vlaming, *Praelectiones,* I, n. 103 bis.

[273] Cf. Cc. 3, 4, 5, 6, X, *de conditionibus appositis in desponsatione vel in aliis contractibus,* IV, 5: JL, nn. 13946, 13162, 15729. However, because of the thorny problems inherent in these decretals, relating to conditions as they effect the *consensus de futuro* and *de praesenti,* it cannot be stated absolutely that decretal law invested conditional espousals with unmistakable legitimacy and legal value, although probably it did. Cf. pp. 37-39 of this

Certainly, nowhere in the present law are conditional betrothals as such disallowed, as long as the condition is morally good.[274] Furthermore, betrothal contracts are rescissible contracts—hence they admit of conditions.[275]

A. The Notion and Division of Condition

The word "condition" has many significations.[276] Generally, it is defined as: "That circumstance annexed to an arrangement on whose existence we wish the validity [of the arrangement] to depend."[277] In this sense it is used quite generally by authors in their reference to espousals as well as to marriage. It is also in this sense that it is applied in a twofold way, namely, strictly and in a broad manner; strictly, for a future possible contingent event; widely, for past and present facts.[278] In both cases it is commonly signified by means of the usual particles and phrases: If, should, so long as, on condition that, etc.[279] The condition that begets a suspensive effect for the future is a genuine and true condition in the strictest sense of the word, because of itself, by its very nature, it is intended to keep in abeyance the effect of an act till the verification or fulfillment of the condition.[280] Yet, the canonical doctrine on conditions, in general, must also consider such as are without this suspensive effect yet make the validity of

---

dissertation, particularly the English works on this topic therein cited, viz.: Petrovits, *New Church Law,* n. 432; Timlin, *Conditional Matrimonial Consent,* The Catholic University of America Canon Law Studies, n. 89 (Washington, D. C.: The Catholic University of America, 1934), 35-69.

[274] Vlaming, *loc. cit.*

[275] Thus, Cappello, *De Sacramentis,* V, n. 99.

[276] Cf. Schmalzgrueber, *Ius Ecclesiasticum,* lib. IV, tit. V, n. 1. Cf. also pp. 61-65 of this dissertation.

[277] ". . . communissime pro circumstantia [sumitur conditio] dispositioni adiecta a cuius existentia dependere volumus valorem illius."—Schmalzgrueber, *loc. cit.*

[278] Cf. Schmalzgrueber, *ibid.,* n. 2; Gonzalez-Tellez, *Commentaria,* lib. IV, tit. V, cap. I, n. 4; Molina, *De Iustitia,* tract II, disp. CCVI, n. 1; Gasparri, *De Matrimonio,* I, n. 79; Cappello, *De Sacramentis,* V, n. 625.

[279] Cf. Canon 39; D'Annibale, *Summula,* I, n. 41.

[280] Cf. Schmalzgrueber, *loc. cit.*

the act *subjectively uncertain,* as in past and present conditions, about which there will be presented a subsequent discussion.

Now, the *circumstance* that is added to an espousal promise (or to marital consent), and on the verification of which the efficacy of the act is made to depend, can be *any kind* of circumstance. It can *depend* on the free will of the party, v.g., "I will marry you on condition that you first purchase a house"; or the circumstance may be *independent* of it, as e.g.: "I promise to contract marriage with you, once the war is over."[281] The circumstance may also be *factual* or *legal, positive* or *negative.* Factual: "I will become engaged to you if peace is declared." Legal: "I will marry you if a dispensation for our marriage is obtained." Positive: "I promise to enter marriage if the war comes to an end." Negative: "I will marry you if you do not enter the armed service this year."

The *circumstance,* in reference to espousals, must limit the promise of future marriage, i.e., the proper function of the condition, whether suspensive or not (past or present), is to make the efficacy, the espousal-producing result of the promise given, *depend for its existence on the verification or the fulfillment or the truth of the condition.* The existence of the very obligation of the betrothment contract is thus made *to depend on the verification* of the condition which is placed by one or both parties. The condition thus becomes a substantial, constitutive element of the betrothal agreement. The act of affiancement, if the condition is suspensive, is not from its very inception perfect and complete. It becomes so, that is, becomes an *absolute* contract, only at the moment of the verification or the fulfillment of the condition. If the condition is past or present in its reference, v.g.: "I will marry you if you have been pure in the past" or "are a pure person now," then the espousal is or is not in existence according as the condition was or is now verified. Conditions subsequent (*conditio resolutiva*), on the other hand, of their very nature, if added to a betrothal contract, *destroy* the given promise of marriage as soon as they are made, v.g.: "I will carry you unless I find a more attractive girl." The condition obviously indicates a lack of sincerity on the part of the promisor to fulfill his promise.

[281] Cf. Timlin, *Conditional Matrimonial Consent,* pp. 81-82.

Conditions are distinguishable according to the different points of view from which they are considered. From the standpoint of the *instant* in which the condition is verified and the espousals exist, conditions are classed as *suspensive* and *subsequent* (*resolutiva*). The *suspensive* condition is had when the *commencement* of the operation of the act is made to depend on the future fulfillment of the condition, v.g.: "I will take you in marriage if my parents consent." A *subsequent* condition is extant when the termination of the operation of the act is made to depend on the occurrence of the condition, e.g.: "I will marry you unless I find a more attractive girl."[282]

The other categories of conditions are easily understood from their very names. Thus, from the viewpoint of time, they are *past*, *present* and *future,* v.g.: "I become betrothed to you if this *was* my father's wish"; "if it *is* his wish"; "if it *will be* this wish." *Impossible* and *possible* conditions are so called according as they can or cannot be fulfilled, v.g.: "I will be your espoused, if you swim the ocean," or "if our parents consent."

Possible conditions, in turn, are subdivided into *necessary* and *contingent*. A *necessary* condition must be verified of its very nature, v.g.: "I will contract espousals with you if tomorrow comes." A *contingent* condition is one which may or may not be verified but which at the same time is not impossible or necessary, as e.g.: "I will enter marriage with you, unless your family objects."

Possible contingent conditions undergo further subdivision. They may be either arbitrative (*potestativa*) or *casual* conditions. The first, arbitrative conditions, depend only on the free will of one or both contractants, v.g., "I become engaged to you only if you stipulate that you will quit gambling." The second, casual conditions, are not uniformly explained; yet it may be stated that they depend on some occurrence or fact coming to pass without reference to the will of either of the contracting parties, v.g., "I will become your bride, if you survive the war."[283] Such a condition may also depend on a third person, v.g.: "I promise to

---

[282] Cf. Gasparri, *De Matrimonio,* II, n. 80; Cappello, *De Sacramentis,* V, n. 629; Schmalzgrueber, *Ius Ecclesiasticum,* lib. IV, tit. V, n. 8.

[283] Cf. Schmalzgrueber, *Ius Ecclesiasticum,* lib. IV, tit. V, n. 4.

marry you if my commanding officer gives me a reprieve", or on a combination of both the occurrence of the fact and the will of a third party, as v.g.: "I will become engaged to you if your father runs for president and is re-elected."[284]

A *mixed* condition is partly casual, partly arbitrative, v.g.: "I will marry you if you come back to me from the war", i.e., it depends on both the good fortune and on the will of the one departing. Reiffenstuel observed that a *mixed* condition depends in part on the party upon whom it is imposed and in part on the will of another, whereas a casual condition depends not on the will of him upon whom it is placed but on the will of a third party, or on God, v.g.: "I promise to contract marriage with you, if the harvest this year is good."[285]

From the viewpoint of *law,* divine or human, if a condition is contrary to these laws, it belongs to the class of *immoral* (*turpis*) conditions; if *consonant* with them, it is said to be morally good (*honesta*).[286]

B. The Mode, Cause and Demonstration

It is of great importance that the concept of a condition be rightly understood, lest it be confused with other similar notions. Thus, the normal effects of a juridic act may be modified by a condition—but this act can also be qualified by other means, v.g., by collateral agreements. Of such modifications which the parties might engraft on the act and which are called "qualifications" of a juridic act, the following three may be enumerated, scil., *mode, cause, demonstration.* None of these, despite their similarity to a condition, can properly be styled a condition in the accepted sense.

A *mode* (*modus*) is an obligation added to the already perfected and completed contract which, if not of immoral content, obliges the other party in justice, v.g.: "I will marry you but you must first become a Catholic."[287]

---

[284] Cf. Schmalzgrueber, *loc. cit.*

[285] *Ius Canonicum,* lib. IV, tit. V, n. 2.

[286] Cf. Coronata, *De Sacramentis,* III, n. 495.

[287] "Modus . . . est adiectio alicuius oneris, ad quod post contractum perfectum obligare volumus contrahentem."—Schmalzgrueber, *Ius Ecclesiasticum,* lib. IV, tit. V, n. 11.

A *cause* (*causa*) is the expression of the very *reason* or *motive* that moves one to contract espousals or marriage with another, v.g.: "I will contract marriage with you because you are pious."[288]

A *demonstration* (*demonstratio*) is a *description,* as it were, of the person, or the pointing out of some quality existing actually or putatively in the other party to the contract, v.g.: "I contract espousals with you who are truly the daughter of our senator."[289]

C. The Effect of Conditions Upon Espousals

The principles underlying conditional espousal promises are the following:

First, if the condition regards the *past* or the *present,* the betrothal is valid or invalid according as the condition is or is not verified.[290] Should doubts arise as to whether or not the condition was fulfilled, inquiry must be made, and if marriage with a third party is contemplated, it must be deferred.[291]

Secondly, if the condition regards a *future impossibility,* the presumption is that the condition was not seriously made, but if it was, there is no real promise of marriage and the engagement is not valid.[292]

Thirdly, if the condition concerns *a necessary future* event, the presumption is that the condition was not seriously made, but if it was, then the betrothment pact is suspended till the condition is fulfilled.[293]

---

[288] "Causa tum apponi contractui dicitur, quando denotatur causa ob quam contrahitur."—Schmalzgrueber, *ibid.,* n. 12.

[289] "Demonstratio fit, quando exprimitur aliqua qualitas, per quam determinatur vel demonstratur persona cum qua contrahitur."—Schmalzgrueber, *loc. cit.*

[290] Cappello, *De Sacramentis,* V, n. 99; Wouters, *Manuale,* II, n. 671; Gasparri, *De Matrimonio,* I, n. 81; Coronata, *De Sacramentis,* III, n. 50; Vlaming, *Praelectiones,* I, n. 103; Davis, *Moral and Pastoral Theology,* IV, 83; Schmalzgrueber, *Ius Ecclesiasticum,* lib. IV, tit. V, n. 19.

[291] Wouters, *loc. cit.*

[292] Cappello, Vlaming and Davis, *loc. citatis;* Schmalzgrueber, *ibid.,* nn. 75-77; Gasparri, *ibid.,* n. 80; canon 1092, 1°.

[293] Cappello, *loc. cit.*

Fourthly, when there is a question of a *contingent future event* subject to qualification by a condition subsequent, v.g., "I will marry you, unless later you change your mind", the betrothment is null and void since an essential element, namely, obligation, is positively excluded. The promise is valueless.[294]

Fifthly, if the condition is *future, contingent, suspensive* and *morally good,* v.g.: "I will marry you when you are baptized," then the validity of the espousals remains suspended till the condition is verified. Once this is so, i.e., once the realization of the condition is attained, then by that very fact the engagement to marry becomes absolute and pure (*absoluta et pura*). There is no need to renew the promise to marry in this case, once the condition has been verified. However, during the time the condition is pending, it would be unlawful for one to recede from the betrothment or to attempt to hinder the fulfillment of the condition. In other words, an obligation arises to await the fulfillment of the condition. Any subsequent espousal would certainly be null were a breach of the first espousal to occur pending the realization of the condition. The non-fulfillment of the condition, on the other hand, terminates and dissolves the engagement, unless the condition was revoked either expressly or tacitly as, for instance, by illicit intercourse with a third party or by culpable obstruction of the fulfillment of the condition.[295]

Sixthly, a *suspensive and immoral* (*inhonesta*), i.e., a sinful condition, v.g.: "I will marry you if you commit sin with me", when seriously made, in no wise gives rise to obligation of awaiting the realization of that condition, i.e., the contract is not binding and the parties are free to enter new espousals, or marriage, with a third party.[296]

However, Pontius (1570-1629), Schmalzgrueber (1663-1735), Reiffenstuel (1642-1703), De Angelis (1824-1881) and other older authors regarded the espousals *valid,* once the fulfillment of

---

[294] Cappello, *loc. cit.*

[295] Cappello, *loc. cit.* To be obliged to wait more than one year for the fulfillment of a condition would surely constitute grounds for breaking off the engagement. Cf. pp. 218-220.

[296] Cappello, *loc. cit.*

the condition had occurred.[297] The reason for this *positive* position, these writers averred, was that, on the verification of a future immoral condition, *other* contracts became valid and binding—hence also betrothals.[298]

Sanchez and nearly all modern canonists maintain the *negative* view and declare the betrothment invalid and in no wise binding.[299] The basis for this viewpoint, which is also endorsed by the writer of this dissertation, is, this: *A contract entered into under an immoral future condition is of no value prior to the verification of that condition.*[300] Consequently, *after* the fulfillment of the condition a contract, already null from the beginning, *remains null* and no obligation can arise from it as from a fulfilled suspensive condition, as is the case in contracts entered into with honorable and moral conditions.[301]

It is difficult to understand, Cappello well observes in this regard, how a contract which is void from its very inception, and which in no manner is qualified with a suspensive operation, can ever be regarded later as valid.[302] The question does not revert, so he continues, to that which according to many authors relates to contracts

---

[297] Reiffenstuel, *Ius Canonicum,* lib. IV, tit. V, n. 58; Schmalzgrueber, *ibid.,* nn. 99-101; Pontius, *De Sacramento Matrimonii Tractatus* (nova ed., Venetiis, 1756), lib. III, cap. V, n. 1 sq. (hereafter cited *De Matrimonio*); De Angelis, *Praelectiones Iuris Canonici* (5 vols. in 9, Romae, 1877-1891), lib. IV, tit. V, n. 4 (hereafter cited *Praelectiones*).

[298] Cf., v.g., Reiffenstuel (*loc. cit.*), who stated: "Ratio est quia reliqui contractus sub turpi conditione de futuro, adimpleta conditione, ut diximus, valent et obligant, ut fatentur omnes . . . ergo etiam sponsalia, utpote specialiter non excepta."

[299] Cf. Sanchez, *De Matrimonii Sacramento,* lib. V, disp. XVII, Santi, *Praelectiones Iuris Canonici iuxta Ordinem Decretalium Gregorii IX* (5 vols. in 1, Ratisbonae, Neo-Eboraci et Cincinnati, 1886), lib. IV, tit. V, n. 28 (hereafter cited *Praelectiones*); Gasparri, *De Matrimonio,* I, n. 80; Vlaming, *Praelectiones,* I, n. 104; Coronata, *De Sacramentis,* III, n. 50; Cappello, *De Sacramentis,* V, n. 99.

[300] ". . . contractus sub conditione turpi initi, *ante* impletam conditionem sunt nullius roboris."—Cappello, *loc. cit.*

[301] "Consequenter, in huiusmodi contractibus nihil ab initio efficitur, i.e., nulla omnino oritur obligatio, ne quidem in suspensivo, uti contingit in pactis honestis."—Vlaming, *loc. cit.*

[302] Cappello, *De Sacramentis,* V, n. 99.

in general, which, when the immoral condition is realized, are commonly said to become firm, i.e., valid and binding, since a contract that is null from its inception cannot become valid later in consequence of the performance of the terms of the contract. A *new* contract supersedes the original invalid one, Cappello states, inasmuch as when the performance of the deed has occurred, there arises a contract known as a *real, innominate contract* (*realis et innominatus contractus*), scil., *"facio ut de."* Hence, if a new contract is to be entered, the solemnity of form must be observed when espousals are concerned; otherwise an invalidity again will result. In other words, the new contract must be reduced to writing, if canonical effects are to follow.[303]

Thus, for instance, if John promised to marry Anne with the condition that she sin with him, the promise would be *invalid* prior to the fulfillment of the condition, first, obviously, because the requisites of canon 1017 were not observed, i.e., when solemnity of form was lacking. Secondly, even if the solemnities were observed, the contract still would be invalid, because the appended immoral contract vitiates the deed, and because such a contract receives no recognition at law as an espousal contract. A new one is necessary.[304]

Seventhly (to conclude the enumeration of valid and invalid espousals consequent upon conditional promises of matrimony), when a *suspensive condition contrary to the substance of betrothment* (or of marriage) is appended to the contract, v.g.: "I will marry you on condition that I be given freedom to marry someone else, should I lose my love for you", the contract is by the very nature of things obviously null and void.[305]

D. The Condition: "If the Holy Father Dispenses From an Existing Impediment"

But what of the condition: "I will marry you if the Holy Father grants us a dispensation for our marriage"? Are those who

[303] Cappello, *loc. cit.* Cf. also Ferreres, *Compendium Theologiae Moralis* (14. ed., 2 vols., Barcinone, 1928), II, n. 938.

[304] Cf. Cappello, *loc. cit.*

[305] Cappello, *loc. cit.;* Gasparri, *De Matrimonio,* I, n. 80; Schmalzgrueber, *Ius Ecclesiasticum,* lib. IV, tit. V, nn. 131-134; Reiffenstuel, *Ius Canonicum,* lib. IV, tit. V, n. 57; Vlaming, *Praelectiones,* I, n. 103 bis.

are canonically impeded by some diriment or prohibitive impediment of ecclesiastical law capable of making a contract of this nature? There are three opinions on the matter.

The first view favors the validity of such a betrothal compact, provided that the impediment in question is among those from which the Roman Pontiff can and is accustomed to grant a dispensation, only when there is present a sufficient cause for the granting of it. St. Alphonsus, De Angelis, Aertneys (1828-1915), Gasparri and others who espoused this view declared that the *condition is thus honest and possible, and that accordingly the pact is valid.*[306]

The second opinion denies validity outright on the score that, prior to the obtaining of the dispensation in question, the parties are *juridically incapable* of contracting the obligations of betrothment. It is only *after* the dispensation has been granted, Reiffenstuel, Pichler, Lehmkuhl and others argue, that the principals are capable at law to contract validly.[307]

The third opinion *likewise denies validity* to espousals when a condition dependent on a papal dispensation is annexed to the contract—but with a certain restriction, i.e., the opinion stands for the nullity of the contract but as flowing not from the nature of things but solely from the positive will of the Church, manifested particularly in the various decisions of the Sacred Congregation of the Council in this regard.[308]

However, according to this opinion, defended by Santi (1830-1885), Wernz-Vidal, De Smet, Vlaming and others, espousals

---

[306] St. Alphonsus, *Theologia Moralis,* lib. VI, n. 859; Aertnys, *Theologia Moralis Secundum Doctrinam St. Alphonsi* (3. ed., 2 vols., Tornaci, 1893), II, n. 426, 725; Gasparri, *De Matrimonio,* I, nn. 62, 104; De Angelis, *Praelectiones,* lib. IV, tit. V, n. 4. Among older authors the following adhered to this first opinion: Sanchez, *De Matrimonii Sacramento,* lib. V, disp. V, nn. 12-13; Engel, *Collegium Iuris Canonici,* lib. IV, tit. III, nn. 16-17; Pirhing, *Ius Canonicum,* lib. IV, tit. V, n. 27.

[307] Reiffenstuel, *Ius Canonicum,* lib. IV, tit. V, n. 23; Pichler, *Ius Canonicum,* lib. IV, tit. V, n. 11; Lehmkuhl, *Theologia Moralis,* II, n. 840; cf. also Schmalzgrueber, *Ius Ecclesiasticum,* lib. IV, tit. V, n. 78; De Lugo, *De Iustitia,* I, disp. XII, sec. II, n. 53.

[308] Cf. pp. 26-31 of this dissertation, where many such decrees are cited and discussed.

entered into under the condition of the obtaining of a dispensation from an existing impediment are not to be spurned or rejected, since they do engender some sort of obligation. This obligation, these same authors hold, is an obligation to seek and await the requested dispensation. It is an obligation, they state, arising, if not from justice, then at least from equity and decency.[309] In other words, this third opinion declares first, that in the given hypotheses, there is no juridic contract of espousals as such extant; secondly, it maintains that there is an obligation present, not because of the espousal contract which here and now is non-existent, but because of a contract in general; thirdly, this opinion maintains that the obligation is to take whatever means are necessary for the lawful procuring of the dispensation; lastly, this obligation is a serious one.[310]

As a consequence, this same opinion continues, affiancement to a third party *pending the appeal* for the dispensation is invalid. *After* the receipt of the dispensation, it insists, renewal of the promise must take place as a condition for a valid betrothal contract, so that, without the renewal, the earlier promises remain without any validity.[311]

For confirmation of its position, this third opinion cites several outstanding decisions which the Sacred Congregation of the Council rendered in the eighteenth and nineteenth centuries.[312]

Of the three opinions, the first, maintaining the validity of the espousal contract but with a suspensive effect, seems the one of greatest probability and thus proves preferable to the present writer. The reasons are the following: First, the *condition* based on the grant of a dispensation from a competent authority capable and

---

[309] "In hac sententia sponsalia sub hac conditione inita, quamvis invalida, tamen non sunt prorsus despicienda, eaque aliqualem inducunt obligationem, si minus iustitiae saltem aequitatis ac decentiae, petendi et expectandi dispensationem."—Vlaming, *Praelectiones,* I, n. 105. Cf. also Wernz-Vidal, *Ius Canonicum,* V, n. 84; Santi, *Praelectiones,* lib. IV, tit. V, n. 12.

[310] Cf. Wernz-Vidal, *loc. cit.*

[311] *Loc. cit.*

[312] E.g.: S.C.C., *in Brugnaten., Sponsalium,* 27 iun. 1709—cited in S.C.C. *in Ianuen., Sponsalium,* 12 dec. 1733—*Thesaurus,* VI (1741), 176-178; S.C.C., *in Sypontina., Sponsalium,* 22 maii 1857—Pallottini, s.v. *Sponsalia,* nn. 27-28; S.C.C., *Beneventana, Sponsalium,* 27 nov. 1858—*Ibid.,* nn. 27, 34.

accustomed to bestow it, when a just cause exists, is a perfectly *licit* one. Secondly, the *object* is *licit,* scil., a promise of marriage in the future, consequent upon the granting of the dispensation. Thirdly, it is not true to assert, as do the two opposing views, that a promise is false when the parties at the time are "juridically incapable" of contracting, because on that score the condition, v.g., "I will marry you if you become baptized," would also have to be regarded as nullifying espousals. Fourthly, the decisions of the Sacred Congregation of the Council, marshalled by the opposing opinion, are not conclusive for two reasons. In these decisions the dispensation was never fully fulminated, i.e., the rescript was never executed exactly and according to law, or there occurred a revocation of the promise. One easily notes, in these cases decided by the Congregation, the reluctance of one of the parties to marry the betrothed, or notices that one of the parties concerned had passed on to other espousals, if not to marriage itself with a third party. It devolves upon the opposing opinions to demonstrate that the aforesaid Congregation declared espousals null after the dispensation had been granted and had gained its effect, and the parties had not renewed their promise. This the opposition cannot do. Rota decisions, also introduced by the negative view, are of no avail since, as Schmalzgrueber pointed out,[313] there are other Rota decisions which manifestly hold to the contrary.[314]

E. The Impact of Modes, Causes, Demonstrations on Espousals

In reference to the rôle played by the *mode,* the *demonstration* and the *cause* in the betrothal agreement, the following principles apply. First, the mode does *not* suspend the contract—precisely because it is a mode and not a condition. Should the mode be of a base (*turpis*) or impossible nature, then it is regarded as not having been annexed to the compact.[315] When the mode is licit

[313] *Ius Ecclesiasticum,* lib. IV, tit. V, n. 86.

[314] Cf. Diana (*Resolutiones Morales* [10 vols. in 5, Venetiis, 1728], II, tract VI, resol. XIX) for a listing and further discussion of these Rota decisions.

[315] Cf. Schmalzgrueber, *Ius Ecclesiasticum,* lib. IV, tit. V, nn. 139-142; Reiffenstuel, *Ius Canonicum,* lib. IV, tit. V, nn. 63-64.

and morally good (*honestus*), the party who appends it, and whose action is thereby required to follow, is bound to fulfill the obligation assumed. The other party has a right to urge the fulfillment, so much so that, if no satisfaction is forthcoming, grounds for receding from the contract are juridically furnished the other party.[316]

Sometimes the parties to espousals either carelessly or ignorantly express in the form of a mode what they internally mean to be a *condition since qua non.* In such instances the principles governing conditions must be applied.[317] Whenever the mode is, as it is said, contrary to the substance of the future marriage, i.e., against any of the three "boons" of marriage, v.g., "I will marry you, but you must practice onanism after we are married", such contracts of betrothment are deemed invalid.[318] Authors rightly see no serious will to enter true marriage in these cases.[319] Schmalzgrueber regarded this view as probable.[320]

Secondly, a demonstration, v.g.: "I promise to marry you, who are a wealthy widow," does not in and of itself (*per se*) affect the validity of the espousals. Hence an engagement to marry is valid, independently of the demonstration appended, even though the promisor may be completely deceived in his expectations. An error regarding person expressed in the demonstration, v.g., "I contract betrothment with you who are Jane Adams" (who is not Jane Adams), would, of course, invalidate the deed, as an error regarding person is contained in the demonstration. The same would obtain if the error concerning quality redounded to an error regarding person, v.g., "I promise to contract marriage with you who are John's eldest daughter" (which is untrue). As for a demonstration which contravenes one of the three "boons" of marriage, only one author of note has claimed that the contract is null and void, namely Navarrus (1493-1586). Navarrus claimed

---

[316] Cappello, *De Sacramentis,* V, n. 100; Gasparri, *De Matrimonio,* I, n. 85; Schmalzgrueber, Reiffenstuel, *loc. citatis.*

[317] *Loc. cit.*

[318] Cf. Sanchez, *De Matrimonii Sacramento,* lib. V, disp. XIX, n. 5.

[319] Cf. Sanchez, *loc. cit.*

[320] *Ibid.,* n. 143.

that true consent appears lacking.[321] Sanchez and others rightly answered that, as such (*per se*), a demonstration, unlike the mode, does *not* suspend or invalidate a contract, no matter what its quality, whether merely base or opposed to the substance of marriage, false or true. It was to be regarded as not having been placed, because a demonstration in itself represents not an act of the will but only of the intellect.[322]

Thirdly, a *cause*, v.g., "I will marry you because you are a fine woman," also leaves a contract unimpaired no matter whether what is contained in the cause is false or unverified, unless the cause contained an error which of its nature renders the espousal promise invalid. Thus, were one to promise marriage to a woman because she is a widow, whereas she is actually married, the erroneous motive invalidates the contract, because of the serious error contained in the cause. All authors agree on this.[323]

A cause contrary to any of the three "boons" of marriage is a point of dispute, just as is the same kind of demonstration, as was explained above. In this similar type of dispute Sanchez and his followers argued for the validity of the engagement promise, even though the cause was opposed to any of the said three "boons" of marriage. Navarrus denied validity, but his opinion does not appear tenable, for the cause is an act of the intellect, not of the will, and as such (*per se*), does not affect the will as expressed in the act of the contracting of a betrothment.[324]

Article 3: The Promissory Oath in Espousals

To strengthen the promise of future marriage and to add to the solemnities of the deed, oaths were common in the past.[325] But the oath is not necessary in itself. Whenever it is made, it is accessory to the contract and therefore partakes of the nature of the contract.[326] Hence, if betrothment is null from the very beginning, the

[321] Cf. Navarrus, *Opera Omnia* (6 vols., Vol. I, 1618, Venetiis, 1618-1821), I (*Manuale*, cap. XXII, n. 62), pp. 369-370.

[322] Sanchez, *De Matrimonii Sacramento*, lib. V, disp. XIX, n. 6.

[323] Cf. Cappello, *De Sacramentis*, V, n. 100.

[324] Cf. the preceding paragraph.

[325] Cf. c. 16, X, *de sponsalibus et matrimoniis*, IV, 1; Potthast, n. 4379.

[326] Cf. Can. 1318, § 1; *Reg. 42*, R. J., in VI°.

oath cannot validate it. When espousals are lawfully contracted, but later justly dissolved, by that very fact whatever obligation derives from the oath is also dissolved.[327] Had the party making the oath expressly intended to obligate himself *independently* of the obligation accruing out of the betrothment, then the oath is regarded not as accessory but as the principal act of the obligor.[328]

An oath gives rise to an obligation in religion. Hence, were one to violate an engagement promise confirmed by an oath, the virtue of religion as well as the virtue of justice would suffer.[329]

Article 4: Espousal Gifts

In the earlier chapters of this dissertation[330] mention was made of the nature and the rôle of gifts (*arrha, iocalia*) in the engagement compact. Gifts have been given and exchanged between lovers on the occasion of their espousals from time immemorial. These gifts fall into two categories.

The first species, called *arrha,* were commonly given by the future husband to his future wife, or given by either or both sets of parents to the pair, or mutually exchanged by the couple as a surety, security, as well as a pledge of non-breach. The basic assumption underlying such gift-making, as a rule, was that, should the giver unjustly fail to fulfill his promise, what he gave would be lost. Should he be the recipient, what he received he would be forced to restore, i.e., were he the cause of the unlawful violation of the betrothal pact.[331] Of themselves presents of this sort are returnable, once the marriage has taken place as promised, unless custom dictates otherwise.[332]

The second species of gifts given or exchanged on the occasion of betrothment are known as *iocalia.* They are usually given by the

---

[327] Cf. De Lugo, *De Iustitia,* disp. XXII, sec. XXXIV; Santi, *Praelectiones,* lib. IV, tit. I, n. 44; Wernz-Vidal; *Ius Canonicum,* V, n. 101.

[328] *Loc. cit.*

[329] *Loc. cit.*

[330] Pp. 4-6; 12-13; 22-24.

[331] Cf. Ferraris, s.v. *Sponsalia, Bibliotheca,* VIII, 417; Sanchez, *De Matrimonii Sacramento,* lib. I, disp. XXXVII, n. 2.

[332] Cf. Noldin, *Summa Theologiae Moralis,* III, n. 535, nota a; Gasparri, *De Matrimonio,* I, n. 89.

fiancé to his fiancée as a token of love and a sign of espousal faith. Such presents are regarded as engagement gifts *pure and simple, when of relatively small* value—hence they become the property of the recipient automatically, irrespective of the outcome of the espousals. In other words, inexpensive gifts are as such (*per se*) regarded as *absolutely* given, i.e., not as calling for a return to the donor.[333]

When betrothment presents given by a lover to his betrothed are of *great* value (in relation to the financial condition of the parties), they are considered as given *intuitu matrimonii,* i.e., in consideration of future marriage. Hence, if the contract of espousals does not terminate in matrimony, the gifts, as a rule (*regulariter*), are to be returned to the donor. The presumption, therefore, is that these material indications of love are conditional, scil., provided marriage ensues.[334] However, should the donor himself be the culpable cause of the breach of the promise, probably (*probabiliter*) the faithful party would be justified in keeping what was given—as compensation for the injury.[335] The embracing of the religious life or the receiving of Holy Orders does not constitute an unjustifiable breach, as this is an implicit reservation understood in every espousal contract.[336] Nonetheless, equity may demand at times that even in these cases some compensation be made.[337]

As for the question of stipulating in the betrothal contract multiple indemnity upon breach of contract, as found formerly in Roman law,[338] with Cappello some opine that, since Canon law alone obtains today, Roman law no longer applies.[339] Moreover, the civil codes, v.g., of Italy, Belgium, Spain, Holland, Germany, England, etc., do not take cognizance of such stipulated penalties

---

[333] Cf. Reiffenstuel, *Ius Canonicum,* lib. IV, tit. I, n. 180; Schmalzgrueber, *Ius Ecclesiasticum,* lib. IV, tit. I, n. 126; Gasparri, *loc. cit.*; Cappello, *De Sacramentis,* V, n. 104; Wernz-Vidal, *Ius Canonicum,* V, nn. 99-100; Noldin, *ibid.,* nota b.

[334] Noldin, *ibid.,* nota b.

[335] Thus Noldin, *loc. cit.;* Gasparri, *De Matrimonio,* I, n. 89.

[336] Cf. Gasparri, *loc. cit.*

[337] Cf. Schmalzgrueber, *Ius Ecclesiasticum,* lib. VI, tit. II, n. 109.

[338] C. (5.1) 1-20; C. Th. (3.5) 11. Cf. also pp. 9-11 of this dissertation.

[339] *De Sacramentis,* V, n. 104.

in betrothment pacts, and hence that law is to be followed. Where Roman law prevails, it should be observed. The Code lays down the ruling that in matters pertinent to contracts the prevailing laws in any given locality obtain, except where the Canon law itself provides for exceptions.[340]

In Anglo-American law the weight of authority holds that any gift to the person to whom the donor is engaged to be married, made in contemplation of marriage, is conditional, and upon breach of the engagement promise by the recipient, the donor may recover the property.[341] In Louisiana, where the *Code Napoléon* is the basic law,[342] it has been held that: "Every donation made in favor of marriage falls, if the marriage does not take place."[343] Hence, in the United States and England the betrothment present needs to be returned not in consequence of *every* factual nonfulfillment of the betrothal contract, but only on culpable breach of the promise to marry by the donee. When the donor himself is the cause of the recession from the promise to marry, he cannot recover the gift, as it passes automatically into the possession of the abandoned party.

Mutual consent to rescind espousals, a New York Court has ruled, does not necessarily have the effect of abrogating the condition upon which the betrothal gift (in this case: an engagement ring) was held. In other words, cancellation of the betrothment promise by mutual consent does not thereby make for the restoration of the gift, but restoration is dependent upon the subsequent condition that recovery is to be had only if marriage is culpably estopped, i.e., if there is culpable breach of the espousal contract.[344]

---

[340] Canon 1529: "Quae ius civile in territorio statuit de contractibus tam in genere quam in specie, sive nominatis sive innominatis, et de solutionibus eadem iure canonico in materia ecclesiastica iisdem cum effectibus serventur, nisi iuri divino contraria sint aut aliud iure canonico caveatur."

[341] Cf. Jacobs (*Cases and Other Materials on Domestic Relations* [2 ed., Chicago, Foundation Press, 1939], pp. 52-55) for a list of cases in which litigation over espousal gifts occurred.

[342] Cf. Sherman, *Roman Law in the Modern World,* I, n. 264.

[343] *Civil Code of the State of Louisiana* (Dart), 1932, sec. 1740.

[344] Cf. Jacobs, *op. cit.,* p. 53, n. 5.

SECTION VI. EFFECTS OF THE BETROTHAL CONTRACT

Article 1: The Obligation to Marry

Authors generally enumerate *six* effects as deriving from canonical betrothals: the obligation of entering marriage as promised, the obligation of associating with the affianced party, the obligation of foregoing company-keeping with anyone other than the affianced, the incapability of validly contracting espousals with a third party, the prohibition of marrying a third party, and the right to sue for damages in the event of breach of contract.

The first effect begets in both parties, in exclusive relation to each other, the obligation of intermarriage in due time, and, if the time is not fixed, whenever either principal reasonably urges fulfillment. Fundamentally, this is an obligation of *commutative justice* and a *grave* one, and it concerns the conscience only. It is an obligation of commutative justice, because every contract between private parties of its nature begets an obligation. It is grave, because the matter in question is grave, marriage in the future.[345] It concerns the conscience *only,* i.e., it is not a juridical obligation, for no action lies in ecclesiastical courts today to enforce the obligation.[346]

Because of this current legislation, whereby the contracting of marriage cannot be urged in the external forum, three opinions today are proffered in explanation of the nature of the obligation arising out of espousals. They are given only a brief notice here, since this question will be treated in great detail in a special article to follow.[347] The three opinions are the following: First, according to Gasparri, the obligation is now only a slight one, and that an obligation of fidelity.[348] Secondly, in the opinion of

[345] Sanchez, *De Matrimonii Sacramento,* lib. I, disp. XXVII, n. 2; Covarruvias, *Opera Omnia,* pars I, cap. IV, § 2, n. 7; Laymann, *Theologia Moralis,* lib. V, tract. X, pars I, cap. I, n. 3; Pirhing, *Ius Canonicum,* lib. IV, tit. I, n. XXV, Ballerini-Palmieri, *Opus Theologicum Morale,* VI, 123; Wernz-Vidal, *Ius Canonicum,* V, n. 93; Cappello, *De Sacramentis,* V, n. 107.

[346] Canon 1017, § 3. Not even original action is granted today to question the reason on which dissolution of the espousals was based. Cf. *PCI,* 2, 3 iun. 1918—*AAS,* X (1918), 345, n. 4.

[347] Cf. Art. 7 of this section (pp. 188-201).

[348] *De Matrimonio,* I, n. 101.

Vidal, the obligation is not absolute but disjunctive, scil., either to marry or to compensate for any damage sustained, i.e., the Church does not recognize a specific and determinate obligation to marry on the part of the two persons betrothed.[349] Thirdly, in Cappello's view, the obligation is certainly not disjunctive, but probably it is a grave one. The obligation to enter marriage is an essential effect of the betrothment contract, whereas the duty to compensate for any resulting damage, accidental.[350]

Marriage is to follow within a reasonable time, once the betrothment has been concluded. Vidal maintains that marriage should take place within a *year* after the signing of the agreement, when no definite date had been agreed on.[351] The reason, obviously, is that all undue familiarity must be precluded, as the danger of incontinence is frequently present. This has also been the mind of the Holy See.[352] Roman law allowed a two-year period, as a maximum, to intervene between the time of the espousals and that of the marriage.[353] The Code is silent on the matter. Custom and other factors relative to the parties and their conditions will, therefore, determine the question in most instances. Writers, however, unanimously teach that parents, pastors and confessors are to see to it that the espoused couple contract marriage *as soon as possible* so that the danger of undue intimacy and incontinence may be effectively forestalled.[354]

Article 2: The Obligation of the Parties to Associate With Each Other

Secondly, betrothal begets an obligation in the engaged pair to associate with each other. Moralists concede to the affianced lovers all the customary signs of affection, as the honorable kiss, embrace and conversation. Even the danger of experiencing sensual

---

[349] *Ius Canonicum,* V, n. 93.

[350] *De Sacramentis,* V, n. 101.

[351] *Ius Canonicum,* V, n. 97.

[352] Cf., v.g., S.C. de Prop. Fide., 13 apr. 1807—*Collectanea,* n 692 ad XXII.

[353] C. (5.1) 2.

[354] Thus, v.g., St. Alphonsus, *Theologia Moralis,* lib. VI, tract VI, n. 845; Schmalzgrueber, *ibid.,* n. 91; etc.

emotions or even a pollution, authors write, is not a deterrent to these acts of affection, as long as all proximate danger of consent to these excitations is kept absent. A just cause exists, they point out, for indirectly allowing these otherwise irregular and improper effects consequent upon the honorable actions mentioned above.[355] Other questions pertinent to moral implications which could arise out of intimacies associated with affianced couples need not be treated here, as the canonical consideration prevails. The above-cited authors and others can be consulted on the matter.

Article 3: The Obligation to Avoid Undue Familiarity With Others

Thirdly, espousals engender an obligation deriving from the virtue of fidelity for the espoused to avoid, first, undue *familiarities* with a third party. Such sins would obviously offend against the virtue of chastity. However, they would not be specifically different from sins of unchastity committed by persons who are not betrothed, as St. Alphonsus and others most commonly teach.[356] Sanchez, De Lugo, Laymann and others, nonetheless regarded such immoral actions as of a different species, because of the added circumstance of espousals intervening between the parties.[357] On the other hand, immorality under these circumstances, it seems, would not be contrary to justice, because, as St. Alphonsus observed, neither party has acquired rights over the body of the other through the betrothal contract.[358]

Espoused couples are, secondly, forbidden to seek *company-keeping* with other persons. Certainly, to pay more attention to another woman than to his betrothed places the man in danger of violating his espousal pledge and of furnishing grounds for future marital unhappiness and dissatisfaction with his now less desirable spouse. Through association with a particular man or several

---

[355] Cf. St. Alphonsus, *ibid.*, n. 854; Sanchez, *De Matrimonii Sacramento,* lib. IV, disp. XLVI.

[356] Cf. St. Alphonsus, *ibid.*, n. 847.

[357] Sanchez, *op. cit.*, disp. XVIII, nn. 6 sq.; De Lugo, *De Iustitia,* disp. XVI, n. 176; Laymann, *Theologia Moralis,* lib. V, tract. X, pars I, cap. I, n. 6.

[358] Cf. St. Alphonsus, *Theologia Moralis,* lib. VI, n. 847.

men, the woman may engender suspicion, distrust and jealousy in her husband-to-be.

The extent to which either one of the affianced pair can seek the association of a third party of the other sex cannot be fixed with finality. Authors do not treat of the question, though it does appear a practical one. To this writer, the conduct of betrothed persons is to be determined and patterned on the general principles of prudence and charity. Customs and conditions, relative to the time, place and character of the people, are also to be considered.

Certainly in the United States broader and so-called liberal views on the matter are entertained, i.e., young people, even when engaged, do not demand exclusive company-keeping with one another. Nor is it uncommon for them to attend dances and to frequent theaters and parties occasionally with others, or at least to be present without their partners. However, should one of the espoused reasonably object to such activity on the part of the other, in charity, if not out of prudence, the other party should desist and acquiesce in the request.

Article 4: Invalidity of Subsequent Espousals

Fourthly, espousals validly and canonically contracted render null and void any espousals with a third person. This would be verified even if the second espousals were made under oath or the act of *copula* had followed upon such a second betrothment. The basis for invalidity of the attempted new engagement is the illicitness of the action. It is unlawful without just cause to enter into a new contract which is adverse to the earlier legally standing contract.[359]

Some authors, however, think that the second betrothment, when confirmed by an oath, is valid, *once the first one is dissolved.*[360] But this appears contradictory and impossible, since the subsequent *sponsalia* are in the case null from very outset

[359] Thus Sanchez, *ibid.*, n. 29; Schmalzgrueber, *ibid.*, n. 85; Laymann, *op. cit.*, lib. V, tract X, pars I, cap. I, n. 5; St. Alphonsus, *ibid.*, n. 848; Wernz-Vidal, *ibid.*, n. 102

[360] Cf., v.g., Sanchez, *op. cit.*, disp. L, n. 5.

(*ab initio*). What is of no juridic value cannot be juridically obligatory later. A new promise of marriage after the lawful dissolution of the first engagement pact would have to be given if the second contract is to revive, for only in this wise can the respective obligation be forgotten.[361]

In some circles[362] it was even taught that, had there occurred a second espousal in which one party was ignorant of the other party's previous espousal, and thereupon copulation between them had taken place, marriage with the second espoused would be obligatory and the first contract dissolved. Authors espousing this opinion thus recognized as valid the second contract and urged the obligation of marriage with the second woman because of her defloration.[363] This reasoning can hardly be defended as is apparent from the identical reason stated above. Inherently (*per se*) the first affiancement perdures. If compensation would be possible only through marriage with the deflowered maiden, then consent to dissolve the earlier betrothal contract would have to be given by the first affianced party.[364] The contracting of marriage with the second woman could be urged—not indeed in virtue of the second espousals, which are null, but in virtue of the principle that demands compensation for the harm done. The case would be different, and no obligation to compensate would be present, had both parties been conscious of the first espousals.[365]

Article 5: Illicitness of Marriage to a Person Other than the Espoused

Fifthly, betrothals have the effect of rendering marriage with a third person *illicit*. Marriage with such a person could, of course, be valid. Under the current discipline the espousals do not constitute an impediment in the canonical sense. They do act as natural obstacles to marriage with a third party in virtue of the promise given to the espoused, i.e., because of the obli-

---

[361] Cf. Cappello, *ibid.*, n. 107.

[362] Cf. St. Alphonsus, *loc. cit.*, for a list of authors comprising this group.

[363] St. Alphonsus, *loc. cit.*

[364] Cf. Sanchez, *De Matrimonii Sacramento*, lib. I, disp. XVIII, n. 5.

[365] Sanchez, *loc. cit.*

gation assumed by the one becoming espoused, as is clear from the discussions above.

The former impediments of public propriety and affinity arising out of valid betrothment[366] are today obsolete and no longer obtain in the present law. Public propriety acts as an impediment, but as a diriment impediment, only when an *invalid marriage,* whether consummated or not, occurs, or when public and notorious concubinage is practiced. Marriage is thus invalid, because of this impediment, in the first and second degree of the direct line between the man and the blood relatives of the woman and vice versa.[367] Affinity arises from a valid marriage only, whether simply ratified or also consummated.[368]

Article 6: Right of Action on Unjust Breach

A. Competency of Church and State

Lastly, the betrothment contract begets a right, not indeed to compel a contracting of the promised marriage, but to obtain redress for injury deriving from the breach of the contract.

The third paragraph of canon 1017 declares:

> "But from a promise of marriage, although it be valid and there be no just cause excusing from its fulfillment, no grounds are furnished for action demanding the celebration of marriage; grounds, however, for bringing suit for damages, if any be due, are furnished."[369]

By this legislation the Church in part approximates the civil law as found in Italy, Belgium, Spain, Holland, Germany, England and

---

[366] Cc. 11, 12, 14, 15; C. XXVII, q. 2; J E ante n. 2159; JL, n. 1954; JK, n. 199; Cc. 1, 2, 4, 6, X, *de eo qui cognovit consanguineam uxoris suae vel sponsae,* IV, 13; JL, nn. 14058; 17661; Potthast, n. 1182.

[367] Can. 1078.

[368] Cf. canon 97 and canon 1077 for its extent.

[369] Writer's translation.

"At ex matrimonii promissione, licet valida sit nec ulla iusta causa ab eadem implenda excuset, non datur actio ad petendam matrimonii celebrationem; datur tamen ad reparationem damnorum, si qua debeatur."—Can. 1017, § 3.

the United States. Italy, v.g., does not recognize as arising out of the espousals any obligation that calls for an enforceable contracting of marriage; however, action is granted whereby the injured party may be indemnified for losses suffered in the wake of a breach of the betrothment.[370]

The same obtains substantially in the codes of Belgium,[371] Spain,[372] Holland[373] and Germany.[374] Although French law is silent concerning the espousal contract, action is nevertheless granted for the recovery of compensation for any damages resulting from a violation of the compact. Swiss legislation does not grant any legal recognition to espousals, and bars all civil action attempted with the hope of obtaining relief when a violation has intervened.[375]

In the United States of America, where the English common law obtains, except in Louisiana,[376] betrothals are recognized as a legal institution.[377] No state, however, requires the promises of marriage in writing, though it has been advocated by some that legislation to this effect be passed. Practically all the states of the Union have adopted the provisions of the English Statute of Frauds (relating to marriage), in which mention is made of

---

[370] "La promesa scambievole di futuro matrimonio non produce obligàzione legale di contrárlo, nè di esuguire ciò che si fosse convenuto per caso di non adempimento della medesima."—Art. 53.

"Se la promessa fu fatta per atto pubblico o per scrittura privata da chi sia maggiore di età, o dal minore autorizzato dalle persone, il concorso delle quali e necessario per la celebrazione del matrimonio, oppure consta dalle pubblicazioni ordinate dall' uffiziale dello stato civile, il promettente che ricusi di esuguirla senza giusto motivo è obbligato a risarcire l'altra parte delle spese fatte per causa del promesso matrimonio. La domanda però non è più ammessa dopo un anno dal giorno in cui la promessa dovea assere eseguita."—Art. 54—Cf. Cappello, *De Sacramentis,* V, n. 109, footnote 11; Vernier, *American Family Laws* (5 vols., Stanford: University Press, 1931), I, 25.

[371] Art. 1382-1383—Cf. Vlaming, *Praelectiones,* I, n. 116, footnote 1.

[372] Art. 43-44—Cf. Vernier, *loc. cit.*

[373] Art. 113—Cf. Vlaming, *loc. cit.*

[374] Art. 1297-1303—Cf. Vernier, Vlaming, *loc. citatis.*

[375] Cf. Cappello, *De Sacramentis,* V, n. 109, footnote 11.

[376] Cf. Sherman, *Roman Law in the Modern World,* II, 250-253, 392-393.

[377] Cf. Vernier, *ibid.,* p. 23.

the need of a writing "to charge any person upon any agreement in consideration of marriage."[378]

However, all American cases hold that this provision does not apply to *mutual* promises of future marriage. As a matter of fact, twenty-one states and Alaska, adopting this rule, expressly provide that it shall not apply to mutual promises of marriage.[379] Moreover, it is debatable whether the words "any agreement" in the Statute of Frauds include the contract *to marry*. Illinois, New York and Maryland have decided in the affirmative.[380] Ordinarily, cases of this nature deal with *property settlements* made in consideration of marriage, on the order of the old Roman antenuptial practices, rather than with promises of marriage.[381]

Unilateral promises of marriage, being simple contracts,[382] require in Anglo-American law a "consideration." The term consideration is defined as "that which moves from the promisee, or a third person, at the request of the promisee, to the promisor or a third person designated by the promisor, at the express or implied request of the latter, in return for his promise."[383] As used in the law of contracts, the term consideration means a "valuable" consideration, something having value in the eyes of the law, and every simple contract has to be based on what the law deems to be a valuable consideration. Hence, the consideration necessary for a contract is the price bargained and paid for a promise, but it may consist in a *return promise,* an act, a forbearance or a change in legal relationship.[384]

---

[378] Vernier, *loc. cit.*

[379] These states are Alabama, Arizona, California, Colorado, Idaho, Kentucky, Michigan, Minnesota, Mississippi, Montana, Nebraska, Nevada, New York, North Dakota, Oklahoma, Oregon, South Dakota, Utah, Washington, Wisconsin and Wyoming.—Vernier, *ibid.,* p. 30.

[380] Thus Vernier, *loc. cit.*

[381] Cf. Jacobs, *Cases and Other Materials on Domestic Relations,* pp. 54-58; Vernier, *op. cit.,* III, 51-65.

[382] As opposed to *formal* contracts which are dependent on *form alone* for their validity, such as contracts of record or contracts under seal.—Cf. Smith, *Elementary Law,* p. 263.

[383] Cf. Smith, *ibid.,* p. 265.

[384] Smith, *loc. cit.* For the origin of consideration and a fuller explanation of it, cf. Williston, *The Law of Contracts* (4 vols., New York, 1920), I, nn. 99-102.

As for breach of promise suits, most states allow such actions, despite much criticism by various jurists,[385] as a carry-over from the traditional common law practice.[386] Courts generally allow recovery not only for financial damages but also for injury to the plaintiff's reputation, for wounded affections, distress of mind and for other causes having the character of a tort action. Since, unfortunately, action of this nature has been employed as an instrument of oppression, blackmail and fraud, rather than for the righting of wrong, the breach of promise suit is growing in disfavor day by day. Ordinaries and pastors must be alert lest these abuses creep into cases tried before diocesan tribunals.

B. The Nature of the Compensation

The obligation of compensating the injured party for the sustaining of grave loss or damage is, according to the principles of justice, serious whenever the betrothal was unjustly prevented from reaching fruition. If the harm was slight, the obligation cannot be said to be grave.[387]

Some authors also believe that even when a *just* cause intervenes to dissolve the contract, v.g., the entry of one party into the religious life or the priesthood, the disappointed and deserted party still has a right to be compensated for any harm sustained because of the severance of the bond.[388] However, unfaithfulness by one party committed with the precise purpose of causing the other party to renounce the engagement and to sue for damages is to be construed as fraud on the part of the one providing such a pretext.[389]

Which tribunal is competent to act in cases involving breach of promise suits? The Pontifical Commission for the Authentic Interpretation of the Code declared a few weeks after the new law went into effect that both the ecclesiastical and the civil court (unless the civil law itself denies such action) enjoy com-

---

[385] Cf. Jacobs, *op. cit.*, pp. 25, 28-29.

[386] The first case recorded, Stretch v. Parker, occurred in 1639—*loc. cit.*

[387] Cf. Noldin, *Summa Theologiae Moralis*, II, n. 547 b, c, d.

[388] Cf. St. Alphonsus, *Theologia Moralis*, lib. VI, n. 869; Schmalzgrueber, *Ius Ecclesiasticum*, lib. VI, tit. VII, n. 107

[389] Cf. Ballerini-Palmieri, *Opus Theologicum Morale*, VI, n. 358.

petence. The action is *mixti fori.*[390] Hence, the Church expressly acknowledges the right to sue for damages in the case of an unlawful breach of the engagement which had been concluded in due canonical form—both in the tribunals of the land and in its own courts.

The question is raised here by Woywood-Smith, although it is moral rather than canonical, whether one could press action for damages when the espousals, *made orally,* were unjustly breached. Some states of our Union admit mutual promises of marriage as valid even when made orally, i.e., without the formality of writing.[391] Woywod-Smith opine that a person could with moral right avail himself of such an opportunity in order to indemnify himself for whatever loss he suffered. It is certain and true that the Church rightfully claims and actually has exclusive jurisdiction over the contract of engagement, as it has over marriage with which the espousals are so closely allied. It is not certain, however, that the Church intends to nullify *absolutely* the *natural* obligation of repairing the harm done by the wanton breach of one's word of honor. The betrothal agreement has at least the nature of a word of honor when entered into without the solemnities of the canonical form. Wherefore, it seems that, though the Church pronounces the informal promise as of no consequence *as a contract,* i.e., *juridically,* yet *in its external forum* this does not destroy the voluntariness of the act, and there seems to be present in the unwarranted breaking of one's informal promise that element and measure of natural injustice that calls for an available redress through the civil law if any damage or loss was sustained. It is to be construed as *fraud* to make such a formless promise of marriage and then violate it—to the prejudice of another.[392]

This opinion, however, does not seem correct. The legislator has expressly enacted the ruling that a promise of marriage is void in *both* the external as well as the internal forum when the juridic form has not been observed.[393] Hence, intrinsically, the

---

[390] *PCI,* 2-3 iun. 1918—*AAS,* X (1918), 345.

[391] Cf. Woywod-Smith, *Commentary,* I, n. 989.

[392] Woywod-Smith, *loc. cit.*

[393] Canon 1017, § 1.

obligation to compensate for the injury resulting from the breaking off of a formless engagement is not recognized by the Code today as binding in conscience or before the tribunal.

If injury occurs because of positive acts of fraud, of violence, or of deceit, an obligation in conscience to remunerate the injured party surely is present, not in consequence of the promise as such, but because of the fraud, violence or deceit. In other words, incidentally (*per accidens*) an obligation of this nature may arise, but intrinsically (*per se*), as stated above, no obligation is extant.[394]

If Woywod-Smith substantially and in reality entertain the same notion as the one explained above, then their doctrine should not be impugned. However, as proposed in its present form, their statement appears to be contradictory to the current Code law.

Now, how is the damage inflicted upon the innocent party to be computed? The amount to be awarded the party who suffered loss or damage, or the nature of the compensation due, is to be determined according to the norms found in theological treatises on restitution. Civil tribunals are to proceed according to the principles of natural justice and equity.

Article 7: The Nature of the Parties' Obligation to Intermarry

In the preceding articles were listed six effects attendant upon the engagement contract. The first and foremost, as there pointed out, was the parties' obligation to enter the marriage as promised in their compact. The betrothal promise, so it appears, binds in conscience and is given acceptance and endorsement in the external forum of the Church. Nevertheless, as canon 1017, § 3, proclaims, the Church will not insist on the contracting of promised marriage, not even when the affiancement has been broken off without sufficient grounds. Now, authors are at pains to explain how the Church recognizes a grave obligation in conscience, arising from canonical espousals, but does not urge its fulfillment in the external forum by means of the contracting of matrimony,

---

[394] Cf. Cappello, *De Sacramentis,* V, n. 115; Coronata, *De Sacramentis,* III, n. 56.

when it seems that to save the parties from sinning grievously the Church should insist upon their intermarriage.

A further difficulty raised is this: If one party refuses to stand by a valid betrothment, a parish priest or the ordinary must admit that this party is free to marry a third party, for the Church will not insist on the marriage between the original betrothed parties when a reluctance with reference to this marriage is manifestly present on the side of even one of the parties.

For a reconciliation of the apparent contradiction, three different opinions have been proposed by authors. Cappello's doctrine points out that there is most probably a grave obligation in conscience *without any sanction in the external forum.*[395] Vidal believed that the obligation deriving from the bilateral or the unilateral betrothal compact is *not of an absolute but of a disjunctive* character: either to marry, or to compensate for the harm ensuing upon the unjustifiable breach.[396] Gasparri thought that by refusing to insist on the contracting of the promised marriage the Church *indirectly* freed the offending party, who had broken off the betrothal, from all grave obligation in commutative justice as far as matrimony is concerned. There remained, nonetheless, an obligation to contract the promised marriage, but this obligation—in itself not a serious one—derived solely through the virtue of fidelity. All damage was to be repaired, if any had ensued, upon any unjustifiable violation of the promise.[397]

The writer here proposes to examine each of these three opinions in detail, beginning with the last mentioned.

A. Gasparri's View

Cardinal Gasparri, defending the third opinion, conceded that under the *ancient* discipline a serious and lawful promise of marriage brought into being *a right in virtue of justice* on the part of the promisee to enter marriage with the promisor, and a corresponding *obligation* on the promisor's part to marry the promisee. The gravity of the obligation, Gasparri further conceded, was

395 *De Sacramentis,* V, n. 110-113.

396 *Ius Canonicum,* V, n. 96.

397 *De Matrimonio,* I, n. 101.

derived from the gravity of the object or the matter to which the obligation bore reference. In this case the obligation was that of entering a serious state of life, matrimony—hence a grave obligation.[398]

Later, however, the famed Cardinal continued, authors taught that a judge could not force a party to contract marriage when that party had unjustly broken his promise and was unwilling to marry. The basis for the non-enforcement of the contract on the part of the judge was the fear that the ensuing nuptials might prove unhappy. But this fear, or more correctly, the certitude, of the failure of the marriage, Gasparri said, was always verified as long as one party did not desire matrimony. Therefore, it would flow from this consideration, Gasparri stated, that the injured and innocent party has a right of demanding from the judge what the judge cannot grant, scil., the enforcement of the betrothal contract. This state of affairs, concluded the Cardinal, became a matter that was not without self-contradiction, of course.[399]

Under the *present* law, Gasparri observed, judicial action urging the contracting of the promised marriage is no longer granted.[400] Consequently, the injured betrothed party has no redress, and this for two reasons. The first reason is the Church's desire to bring its laws on this matter in conformity with the civil law of many nations, which likewise disallow action whereby the contracting of the marriage could be urged. The second reason is the Church's wish to safeguard marriage and preserve it from innumerable bickerings, quarrels and disagreements, the evidence of which appears in so many decisions of the Sacred Congregation of the Council and the Roman Rota.[401]

From the foregoing, Gasparri then drew the conclusion that the legislator in can. 1017, § 1, *directly* suppressed all action that in the *external forum* could seek to compel the celebration of the promised marriage, and *indirectly or consequently relieved the guilty party of all serious obligation in conscience,* as arising from the virtue of justice, to contract the promised marriage. By the

[398] *De Matrimonio,* I, n. 94.

[399] Gasparri, *ibid.,* n. 95.

[400] Cf. can. 1017, § 3.

[401] Cf. pp. 48-52.

same token, the Cardinal also stated that the innocent party was relieved of all serious obligation in conscience to insist on the marriage.[402]

Cardinal Gasparri explained his conclusion by stating that, if a grave obligation in conscience, as arising from the virtue of justice, was engendered through the contracting of espousals, it was hard to see how the Church can deny the innocent party the exercise of his lawful right to petition the judge for an enforcing of the engagement contract and for a bringing about of the marriage. The action of the external forum was surely to be in keeping with the obligation existing in the internal forum.[403]

Secondly, Gasparri continued, the same reasons which held for the suppression of all serious obligation in conscience on the part of the innocent party to insist on the marriage held also for the suppression of all grave obligation in conscience in the other party to enter the marriage. The Church wished, as it was stated before, to bring its laws in line with civil law in this regard. But civil legislation not only disbars the injured party from petitioning matrimony, but also refuses to acknowledge as arising from betrothals any obligation to contract the marriage. Further, coercion in the internal forum, scil., denial of absolution by a confessor and the threat of eternal punishment made to a party who has violated his betrothal pledge, is deemed a *serious* coercion both by the Church and by the faithful at large. The reason for deeming the coercion grave is that the marriage, when forced, will have only unhappy and inauspicious consequences. Hence, all serious obligation on the part of the promisor to contract the promised marriage was suppressed by the legislator (in favor of an obligation arising simply from the virtue of fidelity), just as it was suppressed in reference to the right of the promisee to become married to the promisor.[404]

---

[402] ". . . putamus legislatorem ecclesiasticum in prima parte relati can. 1017, § 1, suppressisse *directe* actionem externi fori partis innocentis ad petendam a iudice ecclesiastica matrimonii celebrationem, uti supra demonstratum est, et *indirecte* vel *consequenter* ipsam gravem conscientiae obligationem ex virtute iustitiae partis iniuste resilientis cum relativo iure partis innocentis."—Gasparri, *De Matrimonio,* I, n. 99.

[403] *Ibid.,* n. 100.

[404] *Loc. cit.*

The third argument employed by the scholarly Cardinal was taken from a decision rendered by the Pontifical Commission for the Authentic Interpretation of the Code on June 2-3, 1918.[405] This Commission answered in the negative to the query whether the celebration of marriage was to be suspended when one of the parties to the nuptials had been previously betrothed legally to a person other than his present love. On the basis of this negative decision, how could the man in question be allowed to marry someone else if there was incumbent upon him a previous and a serious obligation to lead to the altar his first beloved? Were a serious obligation extant, how could the pastor lawfully assist at such a marriage?[406] Consequently, after the promulgation of the Code, it was Gasparri's firm belief that a promise of marriage, whether bilateral or unilateral, brings into being *only a slight obligation*—with but a relative right as arising through the virtue of fidelity—for the contracting of the marriage. The obligation to make recompense for any ensuing damages always remains grave—in virtue of natural justice.[407] Of course, ordinaries, pastors and confessors, Gasparri conceded, can and should exhort the person who has failed to marry, as he promised, to keep his word. Should, however, all charitable and exhortatory measures fail, the confessor cannot deny absolution for a "slight sin," so Gasparri finally concluded, and the ordinary or the pastor cannot "suspend," i.e., prevent the celebration of marriage of the person who has spurned his first love.[408]

B. The Opinion of Vidal

Vidal, defending another opinion, departed from Cardinal Gasparri's view by interpreting the affianced parties' obligation as being *disjunctive* in character, scil., either to marry or to make

[405] *PCI,* 2-3 iun. 1918, ad IV, n. 1—*AAS,* X (1918), 345.

[406] *De Matrimonio,* I, n. 100 (c).

[407] Hinc post Codicis promulgationem promissio matrimonialis sive unilateralis sive sponsalitia est solemnis promissio utrinque facta et acceptata quae utrique parti parit levem obligationem cum relativo iure ex virtute fidelitatis ad matrimonium contrahendum, firma obligatione ex virtute iustitiae reparandi damna, si qua debeantur."—Gasparri, *ibid.,* n. 101.

[408] *Loc. cit.*

recompense for any ensuing evil, if recompense was due. He argued thus: If a contract is rendered null and void for lack of requisite form and in consequence does not engender any obligation, it is not illogical or contradictory to say that in a contract that is valid with respect to the obligation of performing what was promised, scil., marriage, there can be *substituted an alternative obligation.* A contract in such circumstances remains valid, but no obligation relative to the performance is urged in any *specified or determinate* manner. In other words, power is granted to the parties to fulfill their obligation by *substituting something else* in place of the promised marriage, scil., *compensation.*[409]

In this way Vidal concluded, there is excluded from valid espousals all *moral coercion,* engendered by the threat of mortal sin, as long as the party, who otherwise would sin by violating his pledge, is prepared to make restitution. The willingness to indemnify the second or injured party relieves the first party of moral guilt, and thereby prevents an unhappy marriage from ensuing.[410] As a result of this state of affairs, if an affianced party wishes to marry a third party and actually does so, he or she does not commit any serious sin, as long as he or she is capable of compensating the spurned second party. Thus, there is no specific and determined obligation on the part of the two betrothed persons to contract their promised marriage.[411] The pastor, too, under such circumstances can solemnize the marriage of either of the two

---

[409] "Porro, sicut contractus ex defectu formae iure positivo requisitae irritatur et *nullam* producit obligationem, ita non repugnat ut contractus a iure habeatur validus in ordine ad rem promissam praestandam, facultate tamen data alteram rem substituendi, ut, habetur in obligationibus *alternativis seu disiunctivis* et praesertim in facultativis; quo in casu etiam contractus habetur validus et de obiecto promisso, nec tamen urget obligatio *determinate* rem promissam praestandi, sed manet debitori facultas aliam praestandi."—Wernz-Vidal, *Ius Canonicum,* V, n. 96.

[410] ". . . per talem praescriptionem, attenta indole Ecclesiae, valida sponsalia ita directe obligant ad matrimonium promissum, ut sit exclusa etiam illa coactio moralis gravis peccati in eo qui est paratus indemnitatem praestare ob damnum ab altera parte receptum, qua plena libertate non existente facile matrimonium infelicem sortiretur exitum."—Wernz-Vidal, *loc. cit.*

[411] Wernz-Vidal, *loc. ci .*

parties with a third party. He need not await the outcome of the breach of promise suit.

The Pontifical Commission for the Authentic Interpretation of the Code ruled that marriages of this nature are not to be estopped while a suit for damages is pending.[412] Simultaneously with this decision it was decided by the members of the Commission that not only was the marriage not to be hindered when a suit was being pressed concerning the justice of the reason for which the engagement was broken, but the action itself could no longer be introduced in court. Such action was therefore outlawed, i.e., no longer allowed.[413]

Siding with Vidal's doctrine in this regard (among others) were Ferreres (1861-1936),[414] Noldin (1838-1922),[415] and Bouvaert, writing in 1931.[415a]

C. The Opinion of Cappello

Cappello, defending a third opinion, rejects the view of Vidal, scil., that espousals engender a disjunctive obligation, and attacks the opinion of those who claim that no obligation is engendered whatever in the forum of conscience. Thus, first, against those who deny any obligation, he argues: Canon 1017, § 3, speaks of a promise—and of a valid promise at that. Now, the proper immediate and essential effect which inherently (*per se*), and not merely incidentally (*per accidens*), arises out of any promise is an *obligation,* specifically that obligation to which the mind and will have reference at the time of the contract. This obligation, therefore, as it is the proper, immediate and essential effect of a promise, so necessarily flows from the promise that, should all obligation be lacking, by that very fact the very concept of a promise would likewise be lacking, i.e., vanish.[416]

---

[412] *PCI,* 3 iun. 1918, ad IV—*AAS,* X (1918), 345.

[413] *Loc. cit.*

[414] *Compendium Theologiae Moralis,* II, n. 933.

[415] *Summa Theologiae Moralis,* III, 539.

[415a] "De Interpretatione Can. 1017," *Jus Pontificium* (Romae, 1921-1940), XI (1931), 127-132.

[416] Cappello, *De Sacramentis,* V, n. 111. Cf. also his article, "De Obligatione Orta ex Valida Promissione Matrimonii", *Periodica de Re Morali, Canonica, Liturqica* (Brugis, 1927-1936 et Romae, 1937-), XXI (1932), 88-110.

All leading classical authors, so Cappello avers, agree with this reasoning. St. Thomas (1225-1274) for instance wrote: "Honesty demands that a man should keep whatever promise he makes to another, and this obligation is based on the natural law."[417] Molina (1535-1600) taught in no uncertain terms that a true promise always induces obligation.[418] Lessius (1554-1623), Dominicus Soto (1494-1560), Schmalzgrueber (1663-1735), Pirhing (1606-1679) and many others presented a unanimous doctrine on this matter.[419] Sanchez (1550-1610) particularly, in a clear-cut distinction, explained that an obligation arising from the espousal promise may arise *internally, from within* (*intrinsice*), i.e., by reason of the natural precept obliging one to keep one's word, or *extrinsically,* i.e., in virtue of judicial coercion. In other words, it is derived from without when the judge enforces the fulfillment of the promise, or when in virtue of a covenant a penalty is stipulated in case of breach.[420]

Cappello concludes that the following three facts emerge as certain and indisputable from the foregoing consideration: First, every promise *begets* an obligation; secondly, this obligation is such that it *cannot be conceived without the promise* whence it springs; thirdly, this obligation flows from the very essence of the promise, i.e., as Sanchez states it, *from within, intrinsically.*[421] Hence the obligation, by the very fact that it is derived always and necessarily from the essence or nature of a promise, *qua* obligation, regards the same object that the promise regards, namely, future matrimony. Therefore, from a promise of marriage there is always and necessarily engendered an obligation which has reference directly and immediately to the object in question, scil., marriage in the

---

[417] *Summa Theologica,* Ia-IIae, q. 88, a. 3 ad 1.

[418] *De Iustitia,* tract II, disp. CCLXII, nn. 1 sq.

[419] Cf. Lessius, *De Iustitia,* lib. II, cap. XVIII, dub. 1; De Soto, *De Iustitia et Iure Libri Decem* (Salamanticae, 1556), lib. VII, q. i, a. 2 (hereafter cited *De Iustitia*); Schmalzgrueber, *Ius Ecclesiasticum,* lib. V, tit. I, n. 80; Pirhing, *Ius Canonicum,* lib. IV, tit. I, N. 15; Darmanin, "De Promissione Matrimoniali—ad Can. 1017," *Angelicum* (Romae, 1924-), VIII (1931), 369-371.

[420] Cf. Sanchez, *De Matrimonii Sacramento,* lib. I, disp. XXVII, n. 1.

[421] Cappello, *De Sacramentis,* V, n. 111.

future—and that irrespective of whether other obligations arise extrinsically or not.[422]

Therefore, the obligation of restitution, for instance, does not proceed directly and immediately from the promise of marriage, as Vidal would have it.[423] Nor does this obligation come into existence as something intrinsic to the very promise of marriage. At best it is begotten incidentally, Cappello maintains. The proximate cause and immediate source of such an incidental obligation is indemnity (not the promise of future marriage), which, with respect to the obligation of marriage, is merely an occasion. Hence, the origin of the term "incidental" in reference to indemnity.[424]

Besides the obligation of restitution which, as was stated above, is engendered incidentally, and which does not proceed as an immediate and proper effect consequent upon an espousal promise, there must be acknowledged *another* effect which arises of itself and at once (*immediate*) and is of the substance, of the very nature, of the betrothal promise, scil., the obligation to contract the promised marriage.[425] An alternative or disjunctive obligation, such as Vidal defended, can be had only when an option is granted whereby one chooses between two objects. Hence *two* terms are absolutely necessary, so much so that, if one is lacking, then the alternative obligation simultaneously is lacking. But in the case of the betrothment compact, the obligation to make recompense is *not always present,* for the Code speaks of granting action only if it is due (*si qua debeatur*).[426]

When no injury has resulted from the non-fulfillment of the espousal pledge, then no obligation of restitution exists—and hence by that very fact no alternative obligation is present. The reparation of damages, Cappello further insists, is *independent* of the existence and the validity of the espousals. Reparation may be due even when the canonical form was not observed, since reparation is demanded by natural justice, irrespective of the positive pro-

[422] *Loc. cit.*

[423] Cf. Wernz-Vidal, *Ius Canonicum,* V, n. 96. See also the paragraphs above, where Vidal's opinion was scrutinized.

[424] Cappello, *loc. cit.*

[425] Cappello, *loc. cit.*

[426] Cf. Canon 1017, § 3.

visions of civil or canon law. Therefore, if it be independent of the espousal promise, then the obligation of reparation cannot be an alternative obligation at the same time. An alternative obligation cannot be separated from a truly valid promise of marriage.[427]

Cappello supports this view by adverting to the decision of the Pontifical Commission,[428] which declared that action for reparation of damage could be brought before either the ecclesiastical or the civil tribunals. Since this judicial action is a matter for either of the two tribunals (*mixti fori*), i.e., one in which even a lay judge may lawfully adjudicate the point in question, obviously one is dealing with an obligation which *can be separated* from the existence and the validity of the espousal-promise. Were this not true, the civil magistrate would be exercising authority directly or indirectly over the very espousal contract itself—which is certainly outside his competence when the contractants are baptized persons, i.e., subjects of the Church.[429]

Lastly, so Cappello argues, the Code, by using the words in canon 1017, § 3: "But a promise of marriage, although it be valid *and no just cause exists to excuse its fulfillment* . . . ,"[430] proves the contention that a true obligation is engendered when espousals are contracted, because these words "excuse its fulfillment," clearly suppose that the matter treated is a genuine obligation—which must be fulfilled. The word "excuse," as theologians and canonists understand it, postulates a specific circumstance which exempts from the law, from a burden or from some obligation, as Cappello rightly explains. But if there does not exist any obligation of doing,

[427] "Proinde onus resarciendi damna non est effectus necessarius et essentialis *promissionis* sponsalitiae, utpote qui interdum haberi potest etiam independenter a vi atque efficacia eiusdem promissionis. Inde sponte consequitur huiusmodi obligationem reparandi damna, cum sit natura sua *separabilis* ab existentia et valore promissionis matrimonialis, coniungi et acquiparari non posse tamquam *alternativa* alteri obligationi, quae nullo pacto separari potest a vera validaque inita coniugii promissione."—Cappello, *loc. cit.*

[428] *PCI,* 2-3 iun. 1918, ad IV—*AAS,* X (1918), 345.

[429] Cappello, *loc. cit.* Cf. also canons 1553; 87.

[430] "At ex matrimonii promissione, licet valida sit nec ulla iusta causa ab eadem implenda excuset."—Canon 1017, § 3.

giving or omitting something, then there cannot be present any such thing as an "excuse," as there is nothing to be "excused from!" Furthermore, fulfillment or realization, properly considered, regards the obligation of performing or omitting some action, so much so that if no obligation is present, no realization or fulfillment can take place. Finally, a cause, and indeed a just cause, is required in so far as a genuine obligation, whether positive or negative, is concerned. On the contrary, however, if all obligation be absent, then no cause is required for the seeking of relief from the obligation.[431]

In defense of his position Cappello answers several objections for the purpose of reconciling the existence of an obligation in conscience to contract the promised marriage with the fact that no sanction in the external forum is granted by the Church.

Thus, to the objection that the Church can take away natural obligations and does so in the case of betrothals when providing an alternative obligation, Cappello replies as follows: The Church can take away natural obligations, i.e., in conscience, as can the State, in so far as it declares them null and does not recognize any effect in either forum when a specified form was not observed at the time the obligation was contracted. But the Church cannot regard an obligation valid and simultaneously impede its necessary and proper effects. Theoretically this would be contradictory.[432]

A further objection is this, scil., that the Church, by the very fact that it denies judicial action for compelling entry into marriage, even when the promise is valid and no excuse is extant to prevent its celebration, excludes the obligation in reference to the contracting of marriage, for to obligation corresponds a right, and a right is unthinkable unless enforceable through an action. The response of Cappello to this objection is that a right is not always and necessarily protected by the option of judicial action. Canon 1667, for example, states that any right is enforceable not only by a judicial action but also by a judicial exception *unless the contrary is stated*. Hence the Code allows for exceptions. There are many natural obligations, Cappello further remarks, both in the ec-

[431] Cappello, *De Sacramentis,* V, n. 111.

[432] Cappello, *De Sacramentis,* V, n. 112.

clesiastical as well as the civil forum, which cannot be urged with force, i.e., are not enforceable through judicial action, as, for instance, a formless agreement (*nuda pactio*).[433] Denial of action is thus not equivalent to denial of obligation, Cappello insists.[434]

To the observation that the obligation which derives through a betrothal has been abrogated by the Code, Cappello replies that it is true that current legislation has mitigated the sterner measures of the past, but not to the extent that a valid promise of marriage is shorn of its necessary effects. But the *schema* of the Code, on which the present law was based, indicates that the legislator had purposed *to deprive* the espousal promise of binding force in conscience, the opposition further presses. The *schema* under the then tentative canon 1019 declared: "From the promise of marriage, whether unilateral or bilateral, i.e., espousals, no obligation of contracting marriage can be urged, but only the right of demanding reparation of damage, if any is due."[435] Now, since the bishops to whom the *schema* had been sent did not object to this canon as it appeared at the time, the codifiers considered the doctrine sufficiently expressed. Changes in the final draft were made only for the purpose of giving a clearer rendition of the text. This is Gasparri's argument.[436]

To this argument Cappello replies that the final *schema* in no way excluded all obligation *in conscience,* but only excluded the *juridic* obligation in the external forum. The *schema* sent to the bishops, on the other hand, by the words "nulla urgeri potest obligatio" signified that no *external* coercion can be employed by the judge at the instance of the injured party acting as plaintiff. The words are used technically to mean that no action is granted

---

[433] Cappello, *loc. cit.*

[434] *Loc. cit.*

[435] "Ex promissione matrimonii sive unilaterali sive bilaterali seu ex sponsalibus nulla urgeri potest obligatio contrahendi matrimonium, salvo iure exigendi reparationem damnorum, si qua debeatur."—Gasparri, *De Matrimonio,* I, n. 103, footnote 1. An almost identical wording is found in canon 295, § 1, of Gasparri's *Schema Codicis Iuris Canonici* (4 vols. in 2, Romae, 1913), III-IV, p. 125.

[436] *De Matrimonio,* I, n. 102, footnote 1.

for demanding the enforcement of the obligation to contract marriage.[437]

In the light of Cappello's theory and of the solutions he has offered to the arguments of his opponents, a summary under *seven* headings can be made of his view

First, the proper, immediate and essential effect of a valid promise is the existence of an *obligation.* This obligation necessarily proceeds *intrinsically* from the very nature of the promise. Secondly, a valid promise of marriage, in so far as it is made according to the prescript of law, *necessarily* and intrinsically engenders an obligation as its proper, immediate and essential effect. Thirdly, the law cannot change the concept and nature of acts, nor can it destroy their *essential effects,* as long as these acts remain in being. Wherefore, the legislator can indeed declare espousals null and void, v.g., for lack of form, and thus on such grounds deprive betrothals of their obligation in both the external and internal forum, but he cannot expressly acknowledge them as valid, and, notwithstanding their validity, deny them their proper and essential effect, that of a true obligation. Such an act would make, it appears, for a manifest contradiction. Fourthly, the obligation in question cannot be solely an obligation of compensating damages, both because sometimes no damages or disadvantages ensue, and because this effect is neither direct nor immediate but only indirect and accidental, since fundamentally it flows from the indemnity, rather than from the espousal itself. Fifthly, it is irrelevant to the chief issue here whether this obligation is of justice or of fidelity; whether it is grave or slight. The main concern is to safeguard the *genuine notion of a valid promise,* once an obligation has been engendered. Sixthly, *more probably* (*probabilius*), when a promise of marriage, either bilateral or unilateral, is valid, the obligation in the internal forum is *grave* and one that binds in justice, in consideration of all the theological principles and norms governing this and similar contracts. Lastly,

---

[437] "Quae verba [schematum] nullatenus excludunt obligationem conscientiae sed tantum excludunt obligationem iuridicam pro *foro* externo, vel iuxta alterum schema declarant hanc obligationem "urgeri" non posse, scil., exigi externa coactione, iudicis ministerio implorato. Idem quippe est iuridice loquendo, dicere: *obligatio urgeri nequit,* ac dicere, *non datur actio ad petendam, in casu, matrimonii celebrationem."—De Sacramentis,* V, n. 112 (7).

that opinion which asserts that *no* obligation or an alternate obligation is derived from a valid betrothal promise must be regarded as lacking juridic foundation, when the matter is carefully, naturally and thoroughly studied.

D. Conclusions on the Controversy

The present writer concurs with Cappello's view and looks upon his reconciliation of a seeming contradiction between the notion of obligation and the lack of its sanction in the external forum as the best of the three explanations proffered. A grave obligation in conscience arising out of justice is maintained to be the consequence of espousals, since a serious matter is involved, i.e., future marriage. But the withdrawal of a sanction in the external forum is also acknowledged in accord with the mind of the legislator whose aim was the preventing of unhappy unions.[438]

SECTION VII. DISSOLUTION OF THE BETROTHAL CONTRACT

Article 1: Mutual Consent

Unlike marriage, betrothment, whether bilateral or unilateral, by its very nature is rescissible,[439] allowed a dissolution, as in the Germanic law.[440] Hebraic espousals were tantamount to marriage, but as marriage was dissoluble, so too was the promise of marriage.[441] Canon law from earliest times to the present also allowed a dissolution because betrothal was never an indissoluble contract, as is matrimony.[442]

Approximately nine reasons give rise to a dissolution of engagements in the eyes of the law. In this article consideration will first be given to the most common reason, namely, *mutual consent.*

---

[438] Cf. also pp. 227-233 of this dissertation.

[439] Cf. pp. 9-11 of this dissertation. The Roman law also allowed dissolution.

[440] Cf. pp. 15-16 of this dissertation.

[441] Cf. pp. 20-21 of this dissertation.

[442] For legislation on the dissolution of the betrothal promise as found in the *Decretum* of Gratian and in the Decretals of Gregory IX and Boniface VIII, cf. pp. 35, 37-39 of this dissertation.

Since promises of marriage in the future follow the normal laws on contracts, both parties are at liberty to rescind their engagement when both mutually desire it. The principle of law operative here is that rule which states that the causes which give rise to a thing may also terminate it.[443] Canonists are unanimous in concurring with this principle as applied to the engagement compact.[444] Even when it has been sanctioned with an oath, a betrothal is rescissible, once both parties decided on the dissolution, since here the oath is simply accessory to the promise.[445] However, some older canonists doubted that dissolution was possible when the oath was made *principally in God's honor* (*in honorem Dei*) and only secondarily in confirmation of the betrothment promise for the sake of lending it an added binding force. Such an oath was equivalent to a vow, these authors held, and by a vow, in general, there is promised to God something which another cannot renounce.[446] But this theory is not tenable, as the underlying condition of every oath added to espousals is, "unless we mutually resolve to recede from our promise."[447]

In former days, in the event that the espoused persons had not yet reached the age of puberty, a mutual rejection of their affiancement was possible only after their attainment of the age of puberty.[448]

---

[443] "Omnis res, per quascumque causas nascitur, per easdem dissolvitur."—C. 4, C. XXVII, q. 2. Cf. also Reiffenstuel, *Ius Canonicum, De Regulis Iuris,* cap. I, reg. I.

[444] Cf. Sanchez, *De Matrimonii Sacramento,* disp. LII, n. 2; Ballerini-Palmieri, *Opus Theologicum Morale,* VI, n. 275; *Santi, Praelectiones,* lib. IV, tit. I, n. 43; Gasparri, *De Matrimonio,* I, n. 126; Wernz-Vidal, *Ius Canonicum,* V, n. 102; Schmalzgrueber, *Ius Ecclesiasticum,* lib. IV, tit. I, n. 151.

[445] Cf. canon 1318, § 1, and pp. 132-138 of this thesis. *Reg. 42* of the *Regulae Iuris* distinctly states: "Accessorium naturam sequi congruit principalis."—Cf. Reiffenstuel, *loc. cit.*

[446] Cf. De Soto, *De Iustitia,* lib. VIII, a. 9 ad 2; St. Thomas, *Summa Theologica,* IIa, IIae, q. 89, a. 9, ad 2.

[447] Cf. Schmalzgrueber, *ibid.,* nn. 159-160.

[448] Cc. 7, 8, 10, X, *de desponsatione impuberum,* IV, 2; J L, nn. 13767, 13765, 15730; cf. also pp. 35-37 and pp. 45-47 of this thesis.

Article 2: The Condition Subsequent

A second cause justifying dissolution is the *condition subsequent.* In a previous article on conditions,[449] it was said that a condition is subsequent when the termination of the operation of the act is made to depend on the occurrence of the condition, v.g., "I will marry you unless I find a richer girl." Such a condition, because it is directly opposed to the nature of the betrothal, when added to a promise of marriage destroys the promise, provided that it was, first, appended from the very beginning, i.e., at the time the promise was made and, secondly, that it was truly a condition subsequent, and not merely a suspensive one. The principle of law operative and applicable here is: The will governs conditions. In doubt, a condition is *presumed suspensive.*[450]

Article 3: The Election of a Higher State

Espousals are also rescissible on spiritual grounds. Hence, a third reason sufficient for a dissolving of the espousal promise is presented when either party makes a vow of virginity, a vow of perfect chastity, a vow not to marry, or a vow to enter the priesthood or to embrace the religious life. Authors clearly assert that underlying every engagement contract is the conditional clause: "I will marry you unless you should choose a higher state in life."[451] In a unilateral form of espousals the same assumption, therefore, also obtains. As a matter of fact, this clause: "unless you choose a more perfect or higher state", whether tacit or expressed, is so affixed to the betrothment pact that, were it excluded by the principals, this exclusion would be null and void and contrary to the natural law itself.[452]

---

[449] Cf. pp. 161-174.

[450] Cf. Reiffenstuel, *Ius Canonicum,* lib. IV, tit. V, n. 9; Schmalzgrueber, *Ius Ecclesiasticum,* lib. IV, tit. V, n. 18; D'Annibale, *Summula,* I, n. 41.

[451] Cf. Sanchez, *op. cit.,* disp. XLII, n. 2; Schmalzgrueber, *op. cit.,* lib. IV, tit. VI, n. 69; Reiffenstuel, *ibid.,* n. 224; Ballerini-Palmieri, *Opus Theologicum Morale,* VI, n. 335; Sebastianelli, *Praelectiones* (3 vols., Vol. II, *De Rebus,* 2 ed., Romae, 1905-1906), II, n. 24; Gasparri, *De Matrimonio,* I, n. 122; Wernz-Vidal, *Ius Canonicum,* V, n. 105; Noldin, *Summa Theologiae Moralis,* III, 544; Cappello, *ibid.,* n. 119.

[452] Cappello, *loc. cit.*

A. Nature and Division of Vows

A vow dissolves betrothals because by definition it is a free and deliberate promise made to God to do something that is physically and morally possible and, at least for this particular person, better than its opposite, or something that does not hinder the performance of a more perfect act. Hence, a vow to observe perfect chastity or a vow to enter the religious life is better, v.g., than the opposite act of making a promise to enter the state of marriage.[453]

Vows are public when taken before a representative of the Church, and in the name of the Church, v.g., before a bishop or a provincial; they are private when no public authority in the name of the Church receives them, as in the case of one who vows in his own heart to enter the priesthood. Public vows, in turn, are either solemn or simple. A vow is solemn only when recognized by the Church as such, and acts opposed to it are null, if they are capable of being nullified. Simple vows make acts opposed to them illicit. When only the Holy See is capable of dispensing from the vow, it is a reserved vow; otherwise, it is non-reserved. When taken for life or for only a certain length of time, a vow is said to be perpetual or temporary respectively.[454]

It will be assumed here that all the private vows in question are perpetual by nature, i.e., what is promised and vowed to God is to last for life. Hence, the vow of virginity, the vow of perfect chastity, the vow not to marry, and the vows to enter the clerical state and to embrace the religious life, as affecting espousals are *a priori* regarded as taken *in perpetuum*. When the question of revocation occurs, due consideration will be accorded the problem.

When the vows of virginity, perfect chastity and celibacy are *temporary*, it is the opinion of this author, in the absence of the opinion of other authors, that, first, of themselves these vows do not dissolve espousals. Vows of this nature merely *suspend* the

---

[453] Cf. canon 1307, § 1; St. Thomas, *Summa Theologica*, IIa, IIae, q. 88, a. 1; Schmalzgrueber, *op. cit.*, lib. III, tit. XXXIV, n. 3; Ballerini-Palmieri, *op. cit.*, II, n. 1; Cappello, *ibid.*, n. 292; Gasparri, *ibid.*, n 425.

[454] Schmalzgrueber, *ibid.*, n.n. 3 sq.; Ballerini-Palmieri, *op. cit.*, II, n. 2; Cappello, *loc. cit.*

celebration of the promised marriage, provided the other party consents to wait. If this other party is unwilling to wait, he or she may recede from the contract, as a notable change of circumstances has taken place, sufficient to relieve this non-vowing party of the obligation to contract the promised marriage. Secondly, if the vow becomes known to the other party and no opposition is evinced, or if the vow is made with the approval or, at least, without the protest of the other party, the engagement promise remains in a state of suspension till the time of the expiration of the vow. In other words, marriage is mutually postponed till the period of expectancy lapses. Thirdly, when virginity, perfect chastity, or celibacy is vowed for a period which coincides with the duration intervening between the time of the making of the vow and the time fixed for the celebrating of the marriage, then the engagement promise remains unaffected.

Concerning the compensation due because of injury suffered when a vow was made, whereby the espousals became dissolved, equity demands that the one who makes the vow subsequent to the betrothment compensate according to the financial loss suffered, as previously explained.[455] An exorbitant sum should not be exacted by the other party, as this is contrary to Christian charity.

With these general notions in mind, one may now turn to the five private vows: the vow of virginity, the vow of perfect chastity, the vow of the non-contracting of marriage, i.e., celibacy, and the vows of the reception of priestly orders and of the embrace of the religious state. Each will be accorded individual treatment.

B. The Simple Vow of Virginity

The first vow to be considered here is that of *virginity*. Virginity, materially and physically viewed, is the state of bodily integrity present in one who, if a male, has never had a wilful seminal emission; if a female, has not lost her maidenhood deliberately through a disruption of the hymen. The Church considers virginity to be present in a woman who has not had sexual intercourse; in a male who has had no carnal knowledge of a woman. Virginity,

[455] Cf. Schmalzgrueber, *Ius Ecclesiasticum,* lib. VI, tit. II, n. 109. Cf. also pp. 186-188.

as a virtue, i.e., formally viewed, is the will and intention in one who is still either physically a virgin, or whose virginity has not been wilfully violated, of refraining from all deliberate carnal pleasure, both sinful and not sinful, the latter being possible only in the married state. The vow of virginity has in man as its object his abstinence from sexual intercourse or voluntary pollution; in woman, her abstinence from sexual intercourse or unnatural, i.e., culpable infringement of her bodily integrity.[456]

When one of the engaged couple subsequent to the engagement makes a vow of virginity, the betrothal is dissolved in the internal forum. In the external forum, proof must be furnished.[457] Older authors asserted that the ecclesiastical judge in the matter could demand that the person who had made the vow either had to enter religion or the priesthood in demonstration of his claim, or else had to enter the marriage as he had promised.[458] But such a view can hardly be sustained, as one cannot be forced into the religious life on the one hand or, on the other hand, be forced to fulfill his betrothal promise in violation of his subsequent vow of virginity.[459] Sufficient proof by witnesses both in respect of the veracity of the person who made the vow and with regard to the fact that the vow was made, if known to them, should satisfy the bishop acting as judge in the case. If sufficient proof is lacking, the bishop may decide that a just reason exists for declaring the engagement dissolved, v.g., because of the notable change in circumstances, a probable unhappy outcome of the marriage, etc.

A question debated among writers in this regard concerns rescissory action. On whose part is the betrothment contract rescinded? When the vow *preceded* the betrothal agreement, all authors concede that the engagement is null and void at once as far as both parties are concerned. Such a promise of marriage is *de facto* invalid, since virginity was previously promised to God.[460]

---

[456] Cf. Cappello, *ibid.*, n. 299; Gasparri, *ibid.*, n. 427.

[457] Cf. Cappello, *ibid.*, nn. 119, 121; Ballerini-Palmieri, *Opus Theogicum Morale,* VI, nn. 355, 357.

[458] Cf., v.g., St. Alphonsus, *Theologia Moralis,* Lib. VI, n. 869; Ballerini-Palmieri, *loc. cit.*

[459] Cf. Ballerini-Palmieri, *Opus Theologicum Morale,* VI, n. 357.

[460] Cf. St. Alphonsus, *ibid.*, n. 873, dub. 1.

When one of the parties made the vow *after* the contract of betrothment had been drawn up, authors are also generally agreed that the *other party* can rescind the agreement.[461] It is controverted, however, whether the engagement is broken off as far as the one who made the vow is concerned. Pontius, Dominic De Soto, Suarez, and others contended that the contract is rescinded also on the part of the one making the vow because, first, a vow to God is of greater value than a promise to a human being and, secondly, the underlying assumption and tacit condition of every engagement promise is: "I will marry you unless I should choose a higher state in life."[462] Sanchez, Pirhing, Laymann, Schmalzgrueber, and their followers maintained the opposite, declaring first that God does not accept a vow when a promise was previously made to a man or woman, since such a vow operates to the prejudice of that man or woman. Secondly, they claimed, decretal law favored their view.[463] Thirdly, these authors averred, it cannot be proved that a tacit condition to make a vow outside a religious institute which does not enjoy papal approbation underlies the espousals.[464] Both opinions have been called probable.[465] St. Thomas did not distinguish the question as did the above-cited authors; he merely stated that the simple (private) vow of virginity dissolves espousals.[466]

The arguments of Sanchez, Schmalzgrueber, Pirhing and their adherents, who claimed that the promise of marriage is not extinguished by the one vowing virginity, do not appear conclusive. These men gratuitously restrict to religious profession in institutes

[461] Schmalzgrueber, *Ius Ecclesiasticum,* lib. IV, tit. VI, n. 94; Sanchez, *De Matrimonii Sacramento,* lib. I, disp. XLVI, n. 5; Pirhing, *Ius Canonicum,* lib. IV, tit. I, n. XXVIII.

[462] Cf. Pontius, *De Matrimonio,* lib. VI, cap. XII, n. 4; De Soto, *De Iustitia,* dist. XXVII, q. 2, a. 5; Suarez, *Opera Omnia* (28 vols., Parisiis, 1856-1861), V, nn. 805 ff.

[463] Cf. c. 13, X, *de sponsalibus et matrimoniis,* IV, 1; JL, n. 11869.

[464] Cf. Sanchez, *ibid.,* n. 6; Pirhing, *ibid.,* n. XXX, Laymann, *Theologia Moralis,* lib. V, tract X, § 1, cap. II, n. 6; Schmalzgrueber, *ibid.,* n. 93.

[465] Cf. Ballerini-Palmieri, *Opus Theologicum Morale,* VI, nn. 351-357; St. Alphonsus, *Theologia Moralis,* lib. VI, n. 873.

[466] *Summa Theologica, Supplementum,* q. 53, a. 1 ad 1: "Unde propter votum simplex sunt sponsalia dirimenda."

of pontifical approval the tacit supposition that underlies all engagements and speak loosely of the vow supervening the espousals as being prejudicial to the other party. The appeal to decretal law is not peremptory either, since the opposition can also make use of it. Consequently, the reasoning of Pontius, De Soto and Suarez, with which Cappello also agrees today,[467] appears more probable and acceptable to this writer.

C. The Simple Vow of Perfect Chastity

Espousals are also rescinded in consequence of the vow of perfect chastity. This vow excludes all deliberate sexual pleasure, licit or illicit. The former is morally admissible only in marriage. Perfect chastity includes virginal chastity, but does not necessarily demand virginity, as virginity may have been lost prior to the vow of perfect chastity. So-called imperfect chastity excludes illicit sexual pleasure only, hence can be observed even by those who are married.[468]

The same principles that applied to the vow of virginity in reference to betrothals are equally applicable to the vow of perfect chastity. Hence, this vow, if made prior to espousals, dissolves the engagement on the part of either contractant. If the vow was made posterior to the engagement, severance of the engagement is surely permissible to the party who did not make the vow. It is disputed whether or not the one who made the vow is freed of his obligation. As above, the present writer concurs with the opinion of Pontius, de Soto, Suarez and Cappello in maintaining that *no* obligation of this kind exists, as the vow supersedes the promise of marriage, and this further constitutes such a notable change in circumstances that marriage is out of the question. *De facto*, the two states of perfect chastity and marriage are mutually exclusive and incompatible.[469]

---

[467] *De Sacramentis,* V, n. 121.

[468] Cf. Noldin, *Summa Theologiae Moralis,* III, n. 557; Cappello, *ibid.,* n. 300.

[469] Cf. Pontius, *De Matrimonio,* lib. VI, cap. XII, n. 4; De Soto, *De Iustitia,* dist. XXVII, q. 2, a. 5; Suarez, *Opera Omnia,* V, nn. 805.

D. The Simple Vow of the Non-Contracting of Marriage

The same obtains for the vow of the non-contracting of marriage. This vow may or may not include the intention to enter the priesthood or religion. However, the vow to enter the priesthood or religion does include the vow not to contract marriage. When such a vow of not contracting marriage follows upon an engagement promise, the latter, so all agree, is rescinded on the part of the person not making the vow. It is also rescinded on the part of the one making the vow, if one accept the principles enunciated by Suarez, De Soto and Pontius.[470] These authors' viewpoint the present writer espouses for the reasons explained in the foregoing paragraph. When the vow has preceded the engagement, the betrothal is invalid on the part of both, as explained above in reference to the other vows.

E. The Simple Vow of the Reception of Sacred Orders

Two considerations will be here presented, the *vow* of receiving sacred orders and the *actual reception* of these orders. The latter consideration will fall into three categories, scil., the entrance into the seminary, the reception of first tonsure and minor orders, and lastly, ordination to the major orders.

First, the vow itself. Like the other private vows described in the preceding paragraphs, the vow to become a priest rescinds *ipso facto* the promise to contract marriage. The vow of becoming a priest of its nature includes and supposes the vow of not contracting marriage, as previously mentioned. Hence, the principles laid down in reference to the other vows find application here too, in the same manner as described above. More need not be said, as the principles and their application are clear.

Secondly, the reception of sacred orders: The first consideration here must be given to entrance into the seminary. When an engaged man decides to enter the seminary without previously making a vow to that effect, it is the opinion of Cappello, and also the present writer's, that such a step rescinds the espousals irrespective of the consideration as to whether or not the person perseveres in

---

[470] *Loc. cit.*

his resolve. Canon 1363, § 1, indicates that entrance into the seminary must be accompanied with an intention on the part of the seminarian to serve the Church *for life.* The canon warns ordinaries not to admit candidates to the seminary unless these give indications of persevering.[471] Consequently, the state of being betrothed and of preparing for the priesthood are simultaneously impossible.[472] Through the man's entrance into the seminary, the espousals cease to exist on the part of both the betrothed, as was explained in the treatment of the vows in the paragraphs preceding this.

Reception of first tonsure and of minor orders by one who had contracted betrothals while in the world dissolves the contract according to Cappello, but not so according to St. Alphonsus. The celebrated moralist reasoned that the status of a minor cleric was not incompatible with marriage. One could be married and still become a cleric, he argued, as was to be seen in the decretal law.[473] This opinion St. Alphonsus stated, was the more common and the more acceptable one.[474]

With due deference to the scholarly Saint, Cappello offers the opposite view. He maintains that the reasoning of St. Alphonsus can no longer be sustained in the light of the new legislation in effect today. Canon 983, § 1, provides that first tonsure and minor orders are to be conferred only on those who have the purpose of entering the priesthood and who are at the same time deemed worthy of the priesthood.[475] To the statement of St. Alphonsus that clerical life is not of its very nature incompatible with the married state, canon 132, § 2, may be employed by way of a refutation. This canon expressly and distinctly announces that minor clerics may indeed marry, but by that very fact they *lose their clerical status,* unless

---

[471] "In Seminarium ab Ordinario ne admittantur nisi filii legitimi quorum indoles et voluntas spem afferant eos cum fructu ecclesiasticis ministeriis *perpetuo inservituros.*"—Canon 1363, § 1. (Italics inserted.)

[472] Cf. Cappello, *De Sacramentis,* V, n. 120.

[473] Cf. cc. 1-2, *de clericis coniugatis,* III, 2, in VI°.

[474] *Theologia Moralis,* lib. VI, n. 872.

[475] "Prima tonsura et ordines illis tantum conferendi sunt, qui propositum habeant ascendendi ad presbyteratum et quos merito coniicere liceat aliquando dignos futuros esse sacerdotes."—Canon 973, § 1.

force or fear prevented the marriage from being valid.[476] Obviously, then, it is evident that today the clerical state is, by force of the law itself, not compatible with that of marriage. Hence, espousals cease with the reception of the betrothed man into the ranks of the clergy.[477] Thus, if the cleric were to leave the seminary, and discontinued his studies, no obligation would remain requiring him to marry his former fiancée. A new contract would be necessary, if this obligation was to ensue.

As for major orders, these clearly sever the bond created by espousals. Thus, if a cleric had abandoned the clerical state after receiving the last of the minor orders, only to be readmitted to the clerical state later with espousals intervening in the interim, the espousals would be dissolved.[478] In this connection, to hark back briefly to the subject of vows, St. Alphonsus distinguished between the vow to receive holy (major) orders and the actual reception of these orders. In the case of the former, he held that the engagement can be broken off only by the party who did not make the vow, but that, in the case of the latter, it is broken off mutually, i.e., by both principals, once the vow has been put into execution and the man is ordained a subdeacon.[479]

F. The Simple Vow of the Embrace of the Religious Life

Two problems will be discussed here—the vow of entering religion and the actual fact of entrance into the religious state.

First, the *vow* to enter religion. By religion and the religious state is meant that fixed manner of life within a society approved by the legitimate ecclesiastical authority in which the members strive after evangelical perfection by living according to the special

---

[476] "Clerici minores possunt quidem nuptias inire, sed nisi matrimonium fuerit nullum vi aut metu eisdem incusso, ipso iure e statu clericali decidunt." —Canon 132, § 2.

[477] Cf. Cappello, *De Sacramentis,* V, n. 120.

[478] Cf. Ballerini-Palmieri—*Opus Theologicum Morale,* VI, nn. 335-339, 350.

[479] *Theologia Moralis,* lib. VI, n. 873. St. Alphonsus, however, in this n. 873 speaks simultaneously of the vows of chastity and of entering religion—to the confusion of the reader. Cf. Ballerini-Palmieri, *loc. cit.,* for a commentary on this passage of St. Alphonsus.

laws of the society itself through the taking of public vows, either perpetual or temporary, which if temporary are to be renewed when the time of the vows expires.[480] The religious organization to which one aspires is either an order, in which solemn vows are taken,[481] or a congregation, wherein only simple vows are taken.[482] The Franciscans are an example of the former, the Redemptorists of the latter. One may also vow to enter either a lay community in which all or most of the members are not clerics but simply religious, or a clerical institute in which the members enter the priesthood, e.g., the Christian Brothers and Jesuits respectively.[483]

Lastly, a vow may be taken to enter a society of men or of women who lead a community life after the manner of religious under the government of superiors and according to approved constitutions, but without the three usual vows of the religious life. This sort of society is not a religious organization properly so called nor are its members religious in the strict sense of the word (they are often called quasi-religious). It is either lay or clerical according as the members are non-clerics or clerics.[484] The Fathers of the Precious Blood, e.g., are an example of a clerical quasi-religious society.

When *prior* to one's engagement one has vowed to enter religion, obviously, as was seen previously in similar cases, the vow remains in force and the engagement is invalid. A dispensation from the vow is required before an engagement contract can be entered into validly.

When the vow is taken *subsequent* to the espousals, the bond between the two contractants is, in the opinion of all the authors, severed by the one who did not make the vow, but it is disputed whether or not the one vowing is similarly relieved of the obligation to contract the marriage. St. Alphonsus distinguished thus: If the vow was simply that of entering religion, the person who vowed was by no means liberated of the obligation to contract the

---

[480] Canon 488, 1°.
[481] Canon 488, 2°.
[482] *Loc. cit.*
[483] Cf. Canon 488, 4°.
[484] Cf. canon 673.

marriage, whereas his affianced was. When the vow made was not simply that of entering religion, but also that of making religious profession as well, such a vow rescinded the contract also for the vowing person, since he thereby rendered himself juridically incapable of contracting marriage.[485]

However, this distinction, it seems, cannot be justified under the present discipline. One cannot vow to enter the religious life without simultaneously intending to make the religious profession, or, if no profession is had in the institute to which one aspires, then one must purpose to remain in that institute. There must be had an *implicit* or an *explicit* intention to this effect.[486] The Code law presumes that one proposes to remain in religion for life, once he has entered it, through the renewal of temporary profession, and finally through perpetual profession itself.[487] Consequently, it appears that the promise of marriage becomes extinct on the part of *both* parties when it is the purpose of the vow to enter religion or, what is its equivalent, to make religious profession. To vow to enter religion but not to intend to make the profession would be indicative of a lack of sincerity or proper knowledge of the nature of the religious state.[488]

Secondly, the *actual entrance* into religion, apart from the formality of a pre-existing vow to do so on the part of an espoused person, now calls for an explanation. Hence, a consideration will be given to the three phases inherent in the act, scil., entry into the novitiate (or postulancy), the making of the temporary profession and, lastly, the pronouncing of perpetual vows.

The act of becoming a novice or a postulant,[489] analogous to the act of entering an ecclesiastical seminary, as seen in the preceding paragraphs, certainly severs the betrothment contract for the party remaining in the world and *probably* for the novice or postulant,

---

[485] "Certum est . . . quod si quis post sponsalia emittit votum non solum ingrediendi sed etiam profitendi religionem, tunc sponsalia ex parte utriusque dissolvuntur, quia vovens tunc fit omnio inhabilis ad matrimonium contrahendum. . . ."—*Theologia Moralis,* lib. VI, n. 873, 3°.

[486] Cf. Cappello, *De Sacramentis,* V, n. 121.

[487] Cf. canons 488, 1°; 538; 543.

[488] Cf. Cappello, *loc. cit.*

[489] Cf. canons 538-571.

according to Cappello—as against the contrary opinion which is called the more common (*communior*).[490] The same may be said in reference to the temporary profession. Thus, were one to abandon the religious life during or after the postulancy, novitiate or temporary profession, no obligation would remain to marry one's formerly affianced partner. The reasons are, first, that a notable change of circumstances has taken place. Now a notable change in circumstances, as will be seen later, is considered by canonists[491] as furnishing satisfactory and justifiable grounds at law for dissolving the espousal obligation. Secondly, the state assumed by the postulant, novice, or temporarily professed party, is opposed to the married state. Hence, to acknowledge as a fact the dissolution of the engagement also on the part of the one entering religion or making temporary profession, to the extent that this religious is freed of the betrothal bond even though he may later lay aside his habit and return to the world, seems simply to stand by the more acceptable probability.[492]

A fortiori, this view must be maintained in respect to perpetual profession. Authors, generally considered, are one in declaring that the obligation arising out of an espousal agreement is extinguished for both parties by perpetual vows on the part of either party, as in the case of ordination to the major orders. Thus, even were such a professed religious later to quit his religious institute upon obtaining an indult of secularization, he could not be pressed to fulfill the obligation, which previously encumbered him when he became engaged.[493]

G. The Effect of Crime on the Vows

A final problem to be discussed under this heading of the choice of a more perfect state of life has reference to the factor of defloration. What is to be said of the obligation to contract the marriage when the fiancé has had sexual intercourse with his espoused with the understanding that marriage will take place, but later the man

[490] *De Sacramentis,* V, n. 120. Cf. also Gasparri, *De Matrimonio,* I, n. 123.

[491] Cf. Art. 6 of this section, pp. 223-225.

[492] Cf. Cappello, *loc. cit.*

[493] Cf. Cappello, *loc. cit.*

chose to enter the religious state instead? Are the espousals dissolved?

Common opinion has it that such a person is *forbidden* to seek the higher state—because he must by marrying the deflowered woman repair the harm that was done. He is bound by an obligation arising out of the wicked deed perpetrated, scil., to indemnify his fiancée by means of the only adequate remedy under the given circumstances, namely, through marriage.[494] However, had the vow anteceded the nefarious deed, is the man bound to take the woman as his wife? We distinguish: If the woman was aware of the vow taken by her fiancé, then no obligation lies with the man, since his fiancée assumed the risk knowingly and willingly.[495] Had the girl been ignorant of the vow made by the man, the more probable view regards the man as bound to marry her, for no other remedy or reparation is adequate except marriage itself. Authors who think thus also deem dispensation from the vow *unnecessary* for licit nuptials—because of the natural obligation already incumbent upon the sinner.[496]

Article 4: Subsequent Impediments

A. The Perpetual and Non-Dispensable Impediment

A fourth cause sufficient to extinguish an engagement is any diriment or impedient impediment arising subsequent to the affiancement. A *diriment* impediment would render *void* the future marriage; an *impedient* impediment would make for an *illicit* union. When an impediment occurs which by the natural or the positive divine law is perpetual and non-dispensable, or one from which the Church does not customarily dispense, v.g., affinity in the direct line, the marriage having been consummated, the engagement is *ipso facto* dissolved on *both* sides. If one party had contracted the impediment maliciously, the innocent party has a

---

[494] Cf. Sanchez, *De Matrimonii Sacramento,* lib. I, disp. XLV, n. 3; Lessius, De Iustitia, lib. II, cap. X, dub. 32; De Lugo, *De Iustitia,* disp. XII, sec. III, n. 42; St. Alphonsus, *Theologia Moralis,* lib. VI, n. 649.

[495] Cf. Lessius, *loc. cit.;* Sanchez, *ibid.,* n. 45.

[496] Cf., v.g., Lessius, *loc. cit.*

right to compensation for any damage suffered, but not to marriage.[497]

Whether or not espousals are *absolutely* dissolved when marriage with a third party is contracted, so that they have no effect if this marriage is later dissolved, is a question controverted among authors. Some canonists and moralists claim that the obligation to contract the promised marriage is *suspended* for the duration of the actually contracted marriage, but that it revives on the dissolution of the marriage.[498] Other authors see an absolute dissolution of the betrothment, once marriage to a third party has taken place.[499]

This writer maintains the second view for the following reasons, so aptly proposed by the supporting authors, particularly Cappello, scil.: First, marriage of its nature induces a permanent status and an indissoluble bond. This irrevocable status obviously excludes the temporary and dissoluble status, such as is betrothment. Hence, when the marriage takes place, espousal ceases. Secondly, it appears contrary to good morals to regard a married person bound to a third person by an espousal promise *as* a married person. Thirdly, for an espoused person to await the revival of an engagement promise made by a person here and now wedded to someone other than his former espoused is tantamount to awaiting the death of the third party—which is obviously immoral.[500] The situation would, of course, be different, were the marriage *civilly* performed, i.e., were it only an attempted marriage. A civil marriage

---

[497] Cf. Ballerini-Palmieri, *Opus Theologicum Morale,* VI, n. 129; Wernz-Vidal, *Ius Canonicum,* V, n. 104; Feije, *De Imperimentis,* n. 565.

[498] Thus, v.g., Pontius, *De Sacramento Matrimonii,* lib. XII, cap. XIII, n. 4; St. Alphonsus, *Theologia Moralis,* lib. VI, n. 875; De Angelis, *Praelectiones,* lib. IV, tit. I, n. 6.

[499] Sanchez, *op. cit.,* disp. XLVIII, n. 3; Laymann, *Theologia Moralis,* lib. V, tract. X, pars I, cap. II, n. 22; Santi, *Praelectiones,* lib. IV, n. 47; Ballerini-Palmieri, *ibid.,* n. 272; Wernz-Vidal, *ibid.,* n. 107; Sebastianelli, *Praelectiones Iuris Canonici,* II, n. 25; Lehmkuhl, *Theologia Moralis,* II, n. 853; Cappello, *ibid.,* n. 123.

[500] Cf. Cappello, *loc. cit.* Whether the marriage in question was consummated or not is irrelevant. Marriage has been contracted and hence a status of permanence and a bond basically (*per se*) indissoluble has been assumed.

has no recognition before canon law in respect to Catholics.[501] The Sacred Congregation of the Council declared on several occasions that civil marriage with a third party in no way dissolves a still extant engagement to another.[502]

B. The Perpetual but Dispensable Impediment

What of the impediment which by nature is *perpetual but yet dispensable?* A distinction must be made, scil.: If the impediment has been contracted innocently, i.e., through no fault of either party or through the fault of a third party, the affiancement ceases for both parties. If each party was the culpable cause of the impediment, the engagement ceases, i.e., the parties lose their mutual right by mutually creating the obstacle. If only *one* party was guilty of bringing the impediment into being, the innocent party is *ipso facto* relieved of the obligation to enter the promised marriage. The guilty person, however, remains bound, lest he should profit by his action. He should, however, seek a papal dispensation from the betrothal or accept its rescission, if offered by the other party. The burden of seeking such a dispensation urges, even though to do so is a grave inconvenience for the party who brought about the impediment. Clearly, this onerous performance of this duty must not be deferred too long.[503]

C. The Temporary Impediment

When the impediment is temporary, v.g., lack of age, again it is necessary to make a distinction. If the obstacle was not effected by either party, the obligation to contract the promised marriage is suspended till the impediment ceases to exist. If both contractants created the obstacles, the engagement no longer exists, i.e., the principals are free to enter another alliance. If only one of the parties was responsible for the obstruction, the innocent

---

[501] Cf. Can. 1094.

[502] Cf. S.C.C., *Bellunen., Sponsalium,* 20 aug. 1887—*Thesaurus,* CXLVI, 576-584.

[503] Cf. Sanchez, *De Matrimonii Sacramento,* lib. I, disp. LXI, n. 4; St. Alphonsus, lib. VI, n. 868.

espoused is free of the obligation but the guilty party is not. With the cessation of the impediment, the guilty person may pursue his original purpose, if the innocent party acquiesces.[504]

Article 5: Violation of Espousal Fidelity

A fifth reason acknowledged by law, whereby engagements cease to bind, is *violation* of the espousal pledge. It is a rule of law that one fruitlessly demands faith of him in whose behalf one refuses to observe one's own plighted honor.[505]

A. Failure to Fulfill at the Stipulated Time

Violation of betrothal faith occurs, first, when one party refuses to contract marriage on the appointed day or protracts the marriage for too long a period; secondly, when one of the espoused parties marries another, promises marriage to another, or attempts civil marriage with another; thirdly, when an impediment has been culpably induced; fourthly, when sexual intercourse with a third party has taken place.

The first violation admits of a distinction, scil., if the time fixed for the promised marriage has for its purpose the termination of the obligation, then the espousals lapse as the time for the fulfillment lapses. If the time is fixed simply as a means for the urging of them, the espousals remain in effect even though the time that had urged obligation has lapsed, as long as neither party was the culpable cause for the failure in question. Should one party protract the marriage unduly, i.e., without legitimate grounds and beyond the determined time, the innocent party may recede from the contract, as was explained in a previous article.[506]

---

[504] Cf. Cappello, *ibid.*, n. 125.

[505] "Frustra sibi fidem quis postulat ab eo servari, cui fidem a se praestitam servare recusat."—Reg. 75, R. J., in VI°.

[506] Cf. pp. 178-179 of this dissertation. Cf. also pp. 9-11 where Roman legislation on enforcement of espousals is treated. Roman law allowed a two-year period to intervene between the espousal and the marriage, with prolongations from one to three years for exceptional cases. Decretal law too demanded the contracting of the marriage within a reasonable time. Cf. pp. 37-47 of this work.

How is the difference between time fixed for terminating the obligation (*ad finiendam obligationem*) and time fixed for urging the obligation (*ad urgendam obligationem*) to be determined? In the internal forum, the distinction is to be gleaned from the intention that the contractants had in mind at the time of the contract. In the external forum the instrument of the espousal compact must be studied. If the wording is ambiguous, the causes and motives for fixing the time must be probed.[507]

When no time has been decided on, then either of the parties must not prevent the union from taking place for any considerable length of time. If this is done deliberately, the other person may abandon his espoused. If the marriage is postponed for a great length of time, even without fault on the part of one, the other may recede from the pact, since a notable change has taken place, i.e., sufficient to give a right to the injured party to seek union with another. A culpable but brief delay does not dissolve the engagement.[508]

What is a brief delay and what constitutes a notable prolongation is difficult to define. No fixed rule exists for accurately determining such periods. A relative norm alone is possible. Hence, as a matter quite generally accepted, a *three-month wait* appears as a brief period of time. A period of six months or more seems to constitute a longer wait. This reckoning, at least implicitly, appears to have been confirmed by a decision handed down by the Sacred Congregation of the Council in 1723.[509]

A prolonged departure of one of the espoused without the knowledge or contrary to the wishes of the other, which notably postpones the date set for the marriage, constitutes a sufficient reason for the abandoned party to rescind the engagement. Flight from one's country as also a prolonged stay in some distant place also warrants a dissolution. Decretal law acknowledged these factors as reasons sufficient for dissolving the engagement.[510] All

---

[507] Cf. Schmalzgrueber, *Ius Ecclesiasticum,* lib. I, tit. I, n. 196.

[508] *Loc. cit.*

[509] Cf. S.C.C., *in Mediolanen.,* 2 oct. 1827—*Thesaurus,* II (1739), 378. For a summary of the case cf. *Canones et Decreta C. Tridentini a Pelella Edita,* p. 223, n. 20.

[510] Cf. c. 5, X, *de sponsalibus et matrimoniis,* IV, 1; JL, n. 14043.

authors concurred on this matter.[511] Cappello is of the opinion that espousals do lapse in the fashion here described, but not because of the provisions of decretal law but in virtue of the fact that a *notable change of circumstances has taken place.*[512] But this reasoning is not basically contradictory. Although it is true that in virtue of canon 6, 2°-3°, the pre-Code law remains in force, nonetheless, the basis underlying the pre-Code law seems to have been the same that Cappello himself adduces, scil., a grave change of situations in the life of either party. Hence, both opinions ultimately resolve themselves into one.

B. Subsequent Espousal

As for a second espousal, while the first is still effective, this obviously constitutes a breach of betrothment fidelity. Moreover, such espousals are illicit and invalid. The party guilty of the violation of his initial contract is bound to fulfill his first obligation. The innocent party, on the other hand, is freed of the engagement when such unjustifiable second espousals have been attempted.[513]

C. Fornication With a Third Party

Concerning fornication with a third party, several distinctions must be taken into consideration. Thus, if the immoral deed was committed *prior* to the engagement *and known* to the other party, the affiancement perdures; if the act came to light after the compact had been made, the older canonists declared that the *woman* could not recede from the engagement when the man was guilty, but not vice versa.[514] The reasoning behind the statement, again, was

---

[511] Cf. Sanchez, *op. cit.,* disp. LIV, n. 6; Schmalzgrueber, *ibid.,* n. 201; Laymann, *Theologia Moralis,* lib. V, tract. X, pars I, cap. II, n. 13; Santi, *Praelectiones,* lib. IV, tit. I, n. 52; St. Alphonsus, *Theologia Moralis,* lib. VI, n. 866; Ballerini-Palmieri, *Opus Theologicum Morale,* VI, n. 315 ff.

[512] Cappello, *De Sacramentis,* V, n. 127.

[513] Sanchez, *op. cit.,* disp. XLIX, n. 2; Gasparri, *ibid.,* n. 109; Noldin, *Summa Theologiae Moralis,* III, n. 550; Wernz-Vidal, *ibid.,* n. 106.

[514] V.g., Sanchez, *op. cit.,* disp. XLIX, n. 2; Pontius, *De Matrimonio,* lib. XII, cap. XVII, n. 2; St. Alphonsus, *ibid.,* n. 863.

that the man's sin was more condonable than the woman's, i.e., the latter's virginity was a presumed condition of every espousal.[515] It appears preferable, however, to hold to the modern view, which grants liberty to *whoever is guiltless* to recede from the pact, again, on the score of a notable mutation in circumstances.[516]

When the act of fornication took place *after* the betrothment, the non-guilty party had sufficient cause to abandon the faithless partner.[517] If both principals were guilty of sinning with a third party respectively, what was the status of the parties? Three different opinions were proffered by authors in answer to the problem.

The first view looked upon the engagement as still in effect, and the engaged couple as still bound to fulfill their promise to marry each other, as the sin of each has been neutralized. Identical crimes become abrogated by way of mutual compensation.[518] The second opinion regarded the engagement dissolved on the part of *each* contractant, as each had violated the espousal agreement. Hence, in accord with Rule 75,[519] one could not demand fulfillment of an obligation on the part of the other when one himself had failed to fulfill an identical obligation.[520] A third and final viewpoint favored the man by declaring the betrothment to be dissolved on his part but not on the part of the woman, since the crime was more serious in her regard than it was in respect to the man. In other words, this opinion did not see equal compensation as a means by which rescission would be available to both sinners.[521] St. Alphonsus

---

[515] *Loc. citatis.*

[516] Cf. Cappello, *De Sacramentis,* V, n. 129.

[517] Schmalzgrueber, *ibid.*, n. 176 sqq.; Ballerini-Palmieri, *ibid.*, n. 298; Cappello, *loc. cit.*

[518] Cf. Bonacina, *De Magno Matrimonii Sacramento* (Mediolani, 1617), punctum VIII, n. 6; Perez, *Institutiones Iuris Publici Ecclesiastici* (Hispali, 1901), disp. IX, sec. XVI, n. 2.

[519] Reg. 75, R. J., in VI°.

[520] Cf. also Schmalzgrueber, *ibid.*, n. 167; Wiestner, *Iustitutiones Canonicae sive Ius Ecclesiasticum* (Monachii, 1705-1706), lib. IV, tit. I, n. 106.

[521] Cf. Sanchez, *op. cit.*, disp. LV, n. 9; Pontius, *op. cit.*, lib. XII, cap. XVII, n. 3; Laymann, *Theologia Moralis,* tract. X, pars I, cap. II, n. 12; Pirhing, *Ius Canonicum,* lib. IV, tit. I, sect. I, n. 62; St. Alphonsus, *ibid.*, n. 862.

called this third opinion the *more probable* as well as the *common* one.[522]

However, the second view appears more acceptable to the present writer. More recent commentators and theologians prefer it as well. The fundamental reason on which it rests seems to be more proper and logical, scil., espousal fidelity has been violated. One of the effects of engagement, as enumerated in a previous article,[523] is the obligation to refrain from carnal congress and other sexual liberties on the part of each of the espoused. Hence, the preference expressed here for the second view, i.e., dissolution of the contract—because of the sin of both contractants.[524]

D. Immodest Touches

Authors also bring up the question involving improper *touches* committed by an espoused woman with a man who is not her fiancé. It is the common doctrine that the fiancé can rescind the engagement because of his fiancée's behavior. But whether the woman could recede from the engagement when her fiancé was guilty of a similar misdemeanor is controverted. The more common opinion denies that a woman enjoys this prerogative of repudiating her obligation.[525] Modern opinion does not discriminate against the woman. Both the man and the woman may cancel their obligation to each other on the perpetration by the other party of the crime in question.[526] If both participants were guilty of the sin with a third party respectively, what was said above in relation to fornication obtains here as well.

Article 6: Notable Change in Circumstances

Sixthly, a notable change in circumstances supervening on the betrothals dissolves the espousals, if it is of such a nature that

---

[522] *Loc. cit.*

[523] Cf. pp. 180-181.

[524] Cf. Gasparri, *ibid.*, n. 112; Sebastianelli, *Praelectiones*, n. 27. Wernz-Vidal, *ibid.*, n. 107; Cappello, *loc. cit.*, Noldin, *loc. cit*, Coronata, *De Sacramentis*, III, n. 63

[525] Thus Sanchez, *ibid.*, n. 5; St. Alphonsus, *ibid.*, n. 860; Ballerini-Palmieri, *ibid.*, n. 303.

[526] Cf. Wernz-Vidal, Cappello, *loc. citatis.*

the espousals would not have been contracted had these circumstances been present at the time, or had they been known to one or both parties. A notable change consequent upon affiancement does not always liberate from his obligation, the party suffering the change, as will be seen below. It *does* free the other party, as the presumption underlying all espousals is: "I will marry you so long as conditions remain as they are now."

A. Meaning of "Notable Change of Circumstances"

What constitutes a *notable* change of circumstances? Any change that is serious and of some moment morally, not absolutely, considered and that renders the fulfillment of the espousal obligation impossible, or extremely difficult (objectively or subjectively), on the part of either party, constitutes a notable change.

Such a change may affect the mind, the body, the reputation or the financial condition of the party or parties concerned.

B. Changes Affecting the Mind, the Body, the Reputation, and the Financial Status

In respect to changes affecting the *mind,* one may enumerate supervening heresy, apostasy, schism. If it becomes impossible to live with one of the parties because of temper, drink, gambling, or if one of the parties becomes infamous, etc., a change as to the psychological state of the party has also taken place. Subsequent serious dislike, hate, aversion likewise fall into this category.

Mutations which militate against the good of the *body* include such occurrences as the contraction of a serious disease, subsequent deformity or some defect which would prevent one from accomplishing one's marital and family duties later on. It is interesting to note here that it is a matter of debate among canonists whether or not the inability on the part of the woman to nurse a child constitutes a technical change of circumstances in reference to the body. Canonists argue, too, whether or not supervening medically irremediable oral and bodily odors act as notable changes, sufficient to make the contract of espousals rescissible. An affirmative answer appears acceptable in regard to both questions,[527] as the attendant circumstances are such that unsuccessful marriage may be prudently foreseen. In other words, the hope of and the outlook for a happy union is dimmed because of the defects contracted.

As for a serious set-back in financial matters, i.e., reduction from a state of affluence to that of poverty or heavy indebtedness, or the prudent fear of losing one's inheritance contingent upon the fulfillment of the espousal obligation, if each party has undergone such a change, each can rescind the engagement. If only one of the affianced pair suffers such a reversal in fortune, the unfortunate person cannot urge fulfillment on the part of the other. This other party is free to recede from the engagement. Should both parties improve their financial status, neither can repudiate the engagement for that reason. If only one has grown considerably wealthy, the more common view forbids him to abandon his contract. But the contrary opinion, which is espoused by very many authors, particularly modern authors, thinks otherwise.[528]

The doctrine underlying this attitude is that an inequality exists between the two which augurs *ill* for the marriage. The financial difference has engendered a considerable change, such that, had it existed at the time of the affiancing, the engagement would, most likely, have never come into existence.[529] The same view too appears to apply in the case in which one of the parties acquired a title of nobility or was raised to such a high rank that fulfillment of the obligation to marry would become impossible or hazardous to the reputation of the one so elevated.[530]

---

[527] Cf. Schmalzgrueber, *ibid.,* n. 189; Genicot-Salsmans, *Institutiones,* II, n. 447.

[528] Ballerini-Palmieri, *ibid.,* n. 359 sqq.; De Angelis, *Praelectiones,* lib. IV, tit. I, n. 6; D'Annibale, *Summula,* I, n. 378, footnote 12; Bucceroni, *Institutiones Theologiae Moralis* (4 ed., 2 vols., Romae, 1900), II, n. 971; Noldin, *ibid.,* n. 552; Gasparri, *ibid.,* n. 116; Wernz-Vidal, *ibid.,* n. 108; Cappello, *De Sacramentis,* V, n. 130.

[529] Cf. Cappello, *loc. cit.*

[530] Cappellc, *loc. cit.*

C. The Obligation to Reveal One's Defects

Is there an obligation in conscience to reveal one's defect prior to the espousal contract, or prior to the marriage after the promise has been made?

The answer lies in several distinctions. First, if the defect is one that would render the promised marriage null, it *must* be revealed or the marriage must be deferred. Defects of this nature fall into two categories in general: they may be reduced either to defects whose absence the espoused partner demands as a *conditio sine qua non,* v.g., absence of the sin of fornication, the presence of virginity, etc., or to defects which properly constitute a diriment impediment. Secondly, if the defect will render the marriage *injurious* to the other party or will make it rather *difficult,* it also must be made known to the other *sub gravi.* Venereal disease, sterility, widowhood, serious infamy (personal or relating to one's family), difference in religious belief, etc., are examples of such defects which must be brought to the notice of the espoused partner.[531] Thirdly, if the defect is *slight,* i.e., one that does not endanger future marital happiness, but only *lessens* it, the defect may by basic rule be licitly kept a secret.

This is the common opinion, as expressed by Sanchez, Pontius and others, at least in reference to the woman. Obviously, of course, the same applies to the man.[532] The reason for this is that no one is obliged to reveal his shortcomings to the detriment of his reputation, as long as *no* rights of the other party suffer. If the defect becomes known to the other party, and yet that other party offers no objection, then the party with the defect can urge the marriage. Such a defect could be, e.g., a harsh disposition, a proneness to irritability, etc. For incidental reasons, however, the presence of such a defect may give rise to an obligation out of charity to make a disclosure to the unsuspecting party—or else to forego the marriage, lest perhaps the marriage prove unhappy.[533]

---

[531] Cf. Cappello, *De Sacramentis,* V, n. 131.

[532] Cf. Sanchez, *op. cit.,* lib. VI, disp. XXVII, n. 9; Pontius, *De Matrimonio,* cap. XVIII, n. 5; St. Alphonsus, *ibid.,* n. 865; Ballerini-Palmieri, *ibid.,* n. 314.

[533] Cappello, *loc. cit.*

Article 7: Danger of an Unhappy Union

A prudent fear of the probable danger of an *unsuccessful* marriage ensuing out of espousals constitutes a *seventh* cause for the dissolution of betrothals. All attendant circumstances, however, which portend future unhappiness, quarrels, recriminations, family feuds, etc., must be carefully evaluated and weighed seriously before a licit dissolution can follow. Charity here forbids that the engagement should terminate in marriage. There is also the obligation to avoid all foreseen scandal and to safeguard the public morals.[534] Hence, the prospect of an unhappy and unsuccessful outcome of the marriage which was promised in the betrothal contract, when sufficiently foreseen, dissolves the espousals.

Article 8: Parental Dissent

An eighth reason lawfully permitting a disruption of the betrothment is *justifiable and reasonable parental dissent.* When parents have a well-founded basis for opposing an engagement of their minor child, e.g., they have a prudent judgment concerning the unhappy outcome of the future marriage, as outlined above, it is generally agreed that parents not only can but *ought* to declare the pact dissolved.

Pope Benedict XIV (1740-1758) actually listed a father's dissent among the just and reasonable causes for a dissolution of a betrothment. agreement.[535] When parents object *unreasonably* to the engagement, then inquiry must be made into the gravity of the harm that may ensue should the objection be ignored. If it can be prudently foreseen that either or both principals will suffer harm prior or subsequently to the marriage, then *in charity* (to themselves) the contractants should rescind the contract, as long as greater harm does not result from the rescission. When no such ill consequences are envisaged, the contractants are not held, nor can they be held, to recede from their promise to wed each other. Such has been the teaching found in

---

[534] Wernz-Vidal, *ibid.*, n. 109; Noldin, *ibid.*, n. 547; Vlaming, *Praelections,* I, n. 122.

[535] Benedictus XIV, *Institutionum Ecclesiasticarum Libri Tres,* I, insist. XLVI, n. 11. Cf. also Pallottini, XVI, 409, n. 104.

many of the decisions emanating from the Sacred Congregation of the Council on this matter.[536]

This same Congregation also upheld many times the rights of the espoused against undue interference from parents and other third parties, on the basis that the essence of the prenuptial promise lies in the consent of the contractants themselves.[537] Parents, in general, are to refrain as much as possible from interfering with their children's betrothals, unless necessity demands the contrary.

Article 9: Papal Dispensation

A. Exclusive Competence of the Roman Pontiff

Under the ancient discipline, when a just cause other than those enumerated in this section was present for dissolving an engagement, the Roman Pontiff often exercised his prerogative and dissolved the contract even when one party was opposed to the dissolution. All authors agree that if the Supreme Shepherd has power to dissolve ratified but non-consummated marriage, *a fortiori* he enjoys similar prerogatives in reference to the dissoluble bond of affiancement.[538] Rule 53 of the Rules of Law proclaims that the one who can rightfully accomplish the greater can likewise accomplish the lesser.[539] The Roman Pontiff, as authentic interpreter of the natural law and as head of the Church, for justifiable reasons can take away an acquired right and declare this or that obligation in justice as not binding because of some attendant circumstance. This the same writers have often pointed out.[540]

[536] Cf., v.g., S.C.C., *Forolivien., Sponsalium,* 29 nov. 1783—*Thesaurus,* LII (1783), 198-205.

[537] Cf., v.g., S.C.C., *Ostunen., Sponsalium,* 26 ian. 1850—*Thesaurus,* CIX (1850), 13. Cf. also pp. 68-73; 88-97 of this dissertation.

[538] Cf. Sanchez, *ibid.,* disp. LXI; Schmalzgrueber, *ibid.,* n. 54, and tit. IV, n. 49 ff.; De Angelis, *Praelectiones,* lib. IV, tit. I, n. 22; Santi, *Praelectiones,* lib. IV, tit. I, n. 66; Gasparri, *ibid,* n. 107; Wernz-Vidal, *ibid.,* n. 110.

[539] "Cui licet quod est plus, licet utique quod est minus."—Reg. 53, PJ., in VI°.

[540] *Loc. cit.* In regard to the nature of the pontifical power of dispensing, the following may be stated: The power to dispense from the espousal promise is looked upon by canonists as *vicarious* rather than proper, for the Pope does

Ordinaries and other prelates inferior to the Roman Pontiff fundamentally lack the faculty to dissolve espousals. The reason is that a relaxation of an obligation arising under the *natural law* is involved. No one save the supreme authority in society enjoys competence in a matter of this kind.[541] The ordinary's competence is limited to an *investigation* of the validity of the betrothment and to the procedure of questioning whether or not the contract has been dissolved or is rescissible on the part of one or both principals. In no way can one of the parties on his own authority dissolve the alliance.[542]

B. The Need of a Just Cause

A just cause is required before the Holy Father can dissolve betrothals. Absence of a just case would render the dispensation not merely illicit but invalid as well, since a relaxation from an obligation of the natural law is at issue. A just cause is defined here as one which, all things having been carefully considered, will result in a good or in an advantage *greater* than the good or the advantage that would accrue were the affiancement not dissolved. This is usually verifiable in cases in which one of the parties has attempted civil marriage, or proposes to wed in the Church, or cohabits with a third party. Several pronouncements to this effect can be found in some of the decisions rendered by the Congregation of the Council in past years.[543]

---

not directly remove the obligation, which is one of the natural law, but only through the *mediation* of a sort of remission. The circumstances in any given case are such that a remission is in order. Hence, the term "dispensation," when used in reference to espousals and any other contracts of this nature, does not refer to a dispensation in the strict sense, but only to an act that is called thus because it stands as a certain remission granted through the Pope's power of jurisdiction.—Cf. Suarez, *De Legibus* (Lugduni, 1619), lib. II, cap. XIV. For the different divisions of power, cf. canon 197.

[541] Cf. Sanchez, *De Matrimonii Sacramento,* lib. I, disp. LXI, n. 3; Schmalzgrueber, *Ius Ecclesiasticum,* lib. IV; tit. II, n. 53.

[542] Sanchez, Schmalzgrueber, *loc. citatis.*

[543] Cf. S.C.C., *Bellunen., Sponsalium,* 20 aug. 1887—*Thesaurus,* CXLVI, 576-584; *Ostunen., Sponsalium,* 10 sept. 1887—*Thesaurus,* CXLVI, 660-664. Cf. also Santi, *Praelectiones,* lib. IV, tit. I, n. 66; De Angelis, *Praelectiones,* lib. IV, tit. I, n. 22.

Today under the Code, since no obligation arising out of espousals except that of compensation can be urged in the external forum, there is no need to speak of a dispensation. The question of the obligation to contract the promised marriage, as explained in the preceding section of this work, is relegated to the internal forum, i.e., to conscience. For this reason one will seek in vain among canons 1960-1992 for a juridic remedy in this regard. These canons deal with cases involving only marriage; nowhere are espousals mentioned. Hence, the question of seeking a dispensation is more a theoretical than a practical one.

Article 10: Declaration of the Dissolution on Private Authority

A. Nature of the Proof Needed for a Declaration of the Dissolution

This dissertation terminates with one final controversy. The controversy deals with the question of private authority in relation to a declaration of the dissolution of the espousals. Can engagements, it is asked, be declared dissolved by one or other or even a third party when a just cause exists? Obviously, when no just reason is present, no such act is possible. However, when there is a valid basis for the dissolution, i.e., a just cause which is certain and admits full proof to that effect, Santi (1830-1885) and many others replied in the affirmative, teaching that the engagement can be dissolved on private authority. The impediments, impedient and diriment, are, of course, excepted, Santi states.[544]

Cappello disagrees only in one respect. He admits that private authority is competent to dissolve a betrothment when a just cause exists, but he does not call for the presence of the full proof, which Santi demanded, in all cases, except such in which the cause is derived from some attendant impediment. If the cause for dissolution is *certain* or even *probable* a private dissolution can ensue.[545]

---

[544] Cf. Santi, *Praelectiones,* lib. IV, tit. I, n. 67.

[545] "Si causa solutionis est certa, licet, imo etiam si vere probabilis est. Hinc convenire non possumus cum Santi aliisque DD., qui docent requiri plenam causae probationem, praeterquam si causa proveniat ex impedimento sive dirimente sive impediente."—*De Sacramentis,* V, n. 136.

Sebastianelli (+ 1920) advanced an opinion contrary to the two stated above. He opposed the common view by asserting that the various causes sufficient to render betrothals rescissible do not dissolve espousals "unless alleged and proved before a judge, for the dissolution of a duly established obligation is never presumed."[546] This position appears difficult to maintain, since neither the positive nor the natural law bears it out. The positive law has no provision for Sebastianelli's method of disposing of the case. The natural law, basically, likewise fails to confirm such a reasoning. As a matter of fact, the natural law favors the opposite opinion in the sense that one has a right by the natural law to recede from a contract when a just reason dictates such an action. One of the underlying conditions of every espousal agreement is: "I will marry you unless a just cause arises to rescind this engagement."[547]

Today, the question of obligation to contract the marriage as promised pertains more to the *confessor* than to the ecclesiastical judge. Parties should refer the matter to their confessor and act upon his advice. However, they are free in Cappello's opinion, as also in the present writer's, to act upon their own initiative, as long as all semblance of self-deception or fraud is absent. Recourse to an ecclesiastical superior is advisable at times. Thus, first, if the espousals had been publicized to some degree, and yet the cause for the dissolution is occult, then for the prevention of possible or actual scandal the matter would best be brought before the ordinary or some other competent ecclesiastic delegated by him. Secondly, if the question of law or fact about the cause for a dissolution is *doubtful,* appeal to an ecclesiastical superior can be urged, for in cases of a doubt one must not be deprived of the right one has by the natural law.[548]

---

[546] Causae, quas recensuimus, contractum sponsalitium non dissolvant, nisi coram iudice allegentur et probentur, numquam enim praesumitur obligationis semel susceptae dissolutio."—*Praelectiones,* II, n. 30.

[547] Thus, v.g., Sanchez, *op. cit.,* disp. LXIX, n. 3; Navarrus, Opera *Omnia,* I, *De Sacramento Matrimonii,* cap. XXII, n. 28; Pontius, *De Matrimonio,* lib. XII, cap. VIII, n. 8.

[548] Cf. Cappello, *loc. cit.*

How may certitude or solid probability be had before the party or parties may recede from their promise? All authors admit that *one* witness, if he be worthy of credence and can testify from certain knowledge, suffices for the *internal* forum.[549] Public knowledge, i.e., notoriety whether established by word of mouth or by publication, also suffices.[550]

In respect to the external forum, nothing can be said doctrinally, for the current law once again admits no action except that dealing with damages, if any arise.[551] Recourse to the bishop, as explained above, is extrajudicial, and hence the matter is to be determined by the pastor to whom the case has been presented.

B. The Rôle of the Confessor and the Pastor

How are the confessor and the pastor to react to cases laid before them concerning repudiation of the obligation to contract a promised marriage?

First, from the foregoing it is clear that the causes excusing from the obligation are many and varied, and hence a wide latitude in regard to them is accorded by the law to the parties—for the fundamental reason that the legislator does not desire to inflict any unjust disadvantages upon the betrothed in regard to their marriage. Hence, a confessor, as well as a pastor, will hardly ever be faced with a case in which a legitimate cause for a dissolution of the contract is not present.

Those who would wish to render conditions more severe, so as to prevent the evasion of the betrothal obligation, must be mindful of the words spoken by the Sacred Congregation of the Council nearly a hundred years ago: "Indeed, unless an oath has been added, it is permissible to recede from these espousals *also for a light, even a very light, cause,* as [this] Congregation, in accord with the common opinion of the doctors, taught in the *Calaritana, Sponsalium* case, on May 8, 1824 . . ." (Italics inserted).[552]

---

[549] Sanchez, *op. cit.*, disp., LXXIII, n. 2; Schmalzgrueber, *ibid.*, n. 220; Ballerini-Palmieri, *ibid.*, n. 386.

[550] Cf. Canon 1747, 1°.

[551] Canon 1017, § 3.

[552] S.C.C., *Nullius Ferentilli, Sponsalium,* 20 maii 1852—Cf. Cappello, *De Sacramentis,* V, n. 138. (Writer's own translation.)

Thus, when approached by the party desirous of rescinding his or her espousals, a confessor or a pastor should inquire, first, whether the engagement was contracted validly. Secondly, if the answer is affirmative, he must ask for the motives deterring the person from his first resolve. Thirdly, if the cause as given is just, the priest should *immediately* declare that it is lawful for the party to dissolve the pact. "Immediately," it is urged, lest perhaps the anxious inquirer labor temporarily under an erroneous conscience. Fourthly, if no justification of a juridic nature is apparent, the confessor or the pastor is bound to persuade and to encourage the party to stand by his promise.

However, should the penitent or subject refuse to abide by his agreement, the cleric is to persuade the man or woman to come to a settlement with the espoused partner. He should also inquire whether any disadvantage will be suffered by the other party in the event the marriage does not take place and whether the one receding from the engagement can or is willing to make compensation for it. If the penitent or subject replies to these last two questions in the affirmative, the clergyman is to absolve the party, or if he acts as pastor, allow him to pass to new nuptials, the reason being that an unhappy marriage might result if the unwilling party is forced to contract the marriage as he originally promised. Should the response be in the negative, the confessor cannot grant absolution, and if the case is treated outside the confessional, the pastor must warn the person of the guilt that he has incurred because of the breach of contract. The other party should be contacted and asked to relieve his espoused of the obligation.

When the penitent is the injured party himself, the confessor or pastor, as the case may be, is to make an attempt to induce the person to surrender his or her right to marry the unwilling other party, so as to free the latter from sin. If the penitent has suffered any damages, the priest should advise the party of his or her right to seek redress and to be content with that, rather than to seek the marriage once promised in the espousal contract. If no harm has ensued, or if the person waives his right to sue for damages, but still refuses to renounce his right to the marriage, the cleric is to apprise the party of the unhappy outcome of the marriage, were it to take place. Hence, for reasons of *charity* toward himself and to the affianced, the penitent should be persuaded to relinquish his right. Lastly, the confessor or pastor may add that the unwillingness of one party to marry makes for the probability of an unhappy marriage, which probability constitutes just grounds for the *other party* to repudiate and recede from the engagement.[553]

When dealing with either party the priest is to dispense his advice in a prudent, mild and patient manner, so as to safeguard the persons' spiritual security and simultaneously uphold ecclesiastical discipline.

C. Summary of the Problem

To sum up the situation as described above, one can maintain with Cappello, first, that the obligation to contract the promised marriage as deriving from the betrothal is probably a grave one, despite the opposing opinions ably defended by Gasparri and Vidal. However, secondly, there will hardly be a time when the confessor or pastor will not be able to find juridically reasonable grounds justifying a dissolution of the espousal bond, once one of the principals is unwilling to wed in accordance with the promise made. Thirdly, the ordinary causes justifying rescissory action are the improbability of a successful union and the presence of the parties' mutual consent, i.e., once the other party is persuaded by the priest to recede voluntarily from the engagement so as to relieve his or her bethothed of the obligation to contract the marriage. Fourthly, if any compensation is due, the guilty party is to make restitution, since this is an obligation in justice. Lastly, when the legally recognized grounds for a dissolution are discernible, and compensation for the breach is assured, the confessor can at once absolve the unwilling party or, if it is the pastor who is acting, allow him to pass to nuptials with a third party.

---

[553] Cf. Cappello, *ibid.*, n. 138.

CONCLUSIONS

1. No obligation to contract the promised marriage is engendered in the internal forum when a total simulation has taken place. In the external forum the simulation must be proved. (Cf. pp. 98-101.

2. For validity, bilateral promises of marriage must be expressly mutual; in the unilateral arrangement, acceptance of the promise must intervene. (Cf. pp. 101-103.)

3. Unjust grave fear induced by an external agent to extort the promise of marriage probably does not in and of itself invalidate the betrothment. (Cf. pp. 107-110.)

4. Abduction is not a factor which inherently renders espousals null. (Cf. pp. 110-113.)

5. For the validity of the betrothment promise it is indeed necessary but it also suffices to have the same advertence and attention that is required for the commission of a serious sin. (Cf. pp. 113-115.)

6. A habitual intention does not suffice for valid espousals when a party contracts them without the use of intellect and will, as when intoxicated. (Cf. p. 116.)

7. The minimum age of seven years, provided that a full use of reason is present, is required but likewise suffices for a valid espousal. (Cf. pp. 118-125.)

8. The congenitally deaf, dumb and blind are not in simple consequence of these defects incapable of entering espousals. (Cf. pp. 126-127.)

9. Engagements contracted by the insane in a lucid period are to be regarded valid in the absence of express legislation to the contrary. (Cf. pp. 128-129.)

10. Annotation of the *place* of contract is not necessary for the validity of the betrothment contract. (Cf. pp. 133-135.)

11. Inability to subscribe the betrothal contract if it attaches to one of the parties does not in consequence free the other party from subscribing the pact. (Cf. pp. 136-137.)

12. Attestation of the espousals by the local ordinary or by the pastor prior to their canonical installation is invalid, except when they act as private witnesses. (Cf. pp. 142-143.)

13. An excommunicated pastor, provided he is not a *"vitandus,"* acts validly when subscribing espousals in the capacity of an official witness. (Cf. pp. 143-144.)

14. Formless or private espousals are not in themselves illicit, but no obligation of compensation on unjust breach can be urged even in the internal forum. (Cf. pp. 149-150.)

15. Conditional promises of marriage are not forbidden. (Cf. p. 161.)

16. Espousals entered into with the condition: "if the Holy Father grants a dispensation for the ecclesiastical impediment present, from which he can and customarily does dispense" suspends rather than invalidates the espousal promise. (Cf. pp. 167-172.)

17. An attempted espousal along with the act of fornication with a third party does not dissolve the first espousal, unless marriage with the same third party has intervened. (Cf. pp. 181-182.)

18. The obligation of contracting marriage as deriving from the betrothment compact is most probably a grave obligation, binding in conscience through the virtue of justice, but without any sanction in the external forum. (Cf. pp. 194-201; 233.)

19. Engagements are rescissible even though confirmed by an oath *in honorem Dei.* (Cf. p. 202.)

20. The private vows of virginity, perfect chastity, celibacy, reception of the priesthood and entrance into the religious life relieve the vowing party of the previous espousal obligation to contract marriage, irrespective of the outcome of the vows—on the grounds that the promise made to God exerts greater claims and stands incompatible with a promise made to man. (Cf. pp. 205-214.)

21. Entrance into the seminary and into religion similarly relieve the espoused party of his promise to marry his espoused, irrespective of the fact of perseverance in the seminary or in the religious institute. (Cf. pp. 205-214.)

22. Marriage with a third party dissolves espousals with a second party, irrespective of the outcome of the said marriage. The

obligation to marry one's former affianced does not revive upon the dissolution of the marriage with the third party. (Cf. p. 220.)

23. Fornication with a third party, whether committed by the man or by the woman, constitutes grounds for a dissolution. The same obtains for immodest touches. (Cf. pp. 220-222.)

24. A notable change in circumstances affecting one of the parties is a justifiable cause for rescissory action with reference to the betrothal contract. (Cf. pp. 222-224.)

25. Full proof of the existence of a just cause for the rescission of the espousals is not necessary in private declarations of the dissolution of betrothal contracts. (Cf. pp. 229-231.)

BIBLIOGRAPHY

Sources

Acta et Decreta Sacrorum Conciliorum, Collectio Lacensis, 7 vols., Friburgi Brisgoviae, 1870-1892.

Acta Apostolicae Sedis, Commentarium Officiale, Romae, 1909-

Acta Sanctae Sedis, 41 vols., Romae, 1865-1908.

Analecta Ecclesiastica, 19 vols., Romae, 1893-1911.

Augustinus Antonius (Agustin, Antonio), *Quinque Compilationes Antiquae,* Ilerdae, 1576.

Bruns, Hermann, *Canones Apostolorum et Conciliorum Saeculorum IV-VII,* 2 vols., Berolini, 1839.

Canones et Decreta Concilii Tridentini, ed. Sacerdos Joseph Pelella, Neapoli, 1859.

Codex Iuris Canonici Pii X Pontificis Maximi iussu digestus, Benedicti Papae XV auctoritate promulgatus, Romae: Typis Polyglottis Vaticanis, 1917. Reimpressio, 1933.

Codicis Iuris Canonici Fontes, cura Eñi Petri Card. Gasparri editi, 9 vols., Romae: Typis Polyglottis Vaticanis, 1923-1939. (Vols. VII-IX, ed. et cura Eñi Justiniani Serédi.)

Collectanea Sacrae Congregationis de Propaganda Fide, 2 vols., Romae: Typographia Polyglotta S. Congregationis de Propaganda Fide, 1907.

Concilii Tridentini Diariorum, Actorum, Epistolarum, Tractatuum, Nova Collectio, ed. Societas Gorresiana, 13 vols., Friburgi Brisgoviae: B. Herder, 1901-1938.

Corpus Iuris Canonici, ed. Lipsiensis 2., post Aemilii Ludovici Richteri curas ad librorum manu scriptorum et editionis Romanae fidem recognovit et adnotatione critica instruxit Aemilius Friedberg, 2 vols., Lipsiae: ex Officina Bernhardi Tauchnitz, 1879-1771. Editio anastatice repetita, Lipsiae: Tauchnitz, 1928.

Corpus Iuris Civilis, editio stereotypa, 3 vols., Berolini: apud Weidmannos, 1928-1929, Vol. I, *Institutiones,* recognovit Paulus Krueger, ed. 15., 1929; *Digesta,* recognovit Theodorus Mommsen, retractavit Paulus Krueger, ed. 15, 1929; Vol. II, *Codex,* recognovit et retractavit Paulus Krueger, ed. 10, 1929; Vol. III, *Novellae,* recognovit Rudolfus Schoell; opus Schoellii morte interceptum absolvit Gulielmus Kroll, ed. 5, 1928.

Cosci, Christophorus, *De Sponsalibus Filiorum Familias Vota Decisiva,* Romae, 1763.

Decisiones Sanctae Romanae Rotae . . . coram Iacobo Emerix, 3 vols. Romae, 1701.

Decretales D. Gregorii Papae IX, una cum Glossis Restitutae, Romae, 1582.

Decretum Gratiani emendatum et notationibus illustratum una cum glossis, Gregorii XIII, Pont. Max. iussu editum, 2 vols., Romae, 1582.

Epstein, Isidore, *Babylonian Talmud, Kiddushim,* London, Sancino Press, 1936.

Hardouin, Jean, *Acta Conciliorum et Epistolae Decretales ac Constitutiones Summorum Pontificum,* 12 vols., Parisiis, 1714-1715.

Jaffé, Phillipus, *Regesta Pontificum Romanorum ab condita Ecclesia ad annum post Christum natum MCXCVIII,* 2. ed., 2 vols. in 1 correctam et auctam auspiciis Gulielmi Wattenbach curaverunt F. Kaltenbrunner (ad annum 590), P. Ewald (590-882), S. Loewenfeld (882-1198), Lipsiae, 1885-1888.

Le Plat, Josse, *Monumentorum ad Historiam Concilii Tridentini Amplissima Collectio,* 7 vols., Lovanii, 1781-1787.

Liber Sextus Decretalium D. Bonifatii Papae VIII, suae integritati una cum Clementinis et Extravagantibus, earumque Glossis restitutus, Romae, 1582.

Magnum Bullarium Romanum, 8 vols., Luxemburgi, 1727.

Mansi, Ioannes, *Sacrorum Conciliorum Nova et Amplissima Collectio,* 53 vols. in 59. Parisiis, 1901-1927.

Mommsen, Theodorus, *Digesta Iustiniani Augusti,* 2 vols., Berolini, 1870.

Monumenta Germaniae Historica, 188 vols., incompleta, Hannoverae,—*Leges,* 5 vols., Vol. I-IV ed. G. Pertz; Vol. V edd. G. Pertz, G. Waitz, H. Brunner, Hannoverae, 1835-1889—*Legum Sectio I,* tom. I, *Leges Visigothorum,* pars 1, ed. K. Zeumer, 1902; tom. II, pars 1, *Leges Burgundiorum,* ed. L. R. de Salis, 1892; tom. V, pars 1, *Leges Alamannorum,* ed. K. Lehmann, 1888; tom. V, pars 2, *Lex Baiwariorum,* ed. E. von Schwind, 1927—*Legum Sectio II, Capitularia Regum Francorum,* tom. I, ed. A. Boretius, 1883.

Pallavicini, Salvator, *Historia Concilii Tridentini,* trans. a Ioanne Baptista Giattini, 3 vols. in 1, Antverpiae, 1670.

Pallottini, S., *Collectio omnium conclusionum et resolutionum quae in causis propositis apud Sacram Congregationem Cardinalium S. Concilii Tridentini Interpretum prodierunt ab eius institutione anno 1564 ad 1860, distinctis titulis alphabetico ordine per materias digesta,* 17 vols., Romae, 1868-1893.

Potthast, Augustus, *Regesta Pontificum Romanorum inde ab anno post Christum natum MCXCVIII ad annum MCCCIV,* 2 vols., Berolini, 1874-1875.

Sacrae Romanae Rotae Decisiones . . . coram (Alexandro) Caprara, 2 vols., Romae, 1758-1763.

Sacrae Romanae Rotae Decisiones . . . coram (Marcello) Crescentio, 4 vols., Romae, 1725.

Sacrae Romanae Rotae Decisiones . . . coram (Cyriaco) Lancetta, 7 vols., Romae, 1732.

Sacrae Romanae Rotae Decisiones . . . coram (Iosepho) Molines, 5 vols., Romae, 1728.

Sacrae Romanae Rotae Decisionum Recentiorum Tomi XIX, 19 vols. in 25, Romae, 1623-1703.

Schroeder, H. J., *Canons and Decrees of the Council of Trent: Original Text with English Translation,* St. Louis: Herder, 1941.

Thesaurus Resolutionum Sacrae Congregationis Concilii (1718-1908), 167 vols., Vols. I-V, Urbini, 1739-1740; Vols. VI ff., Romae, 1741-1908, Urbini-Romae.

Waterworth, J., *The Canons and Decrees of the Sacred and Oecumenical Council of Trent,* London, 1848.

Zamboni, J. F., *Collectio Declarationum Sacrae Congregationis Cardinalium Sacri Concilii Tridentini Interpretum,* 4 vols., Atrebati, 1860-1868.

Reference Works

Aertnys, Josephus, *Theologia Moralis secundum Doctrinam St. Alphonsi,* 3. ed., 2 vols., Tornaci, 1893.

Ante-Nicene Fathers, trans. by Roberts-Donaldson, 14 vols., New York, 1925.

Aquinas, St. Thomas, *Commentaria in IV Libros Sententiarum,* 4 vols. in 2, Parisiis, 1559.

Aquinas, St. Thomas, *Summa Theologica,* First Complete American Edition, 3 vols., New York: Benziger, 1948.

Augustine, Charles, *A Commentary on the New Code of Canon Law,* 8 vols., Vol. V, 2. ed., St. Louis: Herder, 1920.

Ayrinhac, H.-Lydon, P., *Marriage Legislation in the New Code of Canon Law,* revised ed., New York: Benziger, 1941.

Ballerini, Antonius-Palmieri, Dominicus, *Opus Theologicum Morale,* 3. ed., 7 vols., Prati, 1898-1901.

Barbosa, Augustinus, *Collectanea Doctorum tam Veterum quam Recentiorum in Ius Pontificium Universum,* 6 vols. in 4, Lugduni, 1656.

Benedictus XIV, *De Synodo Dioecesana,* 3 vols., Romae, 1783.

Benedictus XIV, *Institutionum Ecclesiasticarum Libri Tres,* 3 vols. Romae, 1784-1785.

Benedictus XIV, *Opera Omnia,* 12 vols., Romae, 1748.

Bonacina, Martinus, *De Magno Matrimonii Sacramento,* Medoliani, 1617.

Browne, Andrew, *Handbook of Notes on Theology,* St. Louis: Ligourian Fathers, 1948.

Bucceroni, Ianuarius, *Institutiones Theologiae Moralis,* 1. ed., 2 vols. Romae, 1900.

Callan, Charles-McHugh, John, *Moral Theology,* 2 vols., New York, 1929.

Cappello, Felix, *Tractatus Canonico-Moralis de Sacramentis,* 5 vols., Vol. I-II, 4. ed.; Vol. III-IV, 2. ed.; Vol. V, 5. ed., Taurinorum Augustae-Romae, 1942-1947.

Carberry, John, *The Juridical Form of Marriage*, The Catholic University of America Canon Law Studies, n. 84, Washington, D. C.: The Catholic University of America, 1934.

Catholic Encyclopedia, The, 15 vols., Index and 2 Supplements, New York, 1907-1922.

Chelodi, Ioannes-Ciprotti, Pius, *Ius Canonicum De Matrimonio,* Vicenza: Società Anonima Tipografica Editrice, 1947.

Corbett, Percy, *The Roman Law of Marriage,* Oxford: Clarendon Press, 1930.

Coronata, Matthaeus Comte a, *Institutiones Iuris Canonici,* 3 vols., Tourini: Marieti, 1943-1946.

Covarruvias, Didacus, *Opera Omnia,* Antverpiae, 1638.

Cronin, John, *The New Marriage Legislation,* New York, 1908.

Davis, Henry, *Moral and Pastoral Theology,* 5. ed., 4 vols., New York: Sheed & Ward, 1946.

D'Annibale, Josephus, *Summula Theologiae Moralis,* 5. ed., 4 vols., Romae, 1908.

De Angelis, Philippus, *Praelectiones Iuris Canonici,* 5 vols. in 9, Romae, 1877-1891.

De Becker, Julius, *De Sponsalibus et Matrimonio,* 2. ed., Lovanii, 1903.

De Lugo, Ioannes Card., *De Iustitia et Iure,* 4 vols. in 2, Venetiis, 1718.

De Smet, Aloysius, *Betrothment and Marriage,* 2 vols., St. Louis, 1912-1913.

De Smet, Aloysius, *De Sponsalibus et Matrimonio,* 1. ed., 1909; 4. ed., 1927, Brugis, 1909-1927.

De Soto, Dominicus, *De Iustitia et Iure Libri Decem,* Salamantcae, 1556.

Devoti, Ioannes, *Institutionum Canonicarum Libri IV,* Romae, 1830.

Diana, Antoninus, *Resolutiones Morales,* 10 vols. in 5, Venetiis, 1728.

Dillon, Robert, *Common Law Marriage,* The Catholic University of America Canon Law Studies, n. 153, Washington, D. C.: The Catholic University of America Press, 1942.

Dodwell, Edward, *The Time and Place for the Celebration of Marriage,* The Catholic University of America Canon Law Studies, n. 154, Washington, D. C.: The Catholic University of America Press, 1942.

Engel, Ludovicus, *Collegium Universi Iuris Canonici,* 9. ed., Beneventi, 1760.

Epstein, Isidore, *Marriage Laws in the Bible and in the Talmud,* Cambridge: Harvard University Press, 1942.

Epstein, Isidore, *The Babylonian Talmud, Kiddushim,* London: Lancino Press, 1936.

Fagnanus, Prosper, *Commentaria in Quinque Libros Decretalium,* 4 vols., Venetiis, 1696.

Fair, Bartholomew, *The Impediment of Abduction,* The Catholic University of America Canon Law Studies, n. 194, Washington, D. C.: The Catholic University of America Press, 1944.

Feije, Henricus, *De Impedimentis et Dispensationibus Matrimonialibus,* 3. ed., Lovanii, 1885.

Ferraris, Lucius, *Prompta Bibliotheca, Canonica, Iuridica, Moralis, Theologica, necnon Ascetica, Polemica, Rubricistica, Historica,* ed. noviss., 9 vols., Parisiis, 1885-1899.

Ferreres, Ioannes, *Compendium Theologiae Moralis,* 14. ed., 2 vols., Barcinone, 1928.

Freisen, Joseph, *Geschichte des canonischen Eherechts,* 2. ed., Paderborn, 1893.

Gasparri, Petrus Card., *Schema Codicis Iuris Canonici,* 4 vols. in 2, Romae, 1913.

Gasparri, Petrus, *Tractatus Canonicus de Matrimonio,* 2 vols., Parisiis, 1892.

Gasparri, Petrus, *Tractatus Canonicus de Matrimonio,* editio nova ad mentem Codicis, 2 vols., Romae: Typis Polyglottis Vaticanis, 1932.

Gellius, Aulus, *Noctes Atticae,* trans. by John Rolfe, 3 vols., London, 1927.

Genicot, E.-Salsmans, I., *Institutiones Theologiae Moralis,* 8. ed., 2 vols., Bruxellis, 1927.

Gietl, Ambrosius, *Die Sentenzen Rolands,* Friburgi Brisgoviae, 1891.

Giraldi, Ubaldus, *Expositio Iuris Pontificii,* 2 vols., Romae, 1769.

Gonzalez-Tellez, Manuel, *Commentaria Perpetua in Singulos Textus Quinque Librorum Decretalium Gregorii IX,* 5 vols., Lugduni, 1673.

Hostiensis, Cardinalis (Henricus de Segusia), *Commentaria in Quinque Libros Decretalium,* 5 vols. in 3, Venetiis, 1581.

Isidori Hispalensis Episcopi Libri XX, trans. by W. M. Lindsay, 2 vols., Oxonii, 1911.

Jacobs, Albert, *Cases and Other Materials on Domestic Relations,* 2. ed., Chicago: Foundation Press, 1939.

Jewish Encyclopedia, The, 12 vols., New York: Funk and Wagnalls, 1903.

Joyce, George, *Christian Marriage,* 2. ed., London: Sheed and Ward, 1948.

Laymann, Paulus, *Theologia Moralis,* 5 vols., Venetiis, 1630.

Leage, R. W., *Roman Private Law,* 2. ed., London: Macmillan, 1948.

Lehmkuhl, Augustinus, *Theologia Moralis,* 12. ed., 2 vols., Friburgi, 1910.

Lessius, Leonardus, *De Iustitia et Iure,* 3. ed., 4 vols. in 1, Antverpiae, 1612.

Liguori, St. Alphonsus de, *Theologia Moralis,* 2 vols., Augustae Taurinorum, 1879.

Marbach, Joseph, *Marriage Legislation for the Catholics of the Oriental Rites in the United States and Canada,* The Catholic University of America Canon Law Studies, n. 243, Washington, D. C.: The Catholic University of America Press, 1946.

Migne, Jacques, *Patrologiae Cursus Completus, Series Graeca,* 161 vols., Parisiis, 1857-1866.

Migne, Jacques, *Patrologiae Cursus Completus, Series Latina,* 221 vols., Parisiis, 1844-1855.

Molina, Ludovicus, *De Iustitia et Iure, Opera Omnia Tractatibus Quinque Tomisque Totidem Comprehensa,* 5 vols., Coloniae, 1759.

Muirhead, James, *The Law of Rome,* 2. ed., London, 1899.

Navarrus, Martinus de Azpilcueta, *Opera Omnia,* 6 vols., Venetiis, 1618-1621.

Neufeld, E., *Ancient Hebrew Marriage Laws,* New York: Longmans, 1944

Noldin, Hieronymus-Schmidt, A., *Summa Theologiae Moralis,* 3 vols., Vol. I, 17. ed., 1940, Vol. II, 17. ed., 1941, Vol. III, 16. ed., 1940, Oeniponte: Pustet, 1923-1934.

O'Dea, John, *The Matrimonial Impediment of Nonage,* The Catholic University of America Canon Law Studies, n. 205, Washington, D. C.: The Catholic University of America Press, 1944.

O'Donnell, Cletus, *The Marriage of Minors,* The Catholic University of America Canon Law Studies, n. 221, Washington, D. C.: The Catholic University of America Press, 1945.

Ojetti, Benedictus, *Synopsis Rerum Moralium et Iuris Pontificii alphabetico ordine digesta,* 3 vols. et Index, Romae, 1909-1914.

Panormitanus, Abbas (Nicolaus de Tudeschis), *Commentaria super Quinque Libros Decretalium,* 5 vols. in 7, Venetiis, 1588.

Pastor, Ludwig, *History of the Popes,* 38 vols., St. Louis: Herder, 1923-1952.

Perez, *Institutiones Iuris Publici Ecclesiastici,* Hispali, 1901.

Petra, Vincentius, *Commentaria ad constitutiones apostolicas,* 5 vols., Romae, 1705-1711.

Petrovits, Joseph, *The New Church Law on Marriage,* Philadelphia, 1919.

Pichler, Vitus, *Ius Canonicum secundum quinque Decretalium titulos Gregorii Papae IX practice explicatum,* 2 vols., Ravennae, 1741.

Pighi, Ioannes, *De Sacramento Matrimonii,* ed. altera, Veronae, 1921.

Pirhing, Ernricus, *Ius Canonicum in Quinque Libros Decretalium Distributum, Nova Methodo Explicatum, ed. novis.,* 5 vols. in 4, Dilingae, 1674-1678.

Pollock, Frederick-Maitland, Frederic, *The History of English Law before Edward I,* 2. ed., 2 vols., Boston, 1899.

Pontius, Basilius, *De Sacramento Matrimonii Tractatus,* nova ed., Venetiis, 1756.

Raymundus de Pennafort, St., *Summa,* Veronae, 1744.

Regatillo, Eduardus, *Ius Sacramentarium,* 2 vols., Santander: Sal Terrae, 1945-1946.

Reiffenstuel, Anacletus, *Ius Canonicum Universum,* 5 vols. in 7, Parisiis, 1864-1870.

Revue d'histoire et de litterature religieuses, tom. 1-12, 1896-1907; nouv. ser. tom. 1-8, 1910-1922, 20 tom., Paris, 1896-1922.

Richeri, Thomas, *Universa Civilis et Criminalis Iurisprudentia,* 2. ed., 12 vols., Taurini, 1824.

Romani, Sylvius, *Institutiones Iuris Canonici,* 3 vols. in 2, Vol. II, Section II, 1945, Romae: Editrice Iustitia, 1941-1945.

Rufinus, Magister, *Summa Decretorum,* ed. H. Singer, Paderborn, 1902.

Sanchez, Thomas, *Disputationum de Sancto Matrimonii Sacramento Tomi Tres,* Antverpiae, 1626.

Sangmeister, Joseph, *Force and Fear as Precluding Matrimonial Consent,* The Catholic University of America Canon Law Studies, n. 80, Washington, D. C.: The Catholic University of America, 1932.

Santi, Franciscus, *Praelectiones Iuris Canonici iuxta Ordinem Decretalium Gregorii IX,* 2. ed., 5 vols. in 1, Ratisbonae, Neo-Eboraci et Cincinnati, 1886.

Schmalzgrueber, Franciscus, *Ius Ecclesiasticum Universum,* 5 vols. in 12, Romae, 1843-1845.

Sebastianelli, Guilelmus, *Praelectiones Iuris Canonici,* 2. ed., 3 vols., Romae, 1905-1906.

Sherman, Charles, *Roman Private Law in the Modern World,* 2. ed., 3 vols., New York, 1924.

Smith, Walter, *Handbook of Elementary Law,* 2. ed., Hornbook Series, St. Paul: West Publ. Co., 1939.

Smith, William, *Dictionary of Christian Antiquities,* 2 vols., Hartford, 1880.

Suarez, Franciscus, *De Legibus,* Lugduni, 1619.

Suarez, Franciscus, *Opera Omnia,* 28 vols., Parisiis, 1856-1861.

Timlin, Bartholomew, *Conditional Matrimonial Consent,* The Catholic University of America Canon Law Studies, n. 89, Washington, D. C.: The Catholic University of America, 1934.

Van Hove, A., *Commentarium Lovaniense in Codicem Iuris Canonici,* Vol. I, tom. I, *Prolegomena ad Codicem Iuris Canonici,* 2. ed., Mechlinae-Romae, 1945.

Varro, Marcus, *De Lingua Latina,* trans. by Roland Kent, 2 vols., New York: Putnam, 1938.

Vazquez, Gabrielis, *Opera Omnia,* 8 vols. in 7, Lugduni, 1531.

Vecchiotti, Septimius (Soglia, Ioannes Card.), *Institutiones Canonicae ex Operibus Card. Soglia excerptae et ad usum seminariorum accommodatae,* 2 vols., Taurini, 1867-1868.

Vernier, Chester, *American Family Laws,* 5 vols., Stanford: University Press, 1931.

Vlaming, *Praelectiones Iuris Canonici,* Bussum in Hollandia, 1919-1921.

Von Hormann, Walter, *Quasiaffinität,* 2 vols. Innsbruck, 1897-1906.

Wahl, Francis, *The Matrimonial Impediments of Consanquinity and Affinity,* The Catholic University of America Canon Law Studies, n. 90, Washington, D. C.: The Catholic University of America, 1934.

Weller, Philip, *The Roman Ritual,* 3 vols., Bruce: Milwaukee, 1946-1952.

Wernz, Franciscus, *Ius Decretalium,* 6 vols., Vol. IV, Romae, 1904.

Wernz, Franciscus-Vidal, Petrus, *Ius Canonicum,* 7 vols. in 8, Vol. V, 3 ed., a P. Aguirre recognita, 1946, Romae: Apud Aedes Universitatis Gregoriana, 1923-1946.

Wiestner, Iacobus, *Institutiones Canonicae sive Ius Ecclesiasticum,* Monachii, 1705-1706.

Williston, Samuel, *The Law on Contracts,* 4 vols., New York, 1920.

Wouters, Ludovicus, *Manuale Theoloqiae Moralis,* 2 vols., Brugis: Beyaert, 1932-1933.

Woywod, Stanislaus-Smith, Callistus, *A Practical Commentary on the Code of Canon Law,* revised ed., 2 vols., New York: John F. Wagner, 1948.

Periodicals

Angelicum, Romae, 1924-

Apollinaris, Romae, 1928-

Irish Ecclesiastical Record, The, Dublin, 1864-

Ius Pontificium, Romae, 1921-1940.

Periodica de Re Morali, Canonica, Liturgica, Brugis (1927-1936) et Romae (1937-)

Religious Bulletin, Notre Dame, Indiana, 1946-

Revue d'histoire et de litterature religieuses, Paris, 1896-

Articles

Bouvaert, F. Claeys, "De Interpretatione Can. 1017,"—*Ius Pontificium,* XI, 127-132.

Cappello, F., S.J., "De Obligatione Orta ex Valida Promissione Matrimonii," —*Periodica de Re Morali, Canonica, Liturgica,* XXI, 88-110.

Darmanin, A., O.P., "De Promissione Matrimoniali—Ad. Can. 1017,"—*Angelicum,* VIII, 369-371.

Drachman, B., "Betrothals,"—*The Jewish Encyclopedia,* III, 125-128.

Ferraris, L., "Sponsalia,"—*Prompta Bibliotheca Canonica, Iuridica, Moralis, Theologica necnon Ascetica, Polemica, Rubricistica, Historica,* VIII, 417.

Fournier, P. ——————————————————————, *Revue d'histoire et de Litterature Religieusses,* III, 115.

Meehan, A., "Betrothal,"—*The Catholic Encyclopedia,* II, 537-538.

Ojetti, B., "Sponsalia,"—*Synopsis Rerum Moralium et Iuris Pontificii alphabetico ordine diqesta,* III, 3793.

O'Neill, P., "The Obligation of an Informal Promise of Marriage,"—*The Irish Ecclesiastical Record,* XLIII, 529.

Pallottini, S., "Sponsalia,"—*Collectio omnium conclusionum et resolutionum quae in causis propositis apud Sacram Congregationem Cardinalium Concilii Tridentini Interpretum prodierunt ab eius institutione anno 1564 ad 1860, distinctis titulis alphabetico ordine per materias digesta,* XVI, n. 19.

Smith, W., "Arrha," "Betrothals,"—*Dictionary of Christian Antiquities,* I, 124, 203.

Theodori, J., "De Promissionis Matrimonialis Forma,"—*Apollinaris,* VII, 240-242.

Thurston, H., "Marriage,"—*The Catholic Encyclopedia,* IX, 703-707.

Zamboni, J., "Sponsalia,"—*Collectio Declarationum Sacrae Congregationis Cardinalium Sacri Concilii Tridentini Interpretum,* III, 261.

———. "Your Engagement Blessed,"—*Religious Bulletin,* V, no. 21, p. 3.

ABBREVIATIONS

a.—articulus
a.v.—aliis verbis
AAS—*Acta Apostolicae Sedis*
ASS—*Acta Sanctae Sedis*
Bruns—*Canones Apostolorum et Consiliorum Veterum Selecti*
C.—Codex (Iustianus) vel Caput vel Causa vel Concilium
c.—canon seu caput (iuris antiqui)
Can.—Canon (novi Codicis)
cc.—canones seu capita (iuris antiqui)
C. Th.—Codex Theodosianus
col.—columna
Conc. Trident.—Concilium Tridentinum
D.—Digestum (Imperatoris Iustiniani)
DD—Doctores
Decisiones—*Sacrae Romanae Rotae Decisiones seu Sententiae*
decr.—decretum
decr. *de ref. matrim.*—decretum *de reformatione matrimonii*
disp.—disputatio
dist.—distinctio
Fontes—*Codicis Iuris Canonici Fontes*
G.—Gaius
I—Institutiones (Iustiniani)
Jaffé—*Regesta Pontificum Romanorum ad annum MCXCVIII* (ed. by Ewald Kaltenbrunner, Löwenfeld)
JE—Jaffé, *Regesta Pontificum Romanorum* (ed. by P. Ewald; for the years 590-882)
JK—Jaffé, *op. cit.* (*ed. by F. Kaltenbrunner; to the year 590*)
JL—Jaffé, *op. cit.* (*ed. by S. Löwenfeld; to the years 892 to 1198*)
Mansi—*Sacrorum Conciliorum Nova et Amplissima Collectio*
MPG—Migne, *Patrologia, Series Graeca*
MPL—Migne, *Patrologia, Series Latina*
N.—Novelae (Iustiniani)
n.—numerus
PCI—*Pontificia Commissio ad Codicis Canones Authentice Interpretandos*
Potthast—*Regesta Pontificum Romanorum inde ab anno pust Christum natum MCXCVIII ad MCCCIV*
Q.; q.—Quaestio
S.C.C.—Sacra Congregatio Concilii
S.C. de Prop. Fide—Sacra Congregatio de Propaganda Fide
S.C. Neg. Eccl. Extraordin.—Sacra Congregatio pro Negotiis Ecclesiae Extraordinariis
S.C.S. Off.—Suprema Congregatio Sancti Officii
S.R.R.—Sacra Romana Rota
s.v.—sub verbo; sub verbis
Thesaurus—*Thesaurus Resolutionum Sacrae Congregationis Concilii*

BIOGRAPHICAL NOTE

Chester Francis Wrzaszczak was born in Chicago, Illinois, on December 16, 1917. He attended Five Holy Martyrs' Grade School and Quigley Preparatory Seminary in that city. His philosophical and part of his theological training was taken at St. Mary of the Lake Seminary, Mundelein, Illinois, where he received the Bachelor of Arts Degree in 1941. The following year he was incardinated in the Diocese of La Crosse, Wisconsin, and was sent to St. Mary's Seminary, Baltimore, Maryland, where he was awarded the degrees of Bachelor and Licentiate in Theology in 1943 and 1944 respectively. He was ordained to the priesthood on November 17, 1943. After three years of parochial labors he was appointed Secretary of the Diocesal Tribunal and instructor at Aquinas High School, La Crosse. In 1948 he was sent to the Catholic University of America to study in the School of Canon Law. He received the Baccalaureate Degree in Canon Law in June of 1949, and that of the Licentiate the following year. In the intervening summer of 1949 he founded St. Patrick Parish, Onalaska, Wisconsin, and in the summer of 1950 he acted as administrator of Corpus Christi Church at Bakerville, Wisconsin. Currently he is the administrator of St. James Parish, Ferryville, Wisconsin, and Defender of the Bond at the Diocesan Tribunal, La Crosse, Wisconsin.

ALPHABETICAL INDEX

CANON LAW STUDIES*

322. GAFFIGAN, REV. ALOYSIUS J., O.S.F.S., J.C.L., Residence of Religious.
323. CAPPIELLO, REV. LINUS V., O.F.M., J.C.L., De Ordinariorum Dispensandi Facultate ad Normam Canonis 81.
324. CONWAY, REV. WALTER J., J.C.L., The Time and Place of Baptism.
325. KING, REV. JAMES P., J.C.L., The Canonical Procedure in Separation Cases.
326. WRZASZCZAK, REV. CHESTER F., J.C.L., The Betrothal Contract in the Code of Canon Law.

---

*A complete list of the previous numbers of this series will be found in the earlier studies. All the published numbers are available from the Catholic University of America Press, 620 Michigan Avenue, N.E., Washington 17, D. C., except the following: Nos. 1-116 inclusive, 118-123 inclusive, 128, 136, 144, 153, 162, 166, 175, 178, 182, 190 and 198. But the following numbers, now reissued, are obtainable from THE JURIST, The Catholic University of America, Washington 17, D. C., namely: Nos. 5, 7, 11, 17, 18, 19, 26, 28, 30, 34, 42, 44, 51, 52 and 61.

www.ingramcontent.com/pod-product-compliance
Lightning Source LLC
LaVergne TN
LVHW050252080826
844660LV00012B/628

* 9 7 8 0 8 1 3 2 2 4 9 7 8 *